For C.J.:
Here's to a long life of health,
happiness…and more frequent
visits from your brother.

M	T	W	T	F	S		S	M	T	W	T	F	S		S	M	T	W	T	F	S		S	M	T	W	T	F	S
	1	2	3	4					1	2	3	4					1	2	3	4					1	2	3	4
6	7	8	9	10	11		5	6	7	8	9	10	11		5	6	7	8	9	10	11		5	6	7	8	9	10	11
13	14	15	16	17	18		12	13	14	15	16	17	18		12	13	14	15	16	17	18		12	13	14	15	16	17	18
20	21	22	23	24	25		19	20	21	22	23	24	25		19	20	21	22	23	24	25		19	20	21	22	23	24	25
27	28	29	30	31			26	27	28	29	30	31			26	27	28	29	30	31			26	27	28	29	30	31	

BLOG ON

The Essential Guide to Building Dynamic Weblogs

About the Author

Todd Stauffer is the author or co-author of over 25 computer books, including titles on the Internet, web publishing, the Macintosh, PC upgrading, and office applications. He helped conceive and was the founding author of McGraw-Hill/Osborne's *How to Do Everything* series, for which he's written the titles *How to Do Everything with Your iMac* and *How to Do Everything with Your iBook*. Todd is also a magazine writer, web publisher, and the publisher of an upstart city news and culture magazine in Jackson, Mississippi. He can be reached via the website for this book at http://www.blogonbook.com/.

BLOG ON

The Essential Guide to
Building Dynamic Weblogs

Todd Stauffer

McGraw-Hill/Osborne

New York   Chicago   San Francisco   Lisbon
London   Madrid   Mexico City   Milan   New Delhi
San Juan   Seoul   Singapore   Sydney   Toronto

The McGraw·Hill Companies

McGraw-Hill/Osborne
2600 Tenth Street
Berkeley, California 94710
U.S.A.

To arrange bulk purchase discounts for sales promotions, premiums, or fund-raisers, please contact **McGraw-Hill**/Osborne at the above address. For information on translations or book distributors outside the U.S.A., please see the International Contact Information page immediately following the index of this book.

Blog On: The Essential Guide to Building Dynamic Weblogs

1234567890 FGR FGR 0198765432

ISBN 0-07-222712-5

Publisher:	Brandon A. Nordin
Vice President &	
Associate Publisher:	Scott Rogers
Senior Acquisitions Editor:	Jane Brownlow
Project Editor:	Katie Conley
Acquisitions Coordinator:	Tana Allen
Technical Editor:	Rick Ellis
Copy Editor:	Bart Reed
Proofreader:	Emily Rader
Indexer:	Irv Hershman
Computer Designers:	Tabi Cagan, Kelly Stanton-Scott
Illustrators:	Michael Mueller, Lyssa Wald, Melinda Moore Lytle
Series Design:	Mickey Galicia
Cover Design:	Patti Lee

This book was composed with Corel VENTURA™ Publisher.

Contents at A Glance

PART I   **What's a Weblog and How Do I Get One?**

     1   Do I Need a Weblog? 3

     2   Choosing Your Weblog Software and Server 25

PART II   **Using Your Weblog**

     3   The Simple Blog 49

     4   Using a Hosted Weblog 73

     5   Setting Up and Using Greymatter 115

     6   Setting Up and Using Movable Type 147

     7   Setting Up and Using pMachine 187

PART III   **Extending Your Weblog**

     8   Writing, Designing, and Tweaking Your Blog 239

     9   Add-Ons for Your Weblog 271

PART IV   **Publicity and Possibilities**

     10   Publicizing Your Weblog Site 297

     11   Using Weblogs in Organizations 317

Appendix   Internet Resources 335

             Index 345

Contents

Acknowledgments   xv
Introduction   xvii

PART I	**What's a Weblog and How Do I Get One?**	

CHAPTER 1	**Do I Need a Weblog?**	**3**
	What Is a Weblog?	4
	Is This a New Thing?	7
	The Weblog Phenomenon	9
	Why Are Weblogs Different?	11
	How Are Weblogs Updated?	14
	How Do Weblogs Build Community?	16
	Is a Weblog Right for You?	17
	Consider Your Content	17
	Consider Your Goals	18
	Fair Use and Blogging	21
	Call to Action: Get Involved	22

CHAPTER 2	**Choosing Your Weblog Software and Server**	25
	Types of Weblog Software	26
	Basic Weblog	26
	The Automated Weblog	30
	Getting a Web Server for Your Weblog	39
	Weblog Server Jargon and Definitions	39
	Choosing a Good IPP or Hosting Service	42
	More…	45

PART II	**Using Your Weblog**	

CHAPTER 3	**The Simple Blog**	**49**
	Requirements for the Simple Blog	50
	Build a Basic Weblog Page	52
	Upload and Test Your Page	56
	Add New Entries, Images, and Hyperlinks to Your Blog	59

Archive Past Posts   66
Ideas for Extending Your Blog   68
More...   71

CHAPTER 4   **Using a Hosted Weblog** **73**
Choose a Hosted Service   74
The Popular Choice: Blogger   76
Sign Up   77
Add Entries   78
Change the Look   81
Manage Archives   86
Change Settings   87
Community Living: LiveJournal   90
Create a LiveJournal   90
Edit Your LiveJournal   92
Customize Your LiveJournal   97
A Business-Like Presence: Radio UserLand   99
Get Started with Radio   100
Add to Your Weblog   102
Edit and Delete Entries   105
Write a Story   106
Change Your Theme   107
Set Preferences   108
Aggregate News   110
The Radio Application   112
More...   114

CHAPTER 5   **Setting Up and Using Greymatter** **115**
The Greymatter Decision: Features and Requirements   116
Get Started   118
Download and Install Greymatter   119
Configure Greymatter   124
Manage Authors   129
Post and Edit Entries   130
Post an Entry   130
Edit or Close an Entry   132
Administer the Weblog   134
Rebuild Files   134
Upload Files   135
Edit and Delete Comments   136
Ban IPs   137
Edit Templates   138
Download Templates   138
Edit Templates Yourself   138

	Add Static Pages	143
	More...	145
CHAPTER 6	**Setting Up and Using Movable Type**	**147**
	The Movable Type Decision: Features and Requirements	148
	Who Is Movable Type For?	150
	Get Started	151
	Download and Configure	151
	Upload and Set Permissions	154
	Configure Movable Type	155
	Load and Run Movable Type	156
	Post and Edit Entries	159
	Edit the Blog's Core Setup	159
	Post an Entry	160
	Create and Edit Categories	162
	Edit an Entry	164
	Delete an Entry	166
	Power Editing Mode	166
	Upload Files	167
	Administer the Weblog	169
	Manage Authors	169
	Ban IPs	170
	Use a Bookmarklet	171
	Use the TrackBack Feature	171
	Manage Your Archives	174
	Edit the Templates	176
	Syndicate Headlines and Ping Others	176
	Add Your Own Links	178
	Using Downloadable Templates	178
	Add Notifications Entry	180
	Understand MT's Tags	181
	Categories and Template Tags	183
	Change the Look	184
	More...	185
CHAPTER 7	**Setting Up and Using pMachine**	**187**
	The pMachine Decision: Features and Requirements	188
	Get Started	191
	Download and Install	191
	Configure pMachine	196
	Configure Your Weblog	199
	Change the Index's Name	200
	Post and Edit Entries	201

Post an Entry 201
Add an Image 203
Edit an Entry 206
Alter or Delete an Entry 206
Add Categories 207
Add pBlocks 209
Use a Bookmarklet 209
Manage Users and Mailings 214
User Registration 214
The Post Office 218
Dig into the Templates 222
How the Templates Work 222
Built-in Templates 223
Edit the HTML Templates 229
Extras: Static Pages, Blurbs, and Headlines 231
Create a Collective Weblog 234
More... 235

PART III   **Extending Your Weblog**

CHAPTER 8   **Writing, Designing, and Tweaking Your Blog** **239**
What Are You Gonna Say? 240
Have Something to Say 241
Say It Well 244
Brevity Is Your Friend 247
Let Others Play 249
Weblog Netiquette 250
Blogging Ethics 251
Change the Look of Your Site 252
Use a Third-Party Template 252
CSS and Style Sheets 254
Tips for a Blog That Works 269
More... 270

CHAPTER 9   **Add-Ons for Your Weblog** **271**
Set Up a Reply E-mail Account 272
Do You Need a Forum? 275
Add and Manage a Mailing List 282
Add a Poll 286
Add an Image Gallery 288
Add Comments 291
Blogger Editing Tools 291
More... 293

PART IV	**Publicity and Possibilities**	
CHAPTER 10	**Publicizing Your Weblog Site**	**297**
	How to Be Seen	298
	The Art of Conversation	299
	On Being a Joiner	301
	Get Listed and Searched	303
	Link and Ping	305
	Headline Syndication	309
	Publish Your Feed	311
	Read Feeds	311
	Publish Others' Feeds	312
	Get the Media Interested	314
	More...	315
CHAPTER 11	**Using Weblogs in Organizations**	**317**
	Can Weblogs Be Serious?	318
	Blog Advantages for Organizations	319
	Make the Choice	321
	Ideas for Organizational Blogs	323
	Store and Share Knowledge	323
	Collaborate Online	324
	Reach Customers	327
	Grassroots Organizing	328
	Blogs in Education	331
	More...	334
APPENDIX	**Internet Resources**	**335**
	Popular Sites	336
	Blogs	336
	News and Roundup Sites	336
	Weblog Philosophy	337
	Weblog Software and Services	337
	Hosted Blogging Software	337
	Server-Based Blogging Software	338
	Hosting Companies	338
	Domain Name Registrars	339
	Site Design	339
	Templates and Design	339
	HTML and CSS References	339
	Add-ons	340
	E-mail	340
	Hosted Discussion Forum	340
	Server-Side Discussion Forums	340

Mailing List Managers 341
Polls and Surveys 341
Photo Galleries 341
Hosted Comments 341
Blogger API Clients 341
Publicity 342
General Publicity Sites 342
Registries and Directories 342
Webrings 342
Search Engine Submissions 343
Headline Syndication and Readers 343

Index 345

Acknowledgments

After working on nearly 30 book projects so far in my career, this book gave me a wonderful new opportunity. I can now tell people my own version of a classic writer's story—the saga of the 25 or so publishers who *rejected* my book proposal before one finally had the vision to publish it. And it wasn't that bad of a proposal. But, every writer needs such a story to tell at cocktail parties, so I thank those 25 or so editors and publishers who helped make that story possible.

It only follows that I should thank Jane Brownlow at McGraw-Hill/Osborne for seeing the value in this project. Jane was invaluable in helping to name (and rename) the book, organize the people involved, and keep everything moving forward. Thanks also to Tana Allen for world-class editorial coordinating, to Katie Conley for herding me through the project-management phase of the book, with an always pleasant lilt to her e-mail voice, and to Bart Reed for his eagle-eyed copyediting.

This project happened quickly, and I'd like to thank Rick Ellis for a wonderful technical edit. If there's valuable insight or a good tip found anywhere in these pages, there's a good chance it came about at the suggestion of Rick. I know this project took a lot of his time—probably more of his weekends and late nights than he'd bargained for—and I appreciate his efforts to make this book better and more technically accurate.

I'd definitely like to thank Wil Wheaton for the kind words he had to say about this book and his willingness to let us print them. Thanks also to G.K. Nelson for singing our praises. And it would be woefully negligent if I didn't thank Neil Salkind for *pitching* this book to those 25 publishers and—as always—for the support and help of the Studio B literary agency.

On the home front, I'd like to thank Donna Ladd for the support and encouragement, not to mention her strong personal interest in this project, as I was able to set up new blogging software for her during the course of this writing.

I'd also like to thank Stephen Barnette, our man-about-town (and probably a future governor of the state of Mississippi), for his help on other projects (web and otherwise) while I've been up to my ears in this one. And, finally, I'd like to thank Willie and Eddie, partly for the comic relief they provided me on a daily basis and partly because this wouldn't be a true computer geek's acknowledgments if I failed to mention my cats.

Introduction

This might be the question of the decade: *What makes successful websites successful?* What do eBay, Amazon, Yahoo!, The Well, Salon.com, and ePinions all have in common? Actually, it's simple—they're all sites that change content constantly while inviting participation from their users. There's something new to read nearly every time you visit, and there's something that you can *do* as a reader—you can log in, search, comment, vote, and say your piece. The result: You go back, repeatedly.

What's amazing is that building this sort of site has rapidly become possible for nearly any web user, without extensive HTML/XHTML knowledge. Regardless of whether the site is a personal diary, a news commentary site, a corporate tech-support site, or a political action bulletin board, all such sites are exponentially easier to build and maintain thanks to recent offerings in the world of weblog content-management software.

Weblogs (or just *blogs*) are easy to create and maintain, and today's weblog software is as powerful as content-management software that cost tens of thousands of dollars just a few years ago. Many blogging options are free or nearly free, with some requiring little beyond the typical monthly payment that most web authors and small-to-midsize organizations pay to a web hosting company.

Perhaps most importantly, weblog software helps the user apply the two rules of generating web traffic: Update interesting content constantly, and build a community of regular users. With a weblog, the tools for following these rules are built right in.

What Can You Do with a Weblog?

The weblog software and add-ons covered in this book enable you to quickly create an online community in which the author and/or users can perform the following tasks:

- Post articles to the site via a web interface, automatically updating the home page and category pages.

- "Blurb" and link quickly to other sites on the Web for dashing off commentary on news articles and world events as well as alerting the group to action items, stories of interest, and so on.

- Search your local site easily so that older entries can be found via keywords.

- Publish online conversations by adding comments to existing stories or adding new entries to "community blogs," where all users can post entries.

- Enable users to personalize their visit by signing in with a username and password.

- Track a calendar of events and group birthdays.

- Send mailings and electronic newsletters to users.

- Build online forums for more in-depth conversations as well as for multimedia postings, classifieds, and so on.

- Run polls, contests, and display headlines and weather forecasts from professional news outlets.

- Automatically send updates to websites that publicize blogs and export headlines for inclusion on other people's websites.

Regardless of the content, nearly all weblogs take the important step of encouraging comments and contributions from their visitors. As one blogger put it, weblogs are like "pirate radio" for individuals and communities. Gone are the days of the "under construction" personal or organizational site, now that weblogs offer constant updates and interactive communities. That's what makes your site dynamic and keeps users interested and excited about returning to it.

Who Should Use This Book?

If you've never had a website but always wanted one—or if you do have a website but you feel that the time required to edit pages and manage files stifles your desire to keep it updated—then a weblog should be at the top of your list of solutions. If you want to learn *how* to do all this in an approachable, entertaining, "how-to" format, then *Blog On: The Essential Guide to Building Dynamic Weblogs* is the book to use.

I've tried to aim this book directly at the beginning-to-intermediate web author or prospective web author. You don't need a strong grasp of HTML/XHTML, and you don't need to know anything about web programming, CGI scripts, or any sort of web server setup. What you do need is a familiarity with your web browser (Internet Explorer, Netscape, or similar application) and a desire to implement an automated online publishing system. You'll also probably need between 5 and 20 minutes in which to get started, depending on the publishing option you choose.

A weblog provides a great way to publish a personal site, a political site, a community site, a grassroots organizational site, an educational site, or collaborative site for your project group or company. Once it's up and running, the real pleasure of a weblog is that you can post regularly without editing lengthy HTML files, and you don't need to learn the high-end HTML editing tools such as Macromedia Dreamweaver.

Small business owners, managers, and entrepreneurs, regardless of their technical skill level, can benefit tremendously from this quick approach to building and maintaining customer community. The ease with which feedback, discussion, and community can be fostered is perfect for a variety of business situations—whether for sales, tech support, or professional networking.

The weblog community approach is great for teachers and professors, who can encourage feedback and student discussion on lesson topics via the Internet (or an in-school intranet). Instructors or discussion leaders can post hyperlinks, tips, extra reading material, assignments, and homework help, and students can reply, discuss items among themselves, and even submit assignments online.

Finally, weblogs are perfect for charitable organizations, small businesses, civic groups, and political organizers. Nontechnical staff and volunteers, regardless of their physical location, can post news stories, action items, and internal business updates. Indeed, a good portion of the current blogging community on the Web is activist or politically minded, from all across the political spectrum. Those users prove that these tools can be harnessed for any sort of organizational or community-building goals.

What Makes This Book Different?

The key focus of this book is not on weblogging history, theory, or its social significance, although I'll touch on those things throughout the text. Instead, this book is about *doing* something—building your weblog and getting it seen by as many people as possible. This is very much a how-to book, with step-by-step instructions, tips, hints, and help in deciding what type of solution is right for your circumstance.

Blog On: The Essential Guide to Building Dynamic Weblogs will compare a number of different weblog packages, including desktop, hosted, and server-side packages, show you how to choose an ISP for your weblog, and help you create a weblog from scratch or sign onto a hosted weblog solution. If you opt to go for a more advanced server-based weblog, this book will step you through the process of uploading and configuring one of three different weblog packages: Greymatter, Movable Type, or pMachine.

After that, you'll learn to extend and customize the software, alter the appearance of the site, and expand upon your weblog with message boards, chatting capabilities, mailing lists, and other features that help maintain and promote community. You'll also get some advice on weblog content and design, including some tips on Internet etiquette and ways to hone your writing. The book finishes up with tips and advice for promoting the site, including a chapter on using weblogs effectively in business, organizational, and educational environments.

Here's a quick list of key benefits you'll get from this book:

- You'll understand weblog technology and what all the excitement is about, including its purposes, benefits, and limitations.

- You'll discover the fundamentals of weblogging and the specific weblogging options available for implementing your own site.

- You'll get step-by-step instructions for using each of three popular weblog applications, as well as detailed help for a number of the simpler, sign-up-and-go weblogging solutions.

- You'll gain an in-depth understanding of some tricks and tips for customizing your weblog and I'll give you some ideas for designing and augmenting the site.

- You'll pick up strategies to drive traffic to your site using various tools for publicity and participation in the blogging community.

- You'll explore uses for weblogs in businesses and organizations, and you'll get ideas for how to make your organization's online discussions, idea-capturing methods, and project management more efficient.

How This Book Is Organized

This book is divided into three major parts in an attempt to make it as easy as possible for you to move to relevant chapters. The book is largely tutorial, but you probably won't read it cover to cover, because Part II is comprised of standalone chapters that focus on specific tools. Once you've chosen and implemented your blogging tool, you're free to move to Part III, which focuses on using and extending that tool as well as on writing your blog and reaching out to your site's visitors. Here's a quick overview:

- **Part I: What's a Weblog and How Do I Get One?**   In this section you'll be introduced to the concept of weblogs, along with a brief explanation of the history, technology, and reasons for their significance. (In other words, you'll learn why blogs are all the rage.) In these chapters I'll help you make decisions about your website: Is the content you want to put on the Web right for a blog? What sort of blog should you implement? What are the particular tools that are best suited to your goals?

- **Part II: Using Your Weblog**   Part II is where the hands-on, how-to portion of the book really starts. Chapter 3 is a must-read (or at least a must-skim). It covers the very basics of HTML and web documents as well as shows you how a weblog-formatted site can be built without any special tools beyond a text editor and some web hosting space. Then, you've got a decision to make: Chapter 4 covers hosted weblogging solutions (sign-up-and-go solutions) whereas Chapters 5, 6, and 7 dig into the high-end server-based weblog applications that require installation and configuration, but give you unprecedented control and features as a result. Although I certainly encourage you to read each of these chapters, you don't have to. They are standalone modules that can be used as tutorials for the particular tools discussed.

- **Part III: Extending Your Weblog and Going Public**   In Part III you'll find relevant advice, techniques, tips, and information, regardless of the type of blogging software or solution you've chosen. Chapter 8 offers suggestions for coming up with and writing good content for your blog as well as tips for designing and personalizing your site's appearance. Chapter 9 focuses on add-on tools—other automatic stuff you can add to make your site more dynamic, such as discussion forums, polls, mailing lists, image galleries, and so on.

- **Part IV: Publicity and Possibilities**   Chapter 10 offers advice and an explanation of the various tools available to help you publicize your weblog, participate in the blogging community, and drive traffic to your site. Chapter 11 ends the book with a discussion of the different applications for a weblog in a business, educational, or organizational setting, including a look at why the latest class of weblog software may help shape a very interesting future for online collaboration and communication.

■ **Appendix**   For your convenience, I've grouped all the website URLs mentioned in this book in the appendix, along with a few others that may be of interest to you. If there's a particular blog, reference site, or tool you need to explore or download, check the links in this appendix to get a quick start while surfing.

Throughout the text you'll see *tips* (which are meant to add to the discussion by providing advice or additional tidbits), *notes* (which should augment the text or call out important points that bear repeating), and occasionally *warnings* (which are meant to point out situations where you could lose data or open up an Internet security risk). You'll also see sidebars in some of the chapters. These offer additional points or tangential discussions related to a chapter's topic.

For More Information

I have, of course, set up a blog for supporting this book. How active it is remains to be seen—if it's going to be a truly stellar resource, it will require your participation. So, come by http://www.blogonbook.com/ to visit with me, ask questions, offer any tips or advice you may have, and see what other questions and comments have been posted by other readers. In fact, you should feel free to drop by the site even if you don't buy this book or you haven't made a decision about which book to buy. I'll post errata, additional links (or fixed links if those in the book or appendix change), and other interesting tidbits—advice, blogging news, and so forth—at this site. What's more, you'll also be able to get a hold of me if you have questions and comments.

Thank You

Thanks for your interest in this book. I hope it proves to be a valuable resource for you and that whatever weblog solution you choose helps to improve the website or websites you're publishing. Good luck, and *Blog On*!

M	T	W	T	F	S		S	M	T	W	T	F	S		S	M	T	W	T	F	S		S	M	T	W	T	F	S
	1	2	3	4					1	2	3	4					1	2	3	4					1	2	3	4
6	7	8	9	10	11		5	6	7	8	9	10	11		5	6	7	8	9	10	11		5	6	7	8	9	10	11
13	14	15	16	17	18		12	13	14	15	16	17	18		12	13	14	15	16	17	18		12	13	14	15	16	17	18
20	21	22	23	24	25		19	20	21	22	23	24	25		19	20	21	22	23	24	25		19	20	21	22	23	24	25
27	28	29	30	31			26	27	28	29	30	31			26	27	28	29	30	31			26	27	28	29	30	31	

Part I

What's a Weblog and How Do I Get One?

Chapter 1   Do I Need a Weblog?

Chapter 2   Choosing Your Weblog Software and Server

M	T	W	T	F	S		S	M	T	W	T	F	S		S	M	T	W	T	F	S		S	M	T	W	T	F	S
	1	2	3	4					1	2	3	4					1	2	3	4					1	2	3	4	
6	7	8	9	10	11		5	6	7	8	9	10	11		5	6	7	8	9	10	11		5	6	7	8	9	10	11
13	14	15	16	17	18		12	13	14	15	16	17	18		12	13	14	15	16	17	18		12	13	14	15	16	17	18
20	21	22	23	24	25		19	20	21	22	23	24	25		19	20	21	22	23	24	25		19	20	21	22	23	24	25
27	28	29	30	31			26	27	28	29	30	31			26	27	28	29	30	31			26	27	28	29	30	31	

Chapter 1

Do I Need a Weblog?

In this chapter:

- What is a weblog?

- Is weblogging new and does it represent some new phenomenon?

- How are weblogs updated and what makes them technically different from a typical website?

- Should you consider using a weblog?

- What basic elements are necessary for a successful weblog?

O K, so maybe nobody *needs* a weblog. But if having a website is important
to you, and if your requirements for that website fit certain criteria, then
a weblog may be the ideal approach for your website, whether it's a personal,
hobbyist, professional, or organizational site.

And you may certainly *want* a weblog. After all, weblogging can be about
expressing oneself, participating in an online community or documenting
important events as they happen. Some weblogs are about friends and family life.
Some are about organizations, institutions, or news headlines, whereas others
focus obsessively on hobbies, politics, or sports. So, if there's something that you
really *need* to say, and you feel it's best said on the Web, then, maybe—just maybe—
you need a weblog.

Weblogs are impermanent, but archived. They're expressive, but coldly digital.
They're personal, but remote. And maybe some of them are significant. But, more
pragmatically, weblogs happen to be websites that offer uniform presentation and
are content oriented and community focused, making them pass an important
buzzword test—they're *sticky*. If people enjoy liking or disliking you, agreeing or
disagreeing with you, spending time with you or just watching the train wreck that
is your life, they may just stick around when they get to your site—and they'll
come back in the future.

What Is a Weblog?

If you were to leave the definition completely up to me, I'd define *weblog* something
like this: A weblog or *blog* is a website that's designed to be updated with items in
a linear, time-based fashion, similar to a personal journal or diary, except that the
contents are meant specifically for public consumption. Often implemented using
special software, weblogs contain articles or entries that are grouped primarily by
the date and time they are posted. Weblogging—or just *blogging*—is the act of
adding articles or updates to such a site at regular intervals.

NOTE
*The word "blog" is used commonly as a verb, as in "I'm going to blog
today" or "I've got to blog about my date last night," or "I'm blogging on
global warming today," meaning simply that you plan to update your blog
site or weblog.* Blog *and* weblog *are used interchangeably, although* blog
is more of a slang term. (Not that you'd find either in Webster's, yet.)

So how do you know whether a particular site you've visited is a weblog? Clearly,
there are no hard-and-fast rules. If the site's author feels like she is blogging or

offering a weblog, you can go ahead and agree with her. But to get a sense of the overall class of sites we're talking about here, you can look at four different features: format, software, personality, and community.

Probably the best indication of a weblog is its format. Are entries arranged chronologically like a diary, perhaps with secondary topical categories? Do entries come one after another? Are the entries generally only a few paragraphs long? If not, do longer stories have special "more" or "read on" links that take you deeper into a story? Does the site appear to have a mechanism that enables visitors to comment on the stories? If the answer is yes to at least a few of these questions, you're probably looking at a weblog (see Figure 1-1).

In a technical sense, the easiest way to identify a website as a weblog is to note the type of software used to create it. If special weblogging software is used, it's reasonable to consider the website a blog. Common blogging software includes Blogger, Manila, Greymatter, Movable Type, and pMachine. Often, a web author

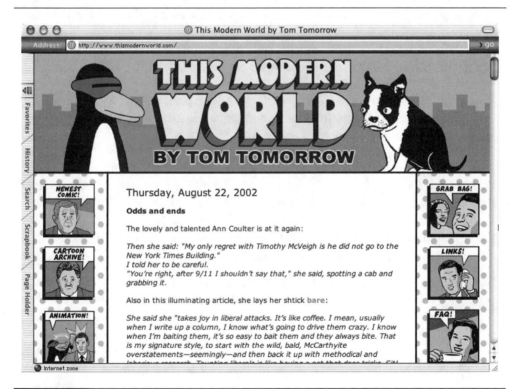

FIGURE 1-1   Although the design can vary greatly, weblogs often have a fairly similar format. Shown here is www.thismodernworld.com, by cartoonist Tom Tomorrow (Dan Perkins).

who uses a blogging tool will include a small image (called a "badge") or a line of text that gives credit to the blogging tool. Of course, software alone doesn't define a weblog—some people blog with just regular web publishing tools or create their own content-management software. But, it's certainly a sign that you're viewing a blog.

Another tip that you're reading a blog is the personal nature of the subject matter—losing jobs, getting jobs, getting out of bed, not getting out of bed, eating, drinking, eating too much, drinking too much, and so on. Likewise, a great many weblogs focus on the author's opinions, whether they're political, philosophical, technical, or spiritual. Again, there's no hard-and-fast rule—not all blogs are about opinions or personal journaling.

A final way to pin down whether a website is a blog is to note the community that it attempts to create or foster, usually in the form of comments posted in response to articles or e-mail sent to (and posted by) the weblog's author. Part of the real magic of the weblog is the fact that it often invites active participation in the discussion, not just passive consumption of the author's writing. But, of course, there are blogs to whom no one ever replies or to which replies are not particularly welcomed or encouraged.

According to Webopedia.com (which may not be the *Oxford English Dictionary,* but it's a place I go when a techie term stumps me), the definition of *blog* is as follows:

Jargon. (n.) Short for *Weblog*, a blog is a Web page that serves as a publicly accessible personal journal for an individual. Typically updated daily, blogs often reflect the personality of the author.

This definition isn't as all-encompassing as I'd like it to be, if only because blogs can certainly be used for something beyond the personal and individual. Companies, organizations, and even cable-news political pundits can use blogs to communicate with their minions or to sell their books. However, it's a good working definition, particularly the "journal" part, because that's the notion that's evoked any time you read a typical weblog (see Figure 1-2).

NOTE   *Some folks make a distinction between an online journal and a weblog, where a journal tends to be about the author and a weblog tends to be the author's observations of the outside world or a "log" of his or her journeys on the "Web." Again, the rules aren't set in stone, but if you find yourself contemplating your dating life, the meaning of life, or your navel, you may be "journaling" more than you are "blogging."*

FIGURE 1-2   Easily one of the more popular weblogs on the Internet is wilwheaton.net, a site run by actor Wil Wheaton, famous for his portrayal of Wesley Crusher on *Star Trek: The Next Generation.* His is certainly a personal blog, discussing life, politics, music, books, and acting.

Is This a New Thing?

Whether or not weblogging is a new thing depends, foremost, on your definition of *new*. Heck, the Web itself has only been around since 1993. So, for adults, most anything we've seen on the Web has a certain newness to it.

Having said that, there are definitely different phases that the Web has gone through in terms of the type of sites we've seen—home pages, resume pages, link pages, portal pages, search engines, and so on. So as an "it" concept or a "killer app," of sorts, blogging is pretty new, having really taken off in the past 12 to 18 months as something that a lot of people are doing.

To me, what's really new about blogging is the sophistication and accessibility of the software tools being used to blog. Plenty of web authors have posted their opinions, ideas, and news clippings in a journal-like fashion for nearly the entire life of the Web (see Figure 1-3).

But the software tools covered in this book—as well as the web-based services that make the tools available inexpensively by subscription—arrived only in the past few months and years. And the power of the software is amazing when put side by side with content-management software of just a few years ago—the sort of back-end code that commercial newspapers and magazines might have used, costing tens or hundreds of thousands of dollars. The fact that you can build an article-centric community with comments, forums, and user management using free or inexpensive software is what may truly be driving this phenomenon.

FIGURE 1-3   Dave Winer (http://www.scripting.com/) not only runs a company that has created popular blogging tools (Manila and Radio UserLand), he was also one of the early weblog proponents and participants.

Of course, the idea of personal journaling is incredibly old—even journaling for public consumption. Consider cave dwellers, Moses, Columbus, Tocqueville, Lewis and Clark, Mark Twain, Anne Frank, May Sarton, and even Captain Kirk (while you're considering, I'll apologize for my painfully Western frame of reference). Although blogging may feel like a totally new thing, it's really only the medium that has changed—even the word "journalism" gives us a clue as to its roots and relationship to the journaling nature of blogging. Newspapers for centuries have offered letters from abroad, letters from readers, travelogues, columns, and opinion pages. The weekly newspaper in America—both the small-town weekly and the big-city alternative and entertainment weekly—is just as much about pushing the editor's opinions and the local reaction to current events as it is about newsgathering and reporting the "five W's" of those events.

Therefore, I'd argue that much of blogging represents some old concepts—personal opinion, gossip, written community discussion, and journalism—brought to a new medium. And even though some users of that medium have engaged in journal-focused web publishing for quite some time, technology and usability have recently coalesced in a significant way for the rest of us. The result is popular, easy-to-use tools that enable pretty much anyone to set up shop on the Web and start publishing this sort of content, while inviting feedback and staking out their own community corner of the Web.

The Weblog Phenomenon

So, weblogs—and particularly web-based journals—haven't exactly burst onto the scene, and they don't necessarily represent a fundamental buzzword-compliant shift in a *paradigm*, in *space-time* or, for that matter, in any sort of *-igm* or *-ism*.

That's not to say that weblogs aren't significant. They are, because they have a popular swell of momentum and some cache in other media. In fact, some other types of media—particularly newspapers and magazines—do seem achingly fascinated by blogging as a phenomenon, probably because newspapers and magazine would have the most to lose if blogging and blog reading became *de rigueur* reading for a large percentage of Internet users. Blogging is hijacking some issues that tend to fall within the jurisdiction of newspapers and magazines—such as opinion and community building—and the thought of those things moving to the Web might prove a bit intimidating.

But why would weblogs have this momentum and significance? The first part of it may be a sense of democratization. The Web has always been pitched to us as the Great Equalizer in democratic publishing, allowing everyone a forum for their ideas with a reasonably low barrier to entry, but the fact is that most personal websites kinda *suck*, whereas many high-dollar commercial sites are kinda *cool*. Weblogging doesn't change that fundamental truth, but it does alter it somewhat—personal sites can now have great tools such as web-based content-management tools, search engines, and mechanisms for registering users and enabling them to comment on stories. Given that some small personal and organizational sites actually manage to transcend *suckiness*, access to this new technology makes them all the more powerful and effective. *Ipso facto ergo*, small sites have the potential to suck less, and a growing number are actually cool.

Second, blogs give people an opportunity to play "editor." An entire class of weblog is out there expressly for the purpose of enabling bloggers to surf the Web, find things that interest—or irritate or nauseate or agitate or tickle—them, create a link, surround it with commentary, and then publish it for the masses. The masses can then, in most cases, comment on the story either automatically or via e-mail. This is something that may not directly intimidate publishers of traditional print media (or nontraditional web media), although it may pique those people's interest a bit. A good blog—or a popular one, or both—can be responsible for redistributing traffic to news sites, commentaries, features, and so on. Eventually, this power may be enough to turn some heads.

Third, blogs are about content. That's not to say that all blogs have good content. Just that the majority of them can't get away with *no* content. The entire journaling format means that fresh ideas or links or thoughts or at least *words* need to be input into the program every few days. Otherwise, the author will never have readers. The entries can be short—in fact, it's encouraged. Readers can generally tell quickly whether a blog has been updated and how often and how actively. The software makes it easier to update the blog, meaning all the author actually has to do is write the entries. Writing is hard, granted, but it's helped along by the technology. And content, as the cliché goes, is king, whether the site is personal or professional. If you don't have content, nobody comes back.

Fourth, blogs are about community. Articles posted on blogs can be revisited quickly, if necessary. They can be commented upon. They can even be edited and reposted or deleted and forgotten. But the most important point is that they encourage community and can do so on a level that a newspaper or magazine cannot. They can promote progressive or conservative ideas. They can be literary. They can be moronic. They can be nice. They can be exclusively about something—*Fahrenheit 451* or Stalag 13 or Matchbox Twenty.

In some combination of these factors, there's a way in which weblogs can be intimate and personal. Again, we're back to the journaling aspect of it—a weblog is often about its author. Even if it's by a political pundit, you may still hear about what he had for dessert or what she did over the weekend or where he's next signing books or how tired she is. In fact, even for famous people, and certainly for the rest of us, blogs are impersonally personal opportunities to express ourselves in an effort to find comfort and acceptance, which can be said another way using a single word: *therapy*.

Now, I don't want to belabor the notion of blogging as therapy, and I'm loathe to make the blogging phenomenon seem more important than it is. But blogging has gained a fair amount of its momentum in North America following September 11, 2001, and in the wake of other significant political and social changes since. Nationally, continentally, and perhaps globally, the geopolitical world has become something that a lot of people want to "talk" about—to share fear, hope, rage or understanding—and some of those people have turned to recent web technologies as part of that answer. Does that mean blogging is a component in some grand movement of Real Significance?

It does seem there's *something* going on, and maybe blogging has a role—but I encourage you to draw your own conclusions and feel free to decide that volunteerism or organized religion or basic cable is much more significant than blogging. Of course, if that's an opinion you hold strongly, and you'd like others to hear about it, then a blog might be the perfect way to publish that opinion on the Web, eh?

Why Are Weblogs Different?

They ain't payin' me for philosophy, so let's move back into the realm of my personal expertise: procrastination. You've already seen that the one factor that makes weblogs obvious to the naked eye is their journaling format, but what truly makes them different—at least, to us weblog authors—is the technology behind them. And the technology is designed, primarily, to give you fewer excuses for procrastinating if your desire is to publish news or stories on the Web.

It negates those excuses by taking away some of the traditional steps required in web publishing—the HTML files, the awkward editing software, sending the updates via FTP—and, instead, uses a server-based application to make it possible for you to update your website via a web browser (see Figure 1-4).

Again, the technology doesn't define the weblog. Therefore, if you wanted to, you could easily forgo all this technology and simply create an HTML document to serve as your main weblog page. Then, you'd open it periodically in a text editor (or an HTML editor, if you've got a decent one) and add a new blog entry. Once you're done, you save the file, launch your FTP program, and upload the

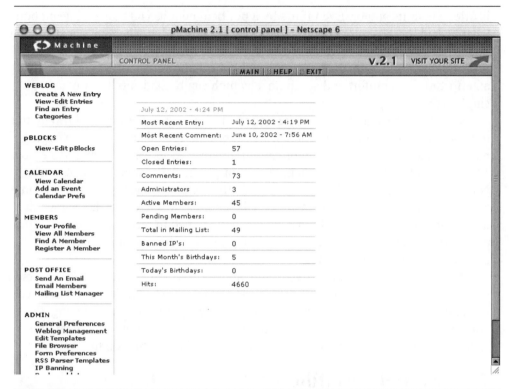

FIGURE 1-4   If you use special weblog server software, you can generally update your site by logging in to it, creating a new article, and editing that article—all from within a web browser.

blog page from your hard disk to the remote web server computer. Soon after it's uploaded, the entry will be available online.

This is simple, cheap, and can be effective—but it's limited. Once you've gotten a few weeks worth of entries, how do you intend to archive them? You could create another HTML document called jan03.html, or some such, and save all your January 2003 entries on that page, while you continue to update your main HTML document. Eventually, you'll have a whole bunch of these archive documents and you'll need to build a page that links to them somehow. Not that doing so is impossible; it's one way people have been putting together this sort of site for years. I've certainly done it this way (see Figure 1-5). It's just tedious.

Tedium aside, let's see what happens when we throw in some twists and try to accomplish this using just HTML and some ingenuity:

1

■ Would you like to be able to search all those entries—or, more to the point, enable your readers to search those entries—looking for a particular keyword or phrase? You can do it, but you'll need to add special search engine software or sign up with a search service.

■ Would you like users to be able to sort the articles by category? Manually, this can be done, but it's a bear.

■ Would you like to be able to have special "jump" or "more" pages so that particularly long articles don't take up screen after screen of your site's index page? Again, the manual approach is grueling—update the new article page, add a blurb to the index page, and then update a special "include" file that stores your navigation menu on the server so that this recently added story appears in the "What's New?" menu.

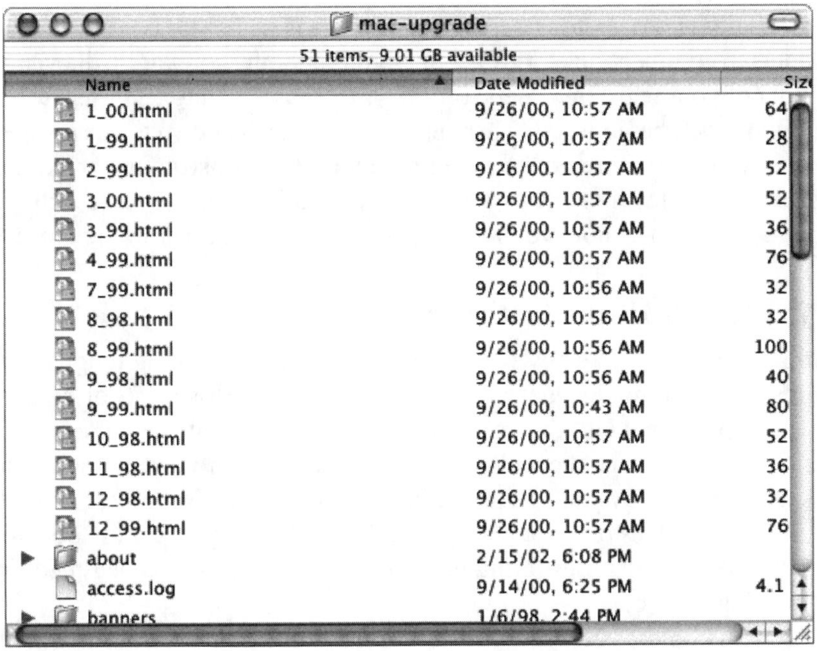

Name	Date Modified	Size
1_00.html	9/26/00, 10:57 AM	64
1_99.html	9/26/00, 10:57 AM	28
2_99.html	9/26/00, 10:57 AM	52
3_00.html	9/26/00, 10:57 AM	52
3_99.html	9/26/00, 10:57 AM	36
4_99.html	9/26/00, 10:57 AM	76
7_99.html	9/26/00, 10:56 AM	32
8_98.html	9/26/00, 10:56 AM	32
8_99.html	9/26/00, 10:56 AM	100
9_98.html	9/26/00, 10:56 AM	40
9_99.html	9/26/00, 10:43 AM	80
10_98.html	9/26/00, 10:57 AM	52
11_98.html	9/26/00, 10:57 AM	36
12_98.html	9/26/00, 10:57 AM	32
12_99.html	9/26/00, 10:57 AM	76
about	2/15/02, 6:08 PM	
access.log	9/14/00, 6:25 PM	4.1
banners	1/6/98, 2:44 PM	

mac-upgrade — 51 items, 9.01 GB available

FIGURE 1-5 Here's a folder listing of a website that I've maintained for years that covered news, tips, and help for upgrading Mac computers. Note the archive pages (4.99.html, 7_99.html, etc.).

All these tasks can be done manually, but, if you're like me, they're tedious enough to discourage you from updating your website as often as you'd like to. You don't feel like opening your web editor and don't feel like updating three different HTML documents just to add one more story or idea to your site. So, maybe you put it off for a day or so until you're ready to really sit at your computer and work on your site for a while. And maybe that day becomes a week or longer.

Without trying to sound too much like a cheesy infomercial (and failing), *wouldn't you like a better way?* Freely available or reasonably inexpensive weblog software, once installed and configured, handles a lot of these tasks automatically. You enter a story—if it's one paragraph, it's dated, signed, and put at the top of your main weblog page. If it's a full-page article, a new page is created and a blurb for that article is put on the front page.

When the month changes over, previous stories are archived, a link to the last month is created, and this month's stories now fill the front page. (Most weblog software can even account for some overlap so that the index page doesn't look barren on the first of every month.)

The ability to search for stories by keywords is generally built in. The ability for readers to comment on stories is often built in. Some software will even maintain a calendar of your registered users' birthdays or enable you to add users to a mailing list or build a web-based forum where users can create their own topics and responses. Ultimately, this software conspires to give you the infrastructure of something approaching a professional news website while freeing you to decide what you want to write about and not how you're going to get it to the server in the correct format.

How Are Weblogs Updated?

Weblog software is generally written in a server-side scripting language that executes on the computer that runs your web server software. (For most of us, that's a computer in a big, dark room somewhere in the data center of an Internet hosting company.) Once the software is installed and configured, you log in to your site the same way you might log in to your personal Yahoo! or MSN home page. Then, to add a story, you look around for a New Story command and click it, which will, in most cases, bring up an interface wherein you begin editing the story (see Figure 1-6).

Depending on the software, you'll be able to decide what portion of the entry will show up on the main blog page and what portion will appear on the "more" or full-article page, and you may be able to choose a category or other options for the story. When you're done editing, you'll generally have the option to preview the

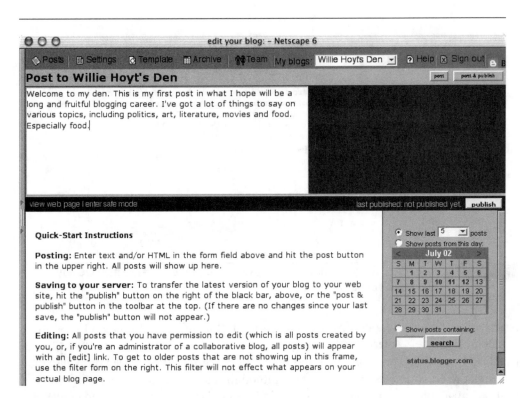

In most cases you'll enter stories via web form entry boxes and buttons.
Shown here is Blogger.com's online editing tool.

story and, if all is well, to post the story to your site. In most cases, it's available
for viewing immediately.

And, as if that weren't sophisticated enough, some weblogging server software
has begun to support editing from actual desktop applications—programs that are
native to your computer's operating system—that you launch and use as you might
a word processing application. Some of them allow you to compose, save, and
return to the document and even check your spelling. What's more, standards are
emerging so that the weblog editing software doesn't have to be written specifically for
the weblog server software—one application can be used to update multiple types
of weblogs (see Figure 1-7). You'll learn more about weblog-editing software in
Chapter 10.

You don't *have* to install and run weblog software on a server computer in
order to have a weblog. You can also subscribe to a service where weblog software

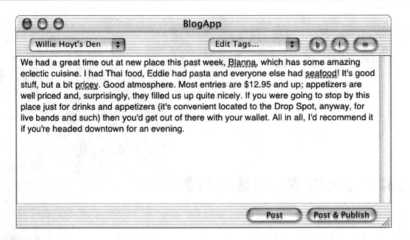

FIGURE 1-7   Third-party applications can be used to edit blogs that are managed by some server packages.

is already installed and, perhaps with a minimum of tweaking, can be put to use in a matter of minutes. Alternatively, you can post a weblog-style page by editing it first (in HTML) on your own computer and then uploading it to the web server. Chapter 3 covers the creation of such a basic site, although it's worth noting that third-party tools are available to help you, such as Radio Userland (http://radio.userland.com/), which I'll bring up again in Chapter 4. (We often call such tools "desktop" tools to differentiate them from tools that are running on a web server and are accessed via a browser.) The only problem with desktop solutions is that they generally don't offer support for user comments, as discussed next.

How Do Weblogs Build Community?

Two elements work together to make a successful website—updated content and tools for community. You may be able to create a community of readers—or at least a following—simply by having something interesting to say or by appealing to a certain niche of users. Beyond that, you can create a sense of community by offering your readers an outlet for their own expression. In blogging, that's done by letting users comment on your blog entries—for that reason, a comment capability it built in to most of the weblog-management software options. When a reader sees something that you've written and wants to respond, she can click the "comment" link, enter a few lines in a web-based form, and click the Send or Submit button.

That comment is then added to the bottom of the article (or otherwise associated with the article) so that others can read what has been written.

Allowing community comments is generally an option—one that you can turn off. There are various reasons for doing so, such as wanting to keep profanity or unproductive comments off your site or simply because you'd prefer not to have all comments made public. Plus, those comments are stored as digital files on your server, adding to the bulk of your site, so even intelligent conversation might become costly in online storage space and ISP charges.

But even if you turn off the commenting feature, you may still want to have a special e-mail account where you can receive messages from readers and perhaps post some of their responses, anonymously or not. (Sometimes posting and responding to e-mail is a great way to generate content that people come back to read.) You might also want to explore creating a web-based forum where users can create topics and chat on issues that may not be directly related to your stories.

With some weblog software you can allow registered members of your site to add their own articles to the blog, thus making for a dynamic *collective* weblog. This is particularly good for an organizational site that has a number of participants and web authors, but it can work for any sort of site—a user group, a news site, a discussion site—where you'd like multiple authors to be able to post. Some of the software lets you specify levels of users, so that some users can post new stories and others can only comment. In fact, you can conceivably make posting open to any reader, with the caveat that you might want to review any posts before they go live on the site. Again, the right software will allow that.

Is a Weblog Right for You?

Now that you've gained a sense of what a weblog is and how one works—at least in broad strokes—you might want to consider whether a weblog is the right choice for you and your website. Then, if not, you can give this book away as a present, which will help cement a friendship while clearing up some shelf space.

Consider Your Content

Easily the most important decision point when considering a website is making sure your content is a good fit. If it isn't, you'll be working a little too hard to fit what you're trying to communicate into the journal format of a weblog.

Weblog software forces your articles into a date-and-time format, and the most recent article you add will always (at least, in a typical configuration) appear at the top of the page. What this means is that weblog software makes it difficult to maintain a static-looking index or home page for your site. It's certainly not impossible, though. With much of the weblog software, you're free to edit the HTML of the underlying page templates. Also, you can always elect to make the blog only part of your site, with your resume, vacation photos, products, and sale literature easily accessible. However, if you don't intend to update your website frequently, or if your intent is to create a website that leans more toward a brochure, a catalog, or an online store, then blogging may not be for you. A blog is good for journal entries, news items, action items, and announcements, not so much for product specification sheets or scientific white papers.

Having said that, I don't mean to suggest that the dynamic content that is managed by your weblog software can't be worked into nearly any type of site. It's certainly possible to have both static elements and blog (dynamic) elements on the same page, if the design works (see Figure 1-8 for an example). This takes a little more effort and at least a little understanding of HTML, but it can definitely be done and will be discussed throughout the book, particularly in Chapters 8 and 9.

The other option you have is to make your blog only part of your site. For instance, say you have the site http://www.*myfullname*.com/, where up until now you have had information about yourself, some examples of your fine artwork, and even some MP3s of your original music available for downloading. Now you want to add to that by starting a blog. You have two choices. First, you can take a hint from Figure 1-8 and make the blog your main page, and then create links all around the edges that point to your other content. That's fairly common. Second, you could create the blog and make it only a portion of your site—perhaps visitors would view the blog at the address http://www.*myfullname*.com/blog/. You could create links from your home page and other static pages, and visitors could read the blog if desired. Neither method is better, although the second approach has the potential to be easier, because you won't have to work as hard to integrate your blog with your other pages and current site design.

Consider Your Goals

Unless you're building a private website designed for project management or similar organizational goals, your number-one goal with a website is probably to attract visitors. Therefore, an important issue to consider is who you expect will be visiting your site. The type of visitor or reader you intend to attract will probably dictate whether you should put the emphasis on a blog for your site or whether

Static content

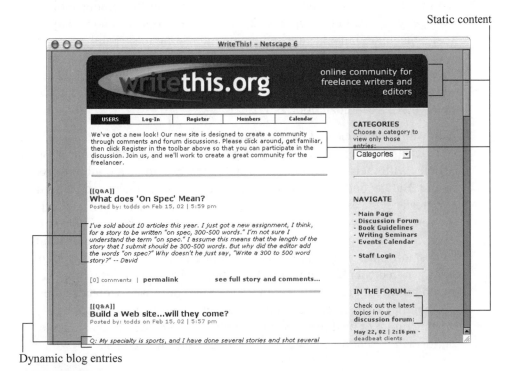

Dynamic blog entries

| **FIGURE 1-8** | Here's an example of a site where dynamic content and static content coexist. |

only a part (or none) of your site should be a blog. Reasons why you could consider using a blog include:

■ **You want to inform.**   If your site is about news and opinion, then a blog is a great format for your site. This is especially true if you're interested in creating debate over topics or trying to convince people of a particular viewpoint. But it's also great if you're simply building a site that links to other sites' content as well as gathering and editing the day's items for a constituency of interested visitors. (You never know—they may actually pay you for the service one day!) This can work for an individual (you're a pro–Green Party advocate and you want others to know about it) or for an organization (you *are* the Green Party, and you want to post recent news events or commentary on the news).

- **You want regular visitors.**   One of the major goals in creating a blog is to get your visitors to come back on a regular basis. You do this by fostering community, having something interesting to say, and saying it with some frequency. What you have to say can vary wildly. If you're great at finding incredible deals on home appliances via the Web, you're a devoted fan of the B52's, or you're a quirky and humorous stock analyst, then you're a candidate for a blog.

- **You want feedback and participation.**   The commenting tools available with weblog server software encourage readers to respond to your opinion articles with their own opinions, which, clearly, can be a double-edged sword. But beyond simple debate, the feedback mechanism can be used for greater good as well. Enabling comments means that others can expand on your articles with their own knowledge—perhaps a reader knows of an even *better* price on PC memory via a website you haven't seen or wants to post information about a political meeting that she's trying to plan in her town to coincide with yours. This one mechanism makes a blog that much better for organizational or educational purposes. Consider the possibilities when people can post their fiction online for critique by a writing group or post their questions online to be discussed by students taking a high school, college, or continuing education course.

These, you'll hopefully agree, are good reasons to start and maintain a weblog, whether the journal-style entries constitute your entire site or simply a portion of it. But there are also some good reasons *not* to use a blog for your site, including the following:

- **You don't have much to say.**   Blogging requires dedication and, although it may be a strong word to use, discipline. As someone who has managed multiple news-oriented websites on topics about which I have tons to say, I happen to know that it's easy to go weeks without posting a thing. And that's not good for a blog, because you'll lose what may already be a fickle audience if you don't keep the content rolling regularly. That's not to say that blogging software won't work for part of a site designed for posting infrequent news or action items—it might fit that bill just fine. But if one entry is dated three weeks ago and the next one is dated a few months before that, as a reader you know you're not looking at much of a blog.

- **You've got tons to say.**   The other characteristic of a blog to bear in mind is that it is often more effective when the entries are short and to the point.

It is certainly true that you *can* have a blog featuring 5,000-word missives, scientific ramblings, or even lengthy fiction. But the key to a good blog is volume of stories and the immediacy of the postings. If you're posting each 5,000-word story weeks or months apart, a blog might not be the right approach. You could opt for a more traditional website, which doesn't lock you into the journaling format.

TIP   *If you are posting exceptionally long articles, then opting for regular HTML postings instead of a blog might give you more flexibility in dividing a longer story up into multiple pages (taking a cue from some of the online magazines that do this professionally). A longer story is easier to digest when it's in multiple chunks of pages, which may not be easy with typical weblog software.*

■ **You want pages individually designed.**   Although blog sites can have outrageously creative designs, overall it's much more difficult to create individual article pages that vary from one to another. Part of the point of using weblog-management software is to make the presentation of many pages of time-based content in a uniform way, thus enabling individual web authors to build sites that look a little more like daily news and opinion outlets. If your goal, instead, is to have a different layout, background color, or look-and-feel for each page that comprises your site, then you'll probably need to edit the documents by hand (or engineer a web-publishing tool that's so creative that it would hurt my head to contemplate it).

In other words, you've got one darn good reason to avoid a weblog: you don't want to be locked into the weblog format. If you need to update your site less frequently or more creatively, then you may well want to look for a different solution for your web-publishing needs.

Fair Use and Blogging

One popular reason to use a blog is to comment on the work of others, whether you've got something to say about new stories, other opinions, art, entertainment, or even other blog entries. Countless blogs out there have story after story that begins or ends (or middles) with either a quote from a story on some other web page, a hyperlink to someone else's work on the Web, or both.

I bring this up because the ease with which the Web enables us to copy other people's work for inclusion in a blog makes it important to consider the legal ramifications. (I'm not a lawyer, so considering legal ramifications with me is something you should only do to pass the time. This isn't legal advice, and if you need some, I recommend that you consult an attorney. My opinions on hockey and Old English literature aren't worth much, either.)

Here's the deal: pretty much any original work that an individual has created is considered immediately copyrighted. That includes items that you and I write and post on the Web, programming code that a smart person puts into a computer application or web-based script, or a photograph you take with your camera. They're all copyrighted immediately, although, clearly, *registering* that copyright makes it stronger.

U.S. copyright law also allows for something called "fair use," which enables people under certain limited circumstances to display or republish someone else's copyrighted work in order to comment upon it, use it for education, or to source the original material, as in a quote of one scientific text in another. The intended purpose of republishing someone's copyrighted work, the attribution, and the relative proportion of the included item are all factors often taken into consideration when determining whether a use is "fair use." There have been interesting cases, however, where publications have lost a fair-use battle—even when reviewing books or commenting on artwork.

The Web makes copying other people's work easier and perhaps a bit enticing, particularly when you're blogging quickly or casting around for something to say. But before going nuts with copy and paste commands, you should always consider whether it's appropriate to do so. In general, you should avoid copying entire news stories or opinion pieces from other websites. If you'd like to refer to something when discussing it, quote as *little* of the piece as you can, attribute the quote (say where you got it), and include a hyperlink to the original story, when possible.

Call to Action: Get Involved

By now you've got a good idea of what a weblog is and whether it's the right thing for you to pursue. The only thing I'll add at this point is a little encouragement: if you've got the inkling to blog, then try it. One of the most exciting things about the blogging concept (and the weblogging software that supports it) is that it encourages you to get participatory on the Web. The tools make it easier for you to say something if you've got something to say, and for others to respond to you.

With a blog, you can be angry, sad, action oriented, rabble-rousing, passive-aggressive, or just detached, witty, and ironic. Most of all, though, you can be a part of the Web as well as a part of something (weblogging) that may, in fact, be a movement. Maybe blogging does represent a new journalism, a new paradigm for democratic thought, an adventure into the future of collective memory, or the next great step in human discourse. Maybe it's a waste of time.

Whatever the case may be, blogs are good for creating community and stickiness. The tools are available, they're low cost, and they're fun to work with. Got something to say? Now is a great time to get a blog and tell us about it—whatever *it* is.

M	T	W	T	F	S		S	M	T	W	T	F	S		S	M	T	W	T	F	S		S	M	T	W	T	F	S
		1	2	3	4					1	2	3	4					1	2	3	4					1	2	3	4
6	7	8	9	10	11		5	6	7	8	9	10	11		5	6	7	8	9	10	11		5	6	7	8	9	10	11
13	14	15	16	17	18		12	13	14	15	16	17	18		12	13	14	15	16	17	18		12	13	14	15	16	17	18
20	21	22	23	24	25		19	20	21	22	23	24	25		19	20	21	22	23	24	25		19	20	21	22	23	24	25
27	28	29	30	31			26	27	28	29	30	31			26	27	28	29	30	31			26	27	28	29	30	31	

Chapter 2

Choosing Your Weblog Software and Server

In this chapter:

- The different types of weblog software
- Should you stick with a basic weblog?
- Can you use a hosted service?
- Consider a community-focused weblog
- What sort of web server or service do you need?
- Advice for shopping and finding an ISP

In Chapter 1, you got a sense of what a weblog is and, hopefully, you're excited about creating one. In this chapter I'd like to present an overview of the different approaches you can take to the technology behind your weblog. This chapter will help you decide which approach makes the most sense for you and how you should get started. In the chapters that follow, I'll introduce you to the progressively more advanced options you have for posting and managing your weblog.

Types of Weblog Software

As mentioned in Chapter 1, the defining visual quality of a weblog, or *blog*, is the fact that it generally looks and reads like a personal or public journal. So, the key features you're looking for, stylewise, are short entries formatted with date lines (or *timestamps*) that say when these messages were authored, in addition to the subject lines and the bodies of text. That, in an oversimplified nutshell, is what defines a basic weblog, at least in terms of how it looks in a web browser.

Of course, many factors differentiate weblogs beyond these basic items. What I just described can be created easily with a text editor such as Windows Notepad or Mac's SimpleText or TextEdit, or even more easily with a graphical web editor such as Adobe GoLive or Macromedia Dreamweaver and some web server space, even if it's just the free space you got with your Internet or America Online account. Where the complexity rears its head, however, is when you decide you want to *manage* those entries over a few months or years.

What most weblog-management software adds beyond the basic do-it-yourself text editor is a system for dynamically storing and retrieving the entries that you add to your site. All of them use a database of some kind to store each blog entry and then display them on the page as is appropriate.

Because the entries are in a database, more than one option is available for outputting those entries; for instance, the software can accept a search keyword from the user and, in response, display only the stories that match that keyword (see Figure 2-1).

Clearly it's these advanced features that make the blogging software enticing. However, to use blogging software, you'll need to sign up for at least an online service that offers hosted blogging software. However, for the fullest amount of control, you'll need to download and install a full server-side blogging software package. Each step is increasingly complex, however, so let's take a look at all the possibilities, including the brand names and relative advantages.

Basic Weblog

If the weblog concept is really nothing but a format for a website, then it certainly doesn't require special server software. If you know anything about HTML, you

Separating Content and Appearance

One reason it's so exciting to see more individuals and small organizations moving to content-management systems and blogging software is that it has increased the number of sites on the Web that separate their content from their *appearance* (that is, the markup that's used to decide the "look" of the page). In the past, web authors have generally embedded the style in their pages by actually typing in not just the text but "hard-coded" instructions for how that text should appear (font, size, and so on).

With content-management systems, the content and appearance are two separate things. The content is mostly text (with *some* markup, but usually for basic emphasis such as bold and italics) filed away in a database. The appearance is managed using templates—one template might be for the site's index page, another template might be for article pages, and a third used for the mid-level category pages, if that's how the site is designed.

This is interesting for two reasons. First, it's easier to change the look of your whole website. All you have to do is change one line in one HTML-based template and that change can be propagated throughout you're entire site. If you've spent any time updating hand-coded websites in the past, you know this is a big deal.

The second reason is that separating the content from the appearance makes that content available for more applications and under more circumstances. Because the content is, for the most part, stored as basic text, it can be repackaged with different templates and sent out in different formats—formats that are readable by different devices or different audience groups. Suddenly, your blog entries can be reformatted for personal digital assistants, cell phones, or browsers designed to assist those with disabilities. Ultimately, a Web that's friendlier to a variety of different devices and uses of the data is a more advanced and useful medium.

already know that putting items in the typical blogging format wouldn't be hard at all. In essence, you'd create a simple Web document and fill in each of the following elements:

- A date line or timestamp that shows the date and date of the entry
- A subject line or headline of some sort that tells the reader what the entry is about
- A body of text, consisting of a few sentence or paragraphs on whatever topic you're writing about
- A dividing line, using white space or a graphical image, that separates one entry from the next

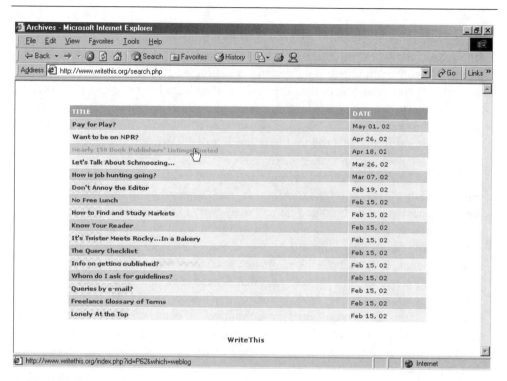

FIGURE 2-1   Here's an example of a search results page for a blog site that is displaying only entries that match a keyword.

This isn't rocket science. It's how the first weblogs were published, and it's how many of them are accomplished today.

In fact, this approach is similar to the way some index pages were maintained even in the early days of the Web. It used to be common to see a dated *changelog* on the index page of a website—that is, a log of updates that had been made to the site. Changelogs are common in software development, where they're used to quickly document the changes between versions (and even incremental releases). From software changelogs came website changelogs, where web authors document the changes to their sites so the return visitor knows quickly if there's anything worth looking at (see Figure 2-2).

Some of the earliest hyperlink-focused weblogs were sort of Internet changelogs—an attempt to provide an editorial function by documenting changes on a variety of websites that would be of interest to the user. These sorts of hyperlink-aggregating sites are still very popular, including round-up news headlines (http://www.thewebtoday.com/), professional interest areas (http://www.thescoop.org/), and hobby news (http://www.macsurfer.com/).

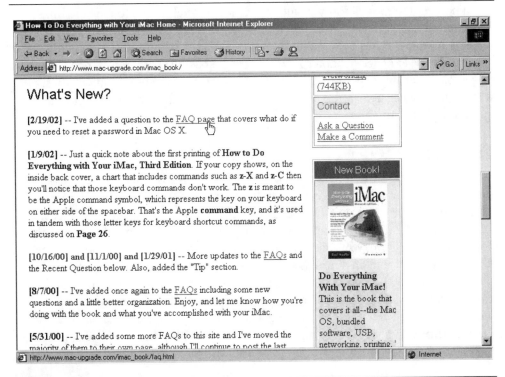

FIGURE 2-2   Here's a typical website changelog. I'm showing changes I've made to a site about one of my books.

Although aggregating links to interesting sites and stories on the Web is certainly one function of the weblog, it isn't the only one. Another way to look at a blog is as a personal or organizational changelog, of sorts, chronicling the updates to your knowledge, hobbies, opinions, or life in general, for everyone to see and comment on. Of course, a "personal changelog" is an overly geeky way of describing the concept of an online diary—essentially a timestamp-based log that's introspective in its nature. This personal approach is the reason many people have blogs—more to talk about themselves and their lives than to talk about other websites or stories posted elsewhere. Ultimately, however, they're quite similar to changelogs.

NOTE   *People disagree on the exact genesis of today's weblogs and whether they started with link-aggregating or with diary-style personal sites. I'll punt. See, for instance, http://www.diarist.net/guide/blogjournal.shtml for some interesting links and thoughts on the history from a journaling perspective. Also, go to Dave Winer's http://newhome.weblogs.com/historyOfWeblogs for a more "weblog as tour guide" perspective.*

Whatever the motivation for building a blog—whether it's to manage links, to comment on the news of the day, to post personal or organizational news, or to create a public diary or personal journal—it can be done with just a text editor and some web server space. Chapter 3 will cover the basic HTML you'll need to know to generate a changelog-style weblog. It won't have all the bells and whistles, but it's a quick way to get started and a great way to integrate a blog-style format into an existing website.

The Automated Weblog

So what's missing from the basic weblog-style site just outlined? Two things. The first thing that's missing is *flexibility*, both in terms of the ways you can retrieve articles and in the complexity of the articles themselves. For instance, the basic weblog would be difficult to archive into, say, entries for last month, the month before that, and so on. Not that it's impossible (again, we'll discuss how to do this in Chapter 3), but an automated weblog-management program would make it much easier. With a basic site, you have to cut and paste stories into an archive page or save the current page as an archive page, re-create a new index page for the current month, and build hyperlinks between the two. Then you have to update the hyperlinks on many other pages in your archive. With the database approach that weblog-management software takes, archive pages are usually created automatically.

Likewise, a basic weblog is much less ideal for managing longer articles. If the story is just a few paragraphs, that's fine, but if it's a few "pages," or screens, you'd probably rather let your users link to the whole story on its own web page. Adding that level of complexity to a hand-coded basic site simply makes things a bit more unwieldy—you'll need to update two pages, or more, instead of simply adding an article to the database.

Even more daunting is dividing your articles up into categories, with a special category page listing the relative stories. Now you're updating two index pages, cutting and pasting between then, while linking to a third article page for each article you decide to write. I promise you'll lose interest. With some of the automated solutions, even a category page can be created on the fly. When you click the category link, the category page is automatically culled from the database and the results are neatly displayed (see Figure 2-3).

NOTE *With some weblog-management software, the pages are prebuilt, so the category page isn't actually generated every time the user clicks a category but rather every time you republish your website. See the sidebar in this section for details.*

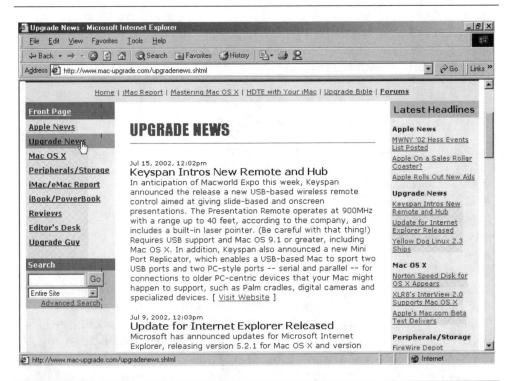

FIGURE 2-3   Another advantage of using content-management software is being able to manage categories dynamically.

The second element that a basic weblog is missing, in most cases, is a *commenting* feature. This feature is a tool that builds your weblog community by allowing others to participate. If your readers can comment on your entries—whether your site is a hyperlink-aggregating site, an opinion site, or a personal journal—they can become more intimately involved. Along with flexibility and convenience, the opportunity to offer a commenting feature is another reason, in my opinion, to look for an automated solution.

NOTE   *Some blog authors don't use commenting features but encourage readers to send e-mail messages that are then quoted and incorporated into posts if the blog author finds them interesting. ("Ronny247 had this to say about....") This a great way to add community to a simple site.*

So, let's assume you're sold on (or at least interested in) an automated weblog. If that's the case, we can move on to the *types* of solutions available: hosted weblogs or server-side weblogs. Hosted weblogs are those that pretty much let you sign up, pick a name, and start blogging. Server-side weblogs are those that require space from an ISP, a download, and an installation and implementation of the site. This may sound like a downer, but the tradeoff is that you tend to have much more power and freedom with a server-side site.

Published Pages vs. Dynamic Pages

Aside from the features and capabilities discussed so far, there's another concept that's worth delving into—published vs. dynamic pages. Different weblog tools take different approaches, and the results have their advantages and disadvantages.

Some weblog tools create *published* pages, meaning the tool is designed to output a finalized HTML document of a particular weblog page, which is then saved to the web server computer. (Some might call this a *static* page, but I'll reserve the term "static" to mean a page that's hard coded in HTML, such as a page that includes your bio or resume.) When a visitor requests that document, the web server simply sends the page over the Internet to the user, and the user's web browser downloads and displays the page, much as it does with any standard HTML document. If the weblog-management tool is designed to create published pages, it will generally ask you to click a "publish" button so that the changed HTML documents can be generated, and those changes will be evident to visitors on the Internet. This step is required because many of your website's files need to be rewritten each time you make a change in order to reflect that change. Although this approach works fine for smaller sites, it can become a problem once you have hundreds or thousands of entries, because this forced rebuild can take a good deal of time and can require a significant amount of a web server's processing power while the update takes place. This extended updating time, introduces opportunities for errors.

This is different from a *dynamic* web management tool, where articles are stored in a database that runs on the web server computer. When a visitor requests the index page of your blog, that request is noted by the web server, which begins to assemble the page by running the scripting code that's embedded within the index document and adding the appropriate headlines, articles, comments, and so on. The document is generated in real time and then sent to the user's computer, where the web browser can read it and display it, just as if it were a static document.

OK, so the two different approaches are established, but why are the differences significant? It's really a matter of the resources used vs. the flexibility of the presentation.

Creating that dynamic page requires a more capable web server, and serving each page tends to take up more of the server's time. Therefore, a dynamic page can take longer than a similar published page to appear in the user's web browser. In some cases, the dynamic approach can also make it more difficult for web-based search engines to catalog your site. (Many, such as Google.com, do a pretty good job with either approach.)

A dynamic page is more flexible, however, with the ability to change immediately when something in the database changes, such as when a new comment is added, a new article is created, or a time-based command is executed. Plus, it's the dynamic solutions that generally offer integrated search engines and community tools.

With a published page, you'll get less of this flexibility. Once the page is published (whether it's an article page or an index) it stays that way until it's republished. That makes it faster to retrieve and send to a visitor's web browser, but it makes it more difficult to incorporate dynamic components, such as comments and community tools. That said, there's one other advantage—published pages require a less sophisticated server, which is often cheaper, easier, and quicker to install and get running.

Should You Use a Hosted Weblog?

Hosted weblog applications offer some attractive pluses: They're cheap or free, you can usually get signed up within a few minutes, and most of them are very attractively designed, letting you focus on words instead of codes and configuration settings. On the downside, they're less "feature rich," some put advertisements on your page (unless you pay for the "privilege" of removing them), and you may not have as much room for growth. If your site becomes the biggest runaway success since televised professional wrestling, a hosted weblog may not give you the flexibility to add new gadgets, scripts, and features to augment and extend your online community.

With a hosted weblog, you'll generally update the site via your web browser, adding stories by typing in HTML form elements (text entry boxes, radio buttons, and check boxes within your web browser window). In some cases, though, you can use standalone applications on your desktop (actual programs written for your computer) to update the site. Hosted solutions generally don't offer community tools (for allowing comments on your articles), although there are exceptions.

Here's a list of hosted weblog-management solutions:

- **Blogger (www.blogger.com)**   Can be used to create a free site at BlogSpot.com or to update your own server space via the hosted tool. Blogger doesn't have a user-comment function (at least in the free version it doesn't) but it's incredible popularity means that a number of third-party tools are available for editing your site, and many higher-end solutions are designed to offer Blogger-friendly tools for importing entries from Blogger or updating entries using Blogger-compatible tools.

- **Radio Userland (radio.userland.com)**   A desktop-based tool that's used to update inexpensive paid space at radio.weblogs.com or space on your own site. You buy a subscription to Radio Userland (currently $39.95), which includes a license for the desktop application and server space for one year. You can opt not to use the server space. If you don't use the space, you can use the Radio Userland editor with your own ISP to post a weblog. Again, no user-comment feature is offered.

- **LiveJournal (www.livejournal.com)**   Similar to Blogger, but with some interesting access rules. You can either pay a small fee ($5 or so to start) to gain an access code or get a free code from someone who is already a member. Once you have access, you can update your site online or via a desktop application for most platforms. The sites created in LiveJournal tend to have a plain design, but comments from your readers are supported.

- **Manila (manila.userland.com)**   A pricey content-management solution that you can buy on your own. It's listed here because it has been implemented by some service providers, such as WebLogger (www.weblogger.com), so that you can use it as a high-end blogging solution. Manila offers clean-looking templates and supports user comments and discussion groups (see Figure 2-4). In fact, it's really an advanced content-management tool (much like the server-side tools described in the next section) but can be used relatively inexpensively, thus enabling your site to grow in complexity.

Should you go with a hosted solution? Clearly, hosted options range from the very lightweight to the rather sophisticated, but they all end up with one basic drawback—lack of control. If you use a hosted solution, you simply have less control over the final product than you do with a server-side weblog. Remember, too, that some of the hosted solutions lack support for photos, user comments, and similar technology, and those that do offer higher-end features tend to charge at least a nominal fee. You'll want to consider whether you can easily leave a hosted solution (can you back up your files and take them to another solution?) if you someday "outgrow" the blog and want to implement a different site.

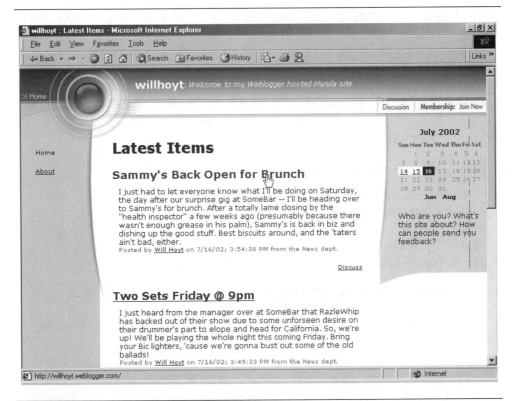

FIGURE 2-4   Manila-based sites offer clean lines and some high-end tools, plus the approach to editing pages is easy to understand, even for people with almost no web publishing experience.

NOTE

Having said all that, many people are using Blogger, Radio Userland, and these other popular hosted tools and, when that happens, people come up with ingenious solutions. You can add comment features, hosted discussion boards, and even image galleries to your hosted blog—it's just a bit more work and, in some cases, you rely on even more hosted services and companies. See Chapter 9 for details.

What you generally trade for the control and high-end features, however, is a freedom *from* the tedium of understanding the tools, which enables you to focus on what you have to say. Most hosted solutions offer some level of customization of the site, at least in appearance, so you can definitely make the site your own. And there's another advantage to a hosted solution: You can get started fast. If you pick a hosted solution and sign up, you could easily have a blog up and running in the amount of time it would take you to read the rest of this chapter.

Whatever the considerations, you may already have a sense that you're a hosted solution–type person, particularly if you're itching to get the site online without worrying about every little detail of how it'll look or how customizable it is. If that's the case, jump straight to Chapter 4, which takes a look at the different options in depth. If you're still unsure, keep reading to learn more about server-side solutions.

Prefer a Server-Side Weblog?

Most people who go with a server-side blog do so for a few basic reasons. See if any of these statements fit your circumstances:

- You already know a little something about web technology or you're interested in learning and customizing your site.

- You already have web server space that offers at least CGI scripting capabilities or you're in the market for some.

- You're integrating the blog into an existing site.

- You want control over your website, including the ability to add other technologies, dig deep into the HTML code, or learn how to tweak and extend the blog software.

- You're setting up an important site and you don't want to be at the whim of a free or cheap service.

If any of these statements ring true for you, you're a good candidate for a server-side weblog-management system. Getting these systems running is a little harder—especially the initial download and installation—but the reward is generally the richest tool available for an advanced website. The downside is that you're going to have to find and pay for Internet service, and you're going to have to do some of the maintenance work yourself. If someone finds a security hole in your site, or if you have trouble with the software and lose data, you'll probably have no one to call on except yourself.

If this all sounds interesting, though, here's a look at a few of the server-side options:

- **Greymatter (noahgrey.com/greysoft/)**   This is the highly regarded package that popularized the server-side approach, and it remains popular with many bloggers. Greymatter includes a comment engine, searching capabilities, image uploading, and more. It's not in active development, as the original author, Noah Grey, has moved on to other projects (he's a photographer). It does have an active community of supporters and users, however, and it's a great tool for a straight personal blog with comments.

- **Movable Type (www.movabletype.org)**   Movable Type (see Figure 2-5) has probably taken Greymatter's place as the most popular tool for personal and celebrity blogs on the Internet. It offers not just blogging and comments, but support for categories, multiple weblogs, multiple authors, images, thumbnail creation, and extras, such as a feature that enables users to mail an article to a friend. Movable Type is free for personal use but costs $150 for commercial use.

- **pMachine (www.pmachine.com)**   This is one of the newest tools for blogging and personal publishing, and it's also one of the most feature rich. Aside from the basics—article management, categories, comments, and support for multiple authors and multiple weblogs—pMachine offers many of the same advantages as Movable Type, including support for images, headline syndication (so other sites can publish your headlines), and the ability to view a "printable" version of an article (as is popular on new commercial sites). Beyond that, pMachine focuses on being software for community building, including tools to create a web-based forum, the ability for readers to become site members, an integrated mailing list manager (for receiving e-mail addresses and sending broadcast e-mail updates), and even an event/birthday calendar for keeping up with the current month's activities for your group. pMachine is offered in two versions: pMachine Free can be used by anyone without a licensing fee, but it offers fewer features. pMachine Pro currently costs $45 for noncommercial use and $125 for commercial sites, but offers support for multiple weblogs, a special discussion forum template, a community activity calendar, and other high-end features.

Certainly other server-side tools are available, although most are more sophisticated tools that fall outside the blogging space as I'm defining it. For instance, one popular variant includes the various server-side tools based on

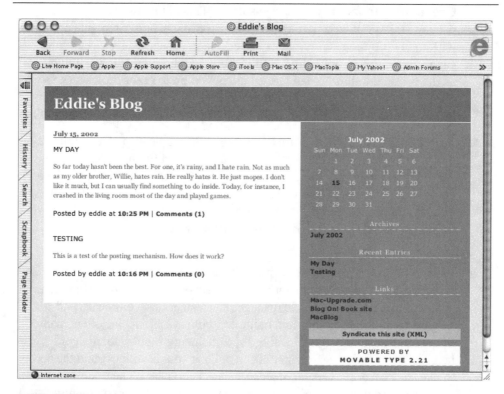

FIGURE 2-5   Movable Type is blogging software that borders on the power of expensive content-management systems used to manage commercial online web magazines and newspapers.

Slashcode (www.slashcode.com), the open-source web application that makes the incredibly popular SlashDot "News for Geeks" website (www.slashdot.org) look and work the way it does.

Similar-looking (and similarly complex) sites can be created and managed using PostNuke (www.postnuke.com), PHPNuke (www.phpnuke.org), or GeekLog (geeklog.sourceforge.net). All these systems—and the many like them—are wonderful for managing information or personal websites in a manner that's very similar to blogging—the only major difference, in my opinion, is that these packages are a bit more difficult to install and work with than the others covered in this book because they target geekier types who like to tinker and want, primarily, a SlashDot-like collaborative news and discussion site. The open-source approach is laudable, and some of the software is outstanding, but most of these solutions simply aren't as personal and user-friendly as the blogging packages I'll focus on.

> TIP
>
> *User-friendliness isn't just important for us as web authors and blog managers—it's important for users as well. One of the nice things about most of the blogging software I'm discussing in this book is that it makes good, clean interface design easy to accomplish. The cleaner and friendlier your blog's interface is, the more likely you are to have people interested in the things you have to write and say. (Of course, if you're building a hard-core computer gaming site, then all bets are off, because the more difficult it is to navigate, the better. You might even experiment with black-on-black text and background, just to be cool.) We'll discuss design considerations in Chapter 8.*

Getting a Web Server for Your Weblog

If you've decided to go with a server-side option, you'll need to get some web server space that you can use with the software. In order to be compatible with one of the server-side solutions, you'll need to make sure the server software complies with some basic requirements. In this section, we'll look at these requirements and what they mean, and we'll consider some basic guidelines you can follow in choosing a good ISP, IPP, or hosting company.

Aside from the server-side options discussed so far, some of the hosted solutions—in particular Blogger and Radio Userland, as well as some third-party blog editors—can be used to update websites hosted by other companies. In fact, both Blogger and Radio Userland can be used with even a basic hosting account elsewhere, because they don't require any special programming or scripting support. Instead, the blogging pages are created within the tool and posted as static pages, not dynamic pages. If you have free space provided by your Internet Service Provider (the one you use for a connection to the Internet) or via some other outlet, you may be able to use it to create a basic published blog. (More on this in Chapter 4.)

Weblog Server Jargon and Definitions

Depending on your level of interest and experience with the Internet, you may be achingly familiar with the terminology or have only a passing relationship with some of it. In any case, I've compiled some important terms here so that you can breeze through them before you begin hunting down the correct service provider for your needs:

- **Web server computer**   This is the computer that runs the software that responds to requests from a visitor's web browser (such as Internet Explorer or Netscape) by sending an HTML document and associated images or other files to the user's computer so that they can be viewed in the web browser. Popular web server applications include Apache, which runs on most Unix and Linux platforms (as well as on Microsoft Windows), Microsoft IIS, which runs on Windows-based servers, and WebStar, which runs on classic Mac OS servers. (Mac OS X features Apache.)

■ **Internet Service Provider (ISP)**   The ISP is the company you use to get access to the Internet, either via a modem (phone line) connection or some form of a broadband connection, whether that's a cable modem, DSL (Digital Subscriber Line) connection, or some form of fixed access to the Internet. In many cases, your ISP will offer you a limited amount of web server space that might be useful for a basic blog.

■ **Internet Presence Provider or hosting company**   If you already have access to the Internet, but your ISP doesn't offer acceptable free web server space, you may want to look into another company that can. These companies don't necessarily offer access to the Internet; instead, they offer you access to their web server computer, where you can set up shop, store your files, upload and configure web applications, and, ultimately, direct your visitors so that they can view your site. In this case, your web server computer is located at the hosting company but is accessible via the Internet (which is how you'll upload files and configure certain settings).

■ **Web hosting account**   This is the type of service you're generally looking for from an IPP, where you get a certain amount of space on one of the IPP's web server computers. Usually you're looking for a *shared* hosting account, where your website is one among many served by a single web server computer (as opposed to a *co-located* or *dedicated* account, where you get your own server computer in the IPP's data center). In most cases, personal and small organizational sites don't require a dedicated web server to handle their traffic requirements. (Once you do have those high-end requirements, no doubt your hosting company will discuss the options with you.)

■ **HTML documents**   Web documents—those that are sent over the Internet and displayed in web browser applications—are written in the Hypertext Markup Language (or, increasingly, XHTML, which is simply the latest version of HTML).

■ **Common Gateway Interface (CGI)**   The Common Gateway Interface provides one way that scripts and applications can be made to interface with HTML documents. In order for any Perl-based server-side solution to work (such as Greymatter or Movable Type), you'll need a web-hosting account that gives you full access to CGI scripting capabilities. Some IPPs offer the ability to run CGI scripts in any directory within your hierarchy; others require that these scripts be stored in a special CGI directory (often called cgi-bin). In my experience, the only web hosts that don't allow some CGI access are some free hosting services.

- **Perl**   Perl is a scripting language popularly used to create CGI scripts. Perl, as a language, is well suited for manipulating text, and most web servers have the Perl interpreter included, so it's a natural solution for dynamic websites. If your weblog software is written in Perl, your web server will need to be running a compatible Perl interpreter. Note that this is not required in other situations, such as with pMachine, which uses the PHP language. (You may, however, still find Perl useful for other add-ons and scripts, as discussed in Chapter 9. Any server that supports PHP most likely offers Perl.)

- **Server-side includes (SSIs)**   SSIs are special commands that can be used in mostly static HTML documents to add dynamic content—anything from simply adding a current date or time to adding the results of a CGI script. Some weblog solutions may require (or allow) the use of SSIs, and many add-ons for websites (such as page counters and special image handlers) also make use of SSIs.

- **PHP Hypertext Processor**   PHP (yes, it's a cute self-referential abbreviation) provides another method for scripting web applications— one created specifically for the web. Unlike Perl, PHP is an "embedded" scripting language, meaning the PHP commands can be written directly into web pages. When a PHP-enabled web document is requested, the web server runs the scripting codes in that document, substitutes the HTML results for those codes, and then sends the dynamically created page to the receiver's computer, where it can be viewed by the user's web browser.

- **MySQL**   MySQL, a web server–based database solution, is popular partly because it's based on IBM's SQL (Structured Query Language) and partly because it's a royalty-free open source implementation. Using this standardized method for accessing database entries appeals to programmers of weblog-management applications, particularly those using PHP. (PHP and MySQL work well together and tend to create responsive database-based sites.) Fortunately, as end users we don't need to know much of anything about MySQL, because the weblog software should take care of the details. You just need to make sure your hosting service includes the ability to create one or more MySQL databases.

Why are these terms significant? You need to know them because you need to know whether your chosen server-side scripting solution requires one or more of them. Some, such as Greymatter, require only that your hosting service allow you to work with Perl CGI scripts, a capability that is fairly common, although some free and inexpensive IPPs don't allow you to use your own CGI scripts. Moveable Type can be run with simple CGI access (and some extension you may need to download and install), but it can also make use of a MySQL database. pMachine requires both PHP and MySQL, so your IPP will need to offer those services as part of your hosting account package. Table 2-1 shows the basic requirements for the different service applications discussed in this book.

> TIP
>
> *For the most part, you're better off using a Unix-based (Linux, BSD, Solaris, SGI, or Mac OS X) as opposed to a Microsoft Windows-based server for weblog software. (Some hosting companies will offer you a choice; I suggest you choose Unix or Linux.) Although any of these server-side weblog-management solutions should run on a Windows server, these packages are generally developed for and better tested in Unix or Linux, and you'll generally have fewer hoops to jump through and problems to work around on a Unix-based server.*

Choosing a Good IPP or Hosting Service

You have an untold number of choices when it comes to a web hosting company, meaning there are certainly a great number of good ones you can use for your weblog. At the same time, there are some not-so-good ones. Therefore, you need a few quick rules to help you avoid the bad ones and find a good one. Keep in mind that you'll need to consider the requirements of the software and any other

Software	Requires Perl?	Requires CGI?	Requires PHP?	Requires MySQL?
Greymatter	Yes, Perl 5	Yes, in the cgi-bin folder	No	No
Movable Type	Yes, Perl 5 (some additional Perl modules are required, some optional)	Yes, either in the cgi-bin folder or in a user-defined folder	No	Optional
pMachine	No	No	Yes	Yes

TABLE 2-1 Server Requirements for Server-Based Blogging Software

personal needs you have, such as a particular billing approach. Here's my list of thoughts on finding a good provider:

- **Choose good customer service**.   In the past, I've chosen inexpensive web-hosting companies that don't post support phone numbers on the theory that I'm a computer expert and therefore don't need their help. I've found, instead, that the majority of IPPs that don't offer phone-based technical support also don't offer phone-based billing support or phone-based explanations as to why their servers have been down for three days running. Go with someone who posts a phone number—preferably a toll-free number—and test it to make sure it and their other customer service options actually work.

- **Look for signs of life**.   I like to visit other sites that are currently using a hosting service that I'm considering, and I like to test those sites on different days at different times. The best way to choose a good service is to get a recommendation from someone using the same blogging software—and with about the same server load (number of visitors and pages viewed)— that you're going to use.

- **Make sure the numbers are up-to-date**.   When you're choosing a weblogging package, check for the latest requirements for that blogging application (in the respective chapter in this book as well as on the software's website) and make sure the IPP supports those version numbers. Although many national IPPs keep up with the latest installations, some local and smaller providers—and particularly ISPs those that focus on selling Internet access instead of web hosting accounts—don't keep up with the latest stuff.

- **Don't get overcharged for extras**.   On Unix-based hosting accounts, it's relatively trivial to allow a user to run PHP scripts and create MySQL databases. Therefore, don't pay a great deal of money per script or per database, unless you're asking for quite a bit of help from the IPP. Of course, they should have limits (don't trust the cheapest IPP that says you can have all the server space you need, either), but avoid a nickel-and-dime provider. Likewise, e-mail accounts, e-mail forwarding, web-based e-mail access, and web-based control panels are all par for the course, not extras, so look for good package prices that include them.

- **Consider a company that focuses on blogging**.   Although they may not offer the cheapest service or the best feature set, a company that focuses on blogging customers should know quite a bit about the tools and how to support them, as well as know some low-priced plans for low-traffic personal sites. For instance, Logjamming.com and Cornerhost.com are two IPPs I've come across that seem to want to help bloggers get their server-side tools up and running. (I haven't worked with them, so I can't guarantee either service.)

■ **Think local**.   If you want the best service and are very interested in phone support, look for a sophisticated local company, particularly one that is interested in helping you with your blog and that shows signs of professional management. Although local companies often can't compete on price, the better ones make up for it by giving the best service possible for their premium. Plus, if things turn ugly, it's much easier to talk personally with or get refunds from a local company with a known address.

■ **Check for a backup strategy**.   Some IPPs back up their servers more regularly than others; some don't back up certain types of data or files, such as MySQL databases. For a personal site, you might be able to accomplish the backing up yourself, or you might not be overly concerned about it. For an organization's site, however, backups may be critical, so ask prospective IPPs about their backup policies and shop for one that offers an effective backup strategy.

With these tips, hopefully you can find a good service provider. For a typical personal site, you may be able to get away with paying $10 or less per month; if you anticipate tens of thousands of page views, you may look for more robust service at $20 or so per month. If you get hundreds of thousands of page views, you may need to look for serious service, which generally costs $35 to $50 a month or more, depending on your traffic level. If you have millions of page views per month, you should buy a server, hire a CTO, and do all of your blog updates from a laptop by the pool. You're famous.

While you're still in the early stages of getting to know your IPP, I recommend that you stay away from long-term contracts and stick with monthly billing, if possible, just so that you can get out of the contract if desired. (I know that some of those annual deals can seem too good to pass up, but I wouldn't sign one unless I had a few personal recommendations for the IPP and felt strongly that they were going to be in business and offer quality customer service.) And, as one final tip, if you'd like your own domain name (www.yourdomainname.com) for your site, you don't need to register it through the IPP (you can if you want, but make sure it's a good price). Instead, you can use any registrar to get your domain name; then you can associate it with your website when you sign up with the IPP. For inexpensive registrars, you have a number of options, including GoDaddy.com, Domainmonger.com, and Namezero.com. The well-known commodities include Register.com and VeriSign (www.netsol.com).

More...

In this chapter you learned the difference between building a basic weblog and using a blogging application of some sort, whether it's a hosted solution or a server-side solution you install and manage yourself. In Chapter 3, you'll read about building your own basic weblog from scratch using a text editor and some web server space. That chapter is also a quick primer on HTML and some other web technologies, so it's a handy chapter to skim, even if you plan to use a special blogging service or server application.

2

M	T	W	T	F	S		S	M	T	W	T	F	S		S	M	T	W	T	F	S		S	M	T	W	T	F	S
			1	2	3	4				1	2	3	4				1	2	3	4				1	2	3	4
6	7	8	9	10	11		5	6	7	8	9	10	11		5	6	7	8	9	10	11		5	6	7	8	9	10	11
13	14	15	16	17	18		12	13	14	15	16	17	18		12	13	14	15	16	17	18		12	13	14	15	16	17	18
20	21	22	23	24	25		19	20	21	22	23	24	25		19	20	21	22	23	24	25		19	20	21	22	23	24	25
27	28	29	30	31			26	27	28	29	30	31			26	27	28	29	30	31			26	27	28	29	30	31	

Part II

Using Your Weblog

Chapter 3 The Simple Blog
Chapter 4 Using a Hosted Weblog
Chapter 5 Setting Up and Using Greymatter
Chapter 6 Setting Up and Using Movable Type
Chapter 7 Setting Up and Using pMachine

T	W	T	F	S		S	M	T	W	T	F	S		S	M	T	W	T	F	S		S	M	T	W	T	F	S
	1	2	3	4				1	2	3	4					1	2	3	4					1	2	3	4
7	8	9	10	11		5	6	7	8	9	10	11		5	6	7	8	9	10	11		5	6	7	8	9	10	11
14	15	16	17	18		12	13	14	15	16	17	18		12	13	14	15	16	17	18		12	13	14	15	16	17	18
21	22	23	24	25		19	20	21	22	23	24	25		19	20	21	22	23	24	25		19	20	21	22	23	24	25
28	29	30	31			26	27	28	29	30	31			26	27	28	29	30	31			26	27	28	29	30	31	

Chapter 3

The Simple Blog

In this chapter:

- ■ Requirements for the homemade blog
- ■ Building a basic page
- ■ Dealing with FTP
- ■ Adding to your blog
- ■ Archiving past posts
- ■ Ideas for extending the site

A s has been discussed in earlier chapters, at least part of what makes a web*site* a web*log* is simply the format. The idea is to keep a website—or at least the index page of a website—up-to-date and timely with little tidbits added frequently. If they're small vignettes about you're life, great. If they're changelog-like entries about your business or organization, that's fabulous.

And if you're not dying to install a bunch of software or sign up for a hosted blog service, you can start out simple, building your own blog with just a tiny bit of knowledge of HTML. You'll also need some web server space (unless you're going to save this website on your hard drive so only you can admire your handiwork), but web server space is usually pretty easy to come by. There are a few more steps, too, but we'll cover them all in this chapter. By the end of it, a mere 20 pages or so from now, you'll have your own homespun blog, ready to present to the world.

Not interested in the "simple" blog? You might skim this chapter anyway, because it's also a quick primer on HTML—the language of web publishing—in disguise. Although most blogging tools can be used in such a way that HTML coding isn't necessary on a daily basis, it's still something that's handy to know, particularly for customizing your weblog. So, if you're not familiar with HTML but want to use a weblog-management tool, page through this chapter quickly and then move on to Chapter 4 or one of the later chapters that focuses on the particular tool you want to use.

Requirements for the Simple Blog

Like any good recipe, we need to start with the ingredients. In order to create a simple HTML-based blog, you're going to need a few items:

- ■ **A text editor** This can easily be the text editor that came with your computer, whether that's Notepad or WordPad in Microsoft Windows, SimpleText or TextEdit in the Mac OS, or one of any number of options available to Unix/Linux users. The key is to make sure the editor saves your files as plain text or ASCII text, not as a Rich Text Format file, a Microsoft Word document, or something similar. (If you're serious about this HTML-based approach to blogging, you should shop around for a good programming- or web-focused text editor because they can offer great features, such as color-coding text and integrating FTP. Many different types of editors are available for downloading on the Web.)

NOTE   *If you use WordPad in Windows or TextEdit in Mac OS X, you need to make sure you save files in Text-Only format (as opposed to Microsoft Word or Rich Text Format) via the Save dialog box.*

■ **An FTP application**   Again, this may be built in to your operating system, particularly if you have an operating system that has a command line or terminal application, such as Microsoft Windows, Mac OS X, or Unix/Linux. If you don't, or if you prefer a graphical FTP program (one designed to run in your computer's windowing environment like a standard Windows or Mac application), you can generally get one as downloadable shareware or even as a freeware application.

TIP   *Not sure where to get shareware? Try http://www.download.com/ and search for keyword "FTP." If you're a go-with-the-crowd type then WS_FTP (http://www.ipswitch.com/), FTP Voyager (http://www.ftpvoyager.com/), and FTP Explorer (http://www.ftpx.com/) are popular choices for Windows, while Fetch (http://www.fetchsoftworks.com/), Transmit (http://www.panic.com), and Interarchy (http://www.stairways.com/) are favorites on the Mac.*

■ **Web server space**   For a simple blog, this can be any sort of web server option that allows you to upload pages via FTP (in other words, the only type not included is a service that requires you to use its own browser-based tools for updating the page). Also, you don't actually need a web server at all if you simply want to test your blog or place it on your in-house network server (if you or your organization has one). But if you have Internet access through an ISP, there's a decent chance you have some free server space you can use for your blog.

NOTE   *You'll also need to know a thing or two about your web server space, although it's all standard info that your ISP should tell you about. You need to know your FTP server address, your username and password for FTP, and the URL for viewing your website online. Print them out, write them down, or do whatever you need to do to keep them handy while you're building your blog.*

That's it! You might consider getting a special HTML-editing application, such as Adobe GoLive or Macromedia Dreamweaver, although this chapter will show you how to edit raw HTML code with the need for a graphical editor. Also, you might want more than the basic web server space offered by your ISP if you intend to do a great deal of blogging, or if you want to be able to use CGI scripts or something similar to add extras to your site, such as page counters (which count how often a page is accessed), online polls, guest books, discussion forums, and so on. More on that kind of stuff in Chapter 9.

Build a Basic Weblog Page

If you're ready to get started, let's do it. The plan is to create, edit, and save your blog's index page—the main page where you'll do your updating. What you'll be doing is creating an HTML document using the text editor application. Before we get there, though, let's quickly define an HTML document. An *HTML document* is a plain-text computer file that includes three things: text to appear on the page, instructions for how a browser should render that text, and other instructions for adding multimedia stuff such as images and animations.

That's pretty much it. The text part is what you want to say on your page, and the instructions are added in the form of *elements*. In HTML, elements are comprised of either one or two *tags*. Elements with one tag are called *empty elements* or *empty tags*. These generally do something special, such as draw a line on the page or add an image to the page from an image file. Elements with two tags are called *containers* because they are designed to contain text and do something to it.

For example, to create a paragraph of text on the page, you can use the <p> and </p> tags, which make up the paragraph element. The paragraph element is a container. It's used to surround a group of words or sentences you want to display as a paragraph in the reader's browser. By contrast, you use a single tag to create a horizontal line on the page; you simply add the <hr /> element, which is the horizontal rule element. It's an empty tag because it isn't designed to do anything to text. It just adds a line.

Create the Page

Open your text editor and enter the following, exactly as shown, in a new, blank text document:

```
<!DOCTYPE html PUBLIC "-//W3C//DTD XHTML 1.0 Transitional//EN"
"http://www.w3.org/TR/xhtml1/DTD/xhtml1-transitional.dtd">
<html>
<head>
<title>Welcome to my Blog</title>
</head>
```

```
<body>
<h1>My Weblog</h1>
<p>Welcome to my weblog. I hope you enjoy your stay.</p>
<hr />
</body>
</html>
```

> **NOTE**
>
> *If you're familiar with HTML but the preceding looks a little odd, that might be because it adheres to some XHTML-based conventions. It's important, going forward, that web documents include a Document Type Definition before the opening <html> tag, as required under the XML/XHTML standards. Also, you may find the lowercase tags and the trailing slash in some of the elements odd (for example <hr />, which used to be just <HR> in the past). In XHTML, both are necessary to make HTML conform with the XML standard, which is all XHTML really is. See Appendix A for links to HTML/XHTML references on the Web.*

When you've got all that entered, you should save the document. Choose File | Save in your text editor and then name the file index.html.

> **TIP**
>
> *In this example, you can customize the text in the <title>, <h1>, and <p> sections. The <title> element is used for the text that will appear in the title bar of the user's web browser; the other text is simply optional introductory text for your weblog, which you can edit to your tastes or just delete.*

You may want to create a new folder in which to place this document, particularly if you intend to have more than one page on your website and/or you plan to have images as part of your blog.

You'll want to maintain the some folder or directory structure on your hard disk that you'll be using for your blog. This will make more sense when we start dealing with images and hyperlinks in a moment.

Now, with the file saved, you can add your first entry. To do that, type the entry between the <body> and </body> tags. The body element defines the portion of the document that will be displayed in your reader's web browser window. Notice that it's a container. It contains all the elements that will appear in the browser window, whereas the <head> element contains items that don't appear in the browser window. For instance, the <head> element contains the <title> container, which surrounds the text that will display not in the browser window area, but in the title bar of most web browsers.

Add Your First Entry

What you type in the body container will look something like this:

```
<h2>June 4th</h2>

<p>Today has been a pretty good day so far; no complaints. For one
thing, I got good news on the home front -- it looks like the
mortgage is going to go through and we're one step closer to being
first-time home owners. Yea! It's been a long time coming, and I
never thought we'd get our little house in the country, but it may
be working out after all. Had a great lunch, too -- I think I'll be
sticking with this diet. I'm surprised that I feel so full and
energetic at the same time. Too cool!</p>
<hr />
```

Figure 3-1 shows you what this listing looks like in a text editor as it's being typed.

Let's take a quick look at what we're doing here. To begin, here's the heading for the entry:

```
<h2>June 4th</h2>
```

In this case, I've simply titled the entry for the current date, given that blogs are pretty date-centric. You could put anything here you want, though, in addition to or instead of the date. The <h2> container is the Heading 2 container. Heading

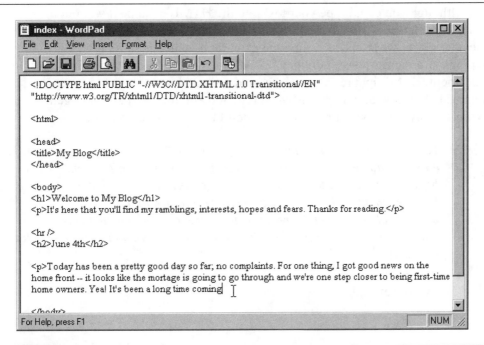

FIGURE 3-1   Here's our simple blog being typed into a text editor.

containers range from Heading 1 all the way through Heading 6; <h1> is the biggest text and <h6> is the smallest. I've chosen <h2> here because of the <h1> used previously to introduce the entire blog. Although it isn't mandatory, a well-formed HTML document uses the <h1>, <h2> … elements in descending order as a sort of outline for the web document. (And, as with an outline, you can have multiple <h2> elements under an <h1> element—it's that type of organizational system.)

Next up:

```
<p> Today has been a pretty good day….</p>
```

In this portion of the entry, I'm adding a paragraph of text. As a rule, any text that is to appear on the page in paragraph form should be inside a <p> container, unless it's inside a different paragraph-level container. (For instance, HTML has a special <div> container that can be used to create paragraph-style "divisions" in your pages, but with additional formatting parameters. More on that in Chapter 8.)

Although you could type your text into the HTML document without the paragraph element—and that text would still appear on the page—the paragraph element places white space around the paragraph, which is something that simply typing extra returns doesn't do in an HTML document. Unlike a word processing document, HTML ignores extra spaces and returns. Even if you add spaces and returns between your paragraphs when typing them, they will all run together when displayed in a web browser if you don't use the paragraph element.

NOTE   *Yes, HTML ignores it when you simply type* RETURN *or* ENTER, *even at the end of a line of text. But using the closing </p> tag isn't the only way to begin a new line of text in your web page. The <br /> element is the line break element and can be used to create a return in the text without using the <p> element, which creates extra space around the elements it encloses. Use <br /> at any point in your text where you'd like a new line to start.*

Finally, we have this:

```
<hr />
```

This empty element adds a horizontal line to the document. Figure 3-2 shows what this looks like in a web browser.

Upload and Test Your Page

If you've finished the basic page just outlined, you can test it in one of two ways. The easy way is to choose File | Open File (or a similar command) in your web browser and then locate the file in the Open dialog box that appears. Once you've found it, click Open. The page should appear in your web browser, where you can give it a good going over.

The other option is to upload the page to your web server and view it over the Internet. In fact, you'll need to do that anyway, at some point, before others will be able to see it.

To upload a file, launch your FTP application. Now, you'll enter the address of the FTP server where you're supposed to send your web document. If you don't know this, you may need to ask your ISP or IPP. If you signed up for web server space specifically for this blog, you probably got all the info from your IPP when you signed up. If your web server space is part of your Internet access account, you may have gotten the info from the ISP back when you signed up for service.

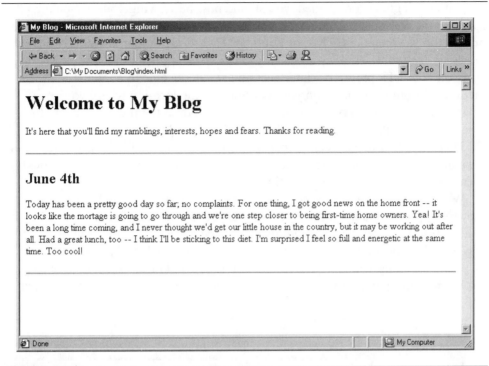

Here's how the blog looks when viewed in a web browser.

You may need to head to the ISP's website to hunt around for the instructions. You'll also need to know your FTP account and password.

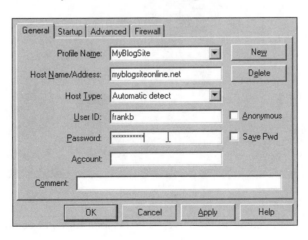

With the login accomplished, you should now be viewing your personal FTP space on the web server computer. In many cases, you'll see a few different folders or directories. Open the HTML or Public_HTML directory, or a similarly named directory, by double-clicking it (usually) in the FTP application. Now, depending again on your FTP program's interface, you should be able to copy the file index.html from its location on your hard disk to the location where you've navigated on the web server. If you can't drag and drop the file from one to the other, look for a Put command, as shown in Figure 3-3.

That's it. The file has been uploaded to the server. (This file is tiny in terms of the amount of disk space it requires, so it should travel to the server very quickly, even over a dial-up modem connection.)

With the file on the web server, you're ready to view it. Launch your web browser application and, in the Address entry box, enter the URL associated with your web server space. Because you've uploaded a file named index.html, your page should appear automatically when you enter the URL and press ENTER or RETURN, assuming your Internet connection is active. For instance, if your URL is http://www.myisp.net/~myname/, your blog page should appear when you enter

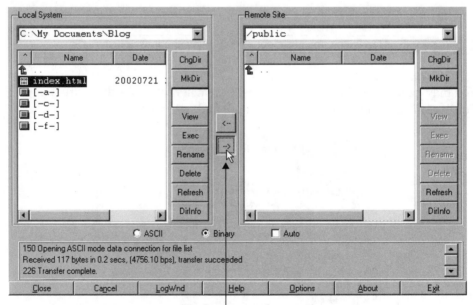

The Put command

FIGURE 3-3   To copy items to the server via FTP, look for a Put command or arrow buttons.

that address in your web browser. If, however, you named the page something other than index.html (such as weblog.html, although it could be pretty much *anything*.html), you'll need to enter that as part of the full address. Here's an example:

```
http://www.myisp.net/~rhondal/weblog.html
```

If you have a registered domain name as part of your hosting service, then you should be able to access your blog using an URL more like http://www.myblogname.com/ or http://www.myblogname.com/weblog.html if you've named the file weblog.html.

Did the page appear? If not, you might have put it in the wrong place on your web server computer via FTP, you might not have actually transferred it, or you might have given it a slightly different name. Check these things and try again. If the page does appear in the window, check it and make sure it looks like the one pictured in Figure 3-2. If not, you might not have typed it exactly the same way. (Of course, there's nothing wrong with changing the content of the example, but all the HTML elements should be in place if you're following this example.) When odd things happen in a web page that you're creating, the first thing to look for is a missing closing tag or any tag that's entered incorrectly. Check them carefully against the examples. Once you find the error, resave the page, send it again via FTP over the Internet to your server, and reload it in your web browser.

Add New Entries, Images, and Hyperlinks to Your Blog

If you're up and running with your weblog, perhaps you've already tasted the sweet nectar of success. At the very least, you might want to get a friend or family member to view your page over the Internet, if only so that you have a witness, for all posterity, to your web publishing venture. Heck, it's fun—I call people every time I put up a new site. (I used to call every time I put up a new entry, but people get annoyed with that, surprisingly.)

Add an Entry

The next step, most likely, is to add another entry or two to your blog. That's easily accomplished. All you need to do is edit, in your text editor, the HTML document you used originally, adding another identical entry. In fact, you might want to highlight and copy the first entry and then paste it again above that entry on the page (see Figure 3-4). Now, edit the new entry by changing the date (if appropriate) and replacing the text with an entry that reflects your latest thoughts.

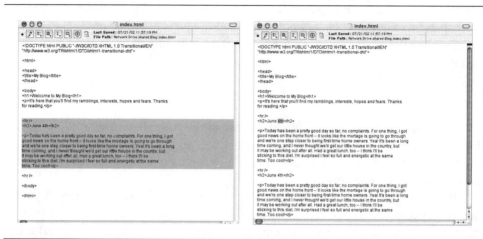

FIGURE 3-4   On the left, copying the originally entry; on the right, pasting it above and preparing to edit it.

Basic Formatting

As you've no doubt seen, a web page can have bold text, italicized text, and other basic emphasis within the text itself. Even if you haven't done any web editing or publishing in the past, you may have already guessed how to change the style of text in your blog entries—by using container elements. For instance, the following sentence uses <b> for bold, <i> for italics, and <tt> for teletype (monospaced font) text, and others elements to create emphasis of different kinds:

```
<p>If there's <i>anything</i> that makes me crazy it's getting a
<b>phone recording</b> from a solicitor telling me <tt>You've just
won...</tt> and then asking <strong>me</strong> to call
<em>them</em> back.</p>
```

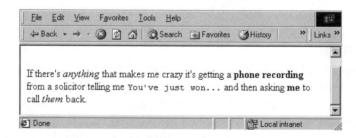

I actually snuck some other elements in there, but for a reason. You'll notice that <strong> and <em> are rendered, in the preceding illustration, as bold and italics, respectively. These elements, which are called *phrase* elements, are actually special elements that you're encouraged to use, because they can be rendered in different types of browsers in different ways. If, for instance, a web browser that's designed to speak the text of web pages (for the visually impaired) encounters an <i> tag, it may have no choice but to ignore that emphasis, because italics is a very specific *visual* style. If, however, the browser encountered the <em> (emphasis) tag, it might be able to communicate that emphasis aurally with the speech processor. The same is true of other *enabled* browsers (Braille or large-text browsers) as well as browsers built in to mobile phones and personal digital assistants (such as a Palm handheld computer) that might not be able to show italics but can communicate emphasis by changing the color or highlighting the text in question.

Many different HTML elements are used to emphasize and alter text (see http://www.w3.org/TR/1998/REC-html40-19980424/struct/text.html for an official list). Table 3-1 shows just a few of them. Note that many of these elements will look similar in a web browser window—for the most part they'll be italic, bold, or monospaced. However, the more specific you are in selecting your emphasis elements, the more portable and accessible your web page will be for different computing (or electronic device) platforms and for special-needs purposes. (We'll talk more about designing for accessibility in Chapter 10.)

Element	What It Does
<b> ,</b>	Makes the text bold
<i>, </i>	Makes the text italic
<u>, </u>	Underlines the text
<tt>, </tt>	Places the text in teletype or monospaced font
<em>, </em>	Adds emphasis (often using italics)
<strong>, </strong>	Adds strong emphasis (often using bold)
<dfn>, </dfn>	Indicates a definition
<code>, </code>	Indicates snippet of programming code
<samp>, </samp>	Indicates a sample of computer output
<cite>, </cite>	Indicates a citation (for instance, you could use this container for a reference to a book or other resource)

TABLE 3-1   A Few Text Markup Elements You Can Use in Your Blog

Add Hyperlinks

Neglected thus far is one of the primary purposes of a weblog—to link to things. You build links using a special container element called the *anchor* element. When combined with a full URL (including an appropriate Internet *protocol*), the anchor element can be used to build links to all sorts of things on the Internet. Let's start with an example:

```
<p>If you're really interested in more news, check out
<a href="http://www.salon.com/">Salon</a> for more coverage
and headlines.</p>
```

The anchor element (<a>, </a>) is special in that it accepts an attribute, href, within the opening tag. The href attribute is used to accept the URL to the item to which you would like to link. The URL that you use with the href attribute will often be a website, as in the preceding example, or it might be the direct address of a particular web page, as shown here:

```
<p>Can you believe what people are saying about our candidate? See
this <a href="http://www.sundaytribshopper.com/jan/02/govback.html">
story</a> in the <i>Sunday Tribune-Shopper</i>.
It's outrageous!</p>
```

NOTE   *Not sure what a URL is? It's a Uniform Resource Locator, which we'll define as "a resource's unique address on the Internet." Web pages have URLs that begin with the protocol http://. Other protocols can be used to access other resources, as discussed in this section.*

The href attribute can accept other sorts of URLs as well. For instance, you can use a relative URL if you're linking to an item that's in the same directory as the page you're creating. For instance, if you store a page called archives.html in the same directory as the weblog page you're editing, you can link to it as follows:

```
Visit our <a href="archives.html">Archives page</a> for
earlier stories.
```

Likewise, URLs can be used to access other sorts of Internet resources. For instance, if you'd like to allow your users to send you an e-mail message, you could use a mailto: protocol to create a link that should open a new message in the user's e-mail application (assuming the user has his web browser configured correctly). Here's an example:

```
Got something to say? <a href="mailto:ryan@mygreatblog.org">Send
me e-mail</a> anytime!
```

Finally, if you're wondering what all these lines and hyperlinks look like, you can see in Figure 3-5 that the text inside the anchor element's tags is rendered in a typical web browser with an underline and a different color (often blue).

Add Images

Although there's a great deal more to HTML, as far as the basics go, you've got two of three covered—text and hyperlinks. The other element to consider is the <img /> element, which can be used to display graphical images in your web documents.

Before you add an image to your weblog, you'll need to have the image on hand. Three different image file formats can be handled by most graphical web

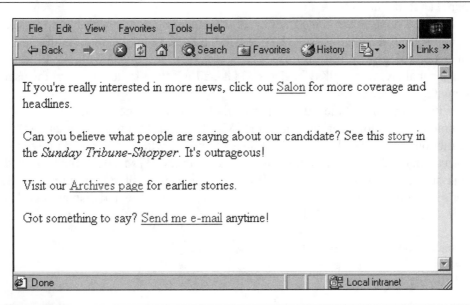

FIGURE 3-5   A series of entries with hyperlinks.

browsers: JPEG, GIF, and PNG. Each format has its advantages. JPEG is best for photographic images, GIF is best for images created in graphics applications, and PNG is a newer format that has many similarities to GIF but isn't quite as universally accepted and can be a problem for older web browsers in particular.

NOTE

Although not universally recognized by web browsers (particularly older versions), PNG is a great format. PNG was designed primarily to be a replacement for the GIF format, which is based on some proprietary technology that, in many cases, requires that the developers of applications designed to create and edit GIF files to pay royalties to do so. PNG doesn't have those restrictions.

Creating images is beyond the scope of this book, but you'll likely want to use a graphics-editing application of some sort, whether it's a professional-level photo-editing application such as Adobe Photoshop, a consumer photo-editing application such as Adobe Elements or Apple iPhoto, or a drawing application such as Macromedia Freehand, CorelDRAW, Windows Paint, or AppleWorks. All these types of applications can be used to create images that you can then add to your HTML documents.

If there's anything to remember when you're creating your web-bound images, it's that images destined for a web page need to be reasonably small, both in dimension (often, you'll want images to be less than 800 pixels wide) and file size (images that are over 100KB in size will take a long time to download to the user's computer, in most cases).

With all that out of the way, you're ready to add an image to your HTML document. I mentioned earlier that an HTML document is a text document with instructions to the web browser. That doesn't change when you're dealing with images. Image files are not somehow embedded in the HTML document. Instead, you issue an instruction (using the <img /> element) that is then interpreted by the user's web browser to mean "locate the following image file and display it at this place when you render the HTML document." So, consider this example:

```
We had a wonderful time hiking today. As you can see, the
vistas around our new home are tough to beat:
<img src="flowers1.jpg" alt="image of flowers and water"/>
```

3

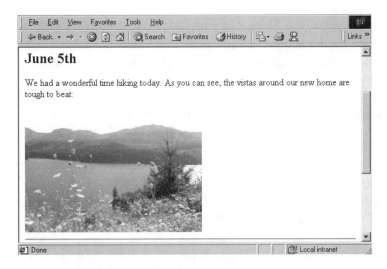

With the <img /> element (which you'll notice is an empty element because it doesn't act on text) comes two important attributes—src and alt. The src attribute is used to specify the URL to the image you'd like to load; in this instance, it's a *relative* URL, which means that the image needs to be in the same directory as the page we created. This is how you'll generally add your own images. Simply upload them to the same directory as the page where the <img /> element appears and then link using a simple relative link. You can also create a subdirectory, such as images, and simply add that subdirectory to the *path* specified in the src attribute, as in:

```
src="images/myimage.gif"
```

The src attribute can accept an entire URL, if desired, as in this example:

```
<img src="http://www.mygreatblog.org/images/flowers1.jpg"
alt="flowers image" />
```

This URL can point to an image file that's on your own server or on another server on the Internet. The only requirement is that the image file actually be stored where the URL says it is; otherwise, the image won't appear on the page.

NOTE

Although the <img /> element enables you to place images from other websites on your own pages, it generally isn't polite (or, at times, could be a legal issue) to link to images on other sites without permission.

The other attribute, alt, is used as a text-only description for web browsers that can't or won't display images. Although this isn't strictly required, it's important to add alternative text if you can, because it helps users of nongraphical browsers to better understand your web page.

> **TIP** *Images added in this way are "inline," so if you want white space around them, you need to use the <br /> element both before and after the images. (Inline images are added to the document just as if they were text, with no special text-wrap characteristics.) You can also use another attribute, align, by adding align="left" and align="right" to the <img /> element. Using one of these two align attribute values causes the image to "float" to the left or right, meaning text will wrap around it. It's a useful effect.*

You can place an image inside an anchor element if you'd like to make the image "clickable." Why do this? It allows your reader to click an image and load another page on the Web (for instance, a picture of a beach leads to a web page about the beach in question), as in this example (the returns are for this book's formatting—you can actually put all of that code on one line in your text editor if you want to):

```
<a href="http://www.bermudabeachliving.com/">
<img src="beach01.jpg" alt="beach were we stayed" border="0" />
</a>
```

> **TIP** *As shown in this example, you can use the border attribute with the <img /> element to determine whether a border will appear around the image and at what size (in pixels, with "0" indicating no border).*

You can also use images to link to other images, as discussed later in the section "Ideas for Extending Your Blog."

Archive Past Posts

You've created a weblog and added to it. Perhaps, after a while, you've added to it *considerably*. What do you do once the main index page becomes a bit unwieldy? Easy enough, at least in theory: you create an archive.

Archiving past entries is what some of the blogging management software is great at, but you can approximate such an archive in simple HTML. Say it's the first day of June and you'd like to put all your May entries into an archive, starting over with a fresh page. Here's one approach:

- Open the index.html document in your text editor.

- Use the File | Save As command in the text editor to save that page with a new name, such as may.html. (In the real world, you might want to include a year, too, as in may2003.html.)

- Load the index.html document in your text editor again (when you used the Save As command, the window changed so that it's now editing the newly created page).

- In the index.html document, you might start by clearing out the existing entries (because they are now in the archives) and then add a new one or two. Next, you can add a link somewhere on the page, perhaps at the bottom, to the new archive page. Here's an example:

```
<hr />
<h2>Archives</h2>
<a href="may.html">May archive</a><br />
```

- Now, users can view the archive link and use it when they get to the bottom of your current page (see Figure 3-6). Plus, as you add more archive pages, each successive link will appear on the index page as well as on the newer archive pages. (For instance, after you get through the next month of entries and create an archive, the June archive page will include the may.html link on it; the July archive will have the may.html and june.html links on it, and so forth.)

Eventually, if you end up blogging for a few years using this approach, you'll end up with a list of archive pages that's very long. If that's the case, you can always create a link on your index page to a page called archives.html (or a page similarly named) that has the sole purpose of storing links to each month of archived posts. This adds an extra step for your readers, but it can take a burdensome list of links off your front page if it turns out you catch blogging fever and you do it for a long time.

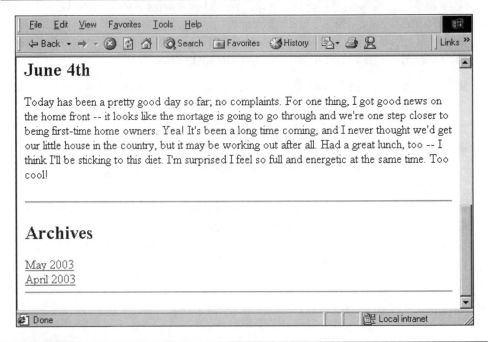

Adding archive links to the bottom of an index page is one way to provide a bridge into the past.

Ideas for Extending Your Blog

As you work with your weblog, most likely you'll get to know quite a bit more about HTML. Aside from this brief primer, there is quite a bit you can learn and do, both within your entries and outside of them, with the rest of your website. Here are a few possibilities you can consider to extend your weblog and use the weblog format for a variety of reasons:

■ **Play with the design.**   You don't have to use <h2> elements for each entry's date, for instance. Instead, you could use the <h2> elements to give each entry a title and then you could put the date in bold right before the text. Anything like that is fine—experiment with the look and feel of your site and explore some online HTML references for other hints on making your page look more exciting. Also, consider creating a banner for your site as an image file, then add it using the <img /> element just inside the top of the <body> element on your page.

3

- **Use thumbnails to link to bigger images.**   With a blog, you generally want to make the main page easy to read. If you add images, they should fit well "inline" with the text, without being too big or taking too much time to download. However, you may have larger images that you'd like your visitors be able to see. The trick is to create a small, inline image that can work as a thumbnail—say, one that's 200 or 300 pixels wide with a height that's proportionate. (You can make those changes to a copy of the original image in most any photo-editing software.) Next, wrap the <img /> tag in an anchor element that points to the larger image, and users will be able to click the image and load the larger version (say, 600 pixels wide or more) in the browser window on its own. Here's an example:

```
<a href="woods01.jpg"><img src="woods01_sml.jpg"
alt="hiking the woods" /></a>
```

- **Learn to use HTML tables.**   The HTML table elements (http://www.w3.org/TR/1998/REC-html40-19980424/struct/tables.html) can be used to create more structure on your page, both within individual entries and for the overall layout of your weblog page.

- **Learn CSS.**   Cascading Style Sheets (CSS) make it easier to change the overall look and feel of your weblog—and, in fact, all the pages on your website. See http://www.w3.org/Style/CSS/ for a primer. We'll discuss CSS in other chapters, particularly Chapter 8.

- **Add static pages.**   Aside from your main weblog page and your archives pages, you might consider creating other pages to which you can link from your weblog, such as a biography, your resume, pages of photos you've taken, your poetry, or anything else you'd like to share with your audience. One standard way to link to such pages is just to separate them using vertical lines, as in:

```
<a href="resume.html">My Resume</a> |
<a href="articles.html">My Articles</a> |
<a href="dog.html">My Dog</a> |
<a href="bio.html">My Bio</a>
<hr />
```

- ■ **Integrate your blog into another site.**   If you already have a website, you might consider adding a blog-format news section to your index page, just to make it more dynamic and inviting to repeat visitors. You could also create a special blog page and link to it from your index page—a technique that's becoming more and more popular. Even if your index page is relatively static, your users can still link to your blog and read what's up on a daily or weekly basis. Not only does this work for individuals, but it's great for organizations, because it's a way to familiarize users with the people involved in your company, whether the blogger is a product manager, business owner, or even the president of the company.

- ■ **Consider using other scripted tools.**   Even if you don't opt for a weblog-management application, you might look into other ways you can automate and script your site. Flip over to Chapter 10 to see some interesting ideas for augmenting any sort of community-oriented site, whether you're handling the publishing tasks yourself or using a weblog tool.

Meanwhile, if you're happy with your blog, go to it and add some content to start wowing your readers. If you're not interested in other blogging tools, skip straight to Parts III and IV of this book, where you can spend some time looking at ways to add to your blog and, after that, to publicize and popularize it.

If you're still interested in using a weblog-management tool, this chapter wasn't a total loss by any stretch of the imagination, because it served as a basic

HTML primer. You'll find that knowledge of HTML is helpful, regardless of whether or not you're using a weblog tool. In Chapter 4, you'll see some of the hosted weblog solutions, including a couple (Blogger and Radio Userland) that can be used not only with the hosted service but also with your own ISP, as was discussed in this chapter. Therefore, if you prefer to use a more sophisticated blogging tool but want to use your own web server space, flip over to Chapter 4 and read on.

More...

In this chapter you learned how to create a blog using just a simple text editor, an FTP application, some web server space, and a little dedication. This chapter also served as a quick HTML primer, which you'll find useful regardless of the blogging tool you choose.

In Chapter 4, you'll learn about the hosted blogging solutions available and, hopefully, get some guidance in choosing and using the correct tool for your blog. If you're content with the simple blog covered in this chapter, however, you can skip to Chapter 8 and beyond, where we'll discuss everything from creative and advanced web publishing tools and techniques, to publicizing your site and using it in an organizational setting.

M	T	W	T	F	S		S	M	T	W	T	F	S		S	M	T	W	T	F	S		S	M	T	W	T	F	S
		1	2	3	4					1	2	3	4					1	2	3	4					1	2	3	4
6	7	8	9	10	11		5	6	7	8	9	10	11		5	6	7	8	9	10	11		5	6	7	8	9	10	11
13	14	15	16	17	18		12	13	14	15	16	17	18		12	13	14	15	16	17	18		12	13	14	15	16	17	18
20	21	22	23	24	25		19	20	21	22	23	24	25		19	20	21	22	23	24	25		19	20	21	22	23	24	25
27	28	29	30	31			26	27	28	29	30	31			26	27	28	29	30	31			26	27	28	29	30	31	

Chapter 4

Using a Hosted Weblog

In this chapter:

- ■ Choosing a hosted weblog service
- ■ Using Blogger, the popular choice
- ■ Digging into the LiveJournal community
- ■ Going pro: Radio UserLand

Wouldn't it be better if someone else could handle all the techie stuff for your blog? It's certainly easier that way. Some of the most popular blogs—and a whole lot of the steam that's been generating the "blogging" movement—have been thanks to Blogger and other hosted blogging solutions. In fact, it's common to see media reports suggest that Blogger started the blogging phenomenon, which really isn't true, although the availability of such an easy (and free!) tool was absolutely a major catalyst.

In this chapter, I'll focus on some of the specifics of working with a hosted weblog service. We'll begin by considering the tradeoff that most (although certainly not all) hosted services bring, in that they tend to give you a little less control, and, in many cases, you'll find fewer community tools—especially with free services. That said, the more you're willing to pay for your hosted service, the more features you'll get. In fact, at the high end, a hosted service can be downright feature heavy.

The rest of the chapter will look at each of three hosted services individually: Blogger, LiveJournal, and Radio UserLand. Throughout, we'll look at some of the interesting ways you can use and augment these tools.

Choose a Hosted Service

Thousands of folks have started their blogs using a hosted service. Indeed, Blogger in particular is one of the foremost tools for creating a blog, and many weblogs that use Blogger succeed wildly. Radio UserLand, although not as popular as Blogger (if only because it isn't free), has an enormous following, and many great weblogs are maintained with that tool. Radio is also the supporting technology for some other blogging services that are popping up, such as the Salon Blogs service (blogs.salon.com), which enables you to host your blog using the popular Salon.com domain name.

The hosted blogging tools to some extent follow the rule: *You get what you pay for*. That's not to say that one of the tools is *better* than another; in fact, some of the costly options might be more than you need for a good blog. What I really mean is that the tools you pay for offer more flexibility and more options, as well as a little more power. But that may not matter to you. Let's look at some specific tools and discuss why you might consider using them:

- **Blogger (www.blogger.com)** Blogger is probably the perfect tool for getting a blog up and running in about five minutes. Although the online editing interface isn't the most intuitive I've worked with, there are a number of shareware and freeware applications you can use to edit your blog online. For free hosting, your site will be placed on Blog*Spot, with your chosen username as the machine name in your URL, as in http://*myblog*.blogspot.com/. It's a hip address, pretty easy to remember and link to, and no one will fault you for starting with Blogger's free services. It's also a reasonably low-risk proposition, because many of the more sophisticated blogging tools will import Blogger entries if you decide to move to them. Blogger has some limitations, including the lack of image hosting, some iffy archiving capabilities, and no built-in comment mechanism or community tools. Also, when your blog is hosted on Blog*Spot, an ad appears at the top of the page, although you can get rid of it for a nominal fee (currently $12 per year).

NOTE   *The Blogger Pro Edition is available for, currently, $50 per year. It adds many of the most requested features, including a spell-checker, the ability to save a post as a draft, the option of sending posts as e-mail, and even priority placement on the Blogger web servers.*

- **LiveJournal (www.livejournal.com)**   Offering some of the advantages of Blogger, LiveJournal.com is a popular service that is a little more community focused. It offers support for comments, a community of users, and a directory of member sites. And, you can edit your entries with desktop editing tools. It's free, too, but only if you get a code from an existing user; otherwise, you have to pay a nominal fee. Paid accounts have the advantage of a personalized URL (http://*yourname*.livejournal.com/), e-mail forwarding, and, if desired, support for forwarding a domain name, such as http://www.*yourname*.com/ to your LiveJournal site.

- **Radio UserLand (radio.userland.com)**   This tool is popular in part because of its unique implementation. Part desktop application and part web tool, Radio allows you to use a web browser to edit your stories, but those stories are actually edited (and stored) on your local computer and then published at your command. Radio gives you control over the appearance of your pages and templates, making it a flexible alternative. You're also free to publish to a different web server, if desired, making it useful beyond its hosted component.

> **NOTE** *Also written by UserLand, Manila is a higher-end tool for website management that retails for about $900. However, a number of Manila-based hosts are available for a reasonable monthly fee, giving you access to some fairly extraordinary tools. Manila is more than a blogging tool; it's a content-management tool designed for both static-style and blog-style pages. It includes some impressive community management tools as well, along with support for comments and online discussion forum topics. Fortunately, you only have to dig as deep as you want to. For typical blogging, Manila works great and, even better, offers community tools for comments and forum discussions. Check out http://manila.userland.com/ and http://www.weblogger.com/ for more on creating a Manila site.*

■ **Others**   If you're interested in a simple, free blog or diary-like site—and Blogger doesn't quite do it for you—there are some other options. All of these are no-cost, and mostly no-frills, but any is a decent option for a basic blog. Just choose the one that seems to fit your personality. Pitas.com offers a free service that enables you to post a basic blog, including basic support for images and links. Crimsonblog.com is a relatively new service (at the time of writing), offering a basic blog for personal use. The service offers a number of good-looking templates and the ability to edit your site's templates. Diaryland.com is focused on daily entries. Unlike a typical blog, there isn't a list of recent posts or a calendar approach, but most members have attractive pages aimed at personal, diary-style blogging.

As you can see, there are numerous choices—and this isn't a complete list. If you'd like to look into additional possibilities, try http://directory.google.com/Top/Computers/Internet/On_the_Web/Weblogs/Tools/. In the meantime, let's take a closer look at some of these hosted tools and services.

The Popular Choice: Blogger

Blogger is certainly the tool that defines the rule, so to speak, even if it really isn't the most powerful or comprehensive weblogging tool available. It's still immensely popular, which is indicated not only by the fact that it's credited with helping spur on the blogging phenomenon but also by the availability of any number of add-ons to make a Blogger-powered site better.

When you sign up for Blogger, you can select to have your site hosted for free on the ad-support Blog*Spot service, or you can point Blogger at your own FTP server, where it can be used to post a Blogger-formatted site. Either option lets you get up and running with a blog very quickly, and, as you'll see later, you can switch from Blog*Spot to your own server in the future if you'd like to graduate to self-hosted at some point.

> NOTE   *Blogger doesn't have the built-in ability to support user comments, but that doesn't mean you can't add them. See Chapter 9 for details on some of the different hosted services that help you add comments to Blogger sites.*

4

Sign Up

To sign up, head to http://www.blogger.com and click the Start Now button. (If there isn't a Start Now button, then things have changed, which is always a risk with a Web-based application. Look for a way to sign up.) You'll be asked for a username, password, and e-mail address and to confirm that you've read the terms of service. When you've done all that, you'll be asked to give your blog a name and a description as well as whether it should be a public blog. (A public blog is simply one that is listed in the directory accessible on the Blogger website.)

Your final decision will be whether you'd like to host the site at blogspot.com (for free, or for a low cost if you'd prefer the hosting without ads) or you'd like to use the Blogger tool to update your own site:

■   **FTP**   If you select FTP, you'll need to know the correct FTP address, username, and password for the site in question. It's also important that the path to your site already exist—for instance, if you plan to post the site at http://www.*yoursite*.com/blog/, you need to make sure that the "blog" directory already exists on your FTP server. Finally, you're asked to specify the name that you'd like to use for the main page of your Blogger site. (Although blogger.html is suggested, you might consider using index.html if this page will be the index page of your website.)

FTP path | /public_html/eddie/

Optional. This is the directory on your FTP server where you want to put your blog. For example: "weblog/". If you want to make your blog your home page or place it elsewhere in your root directory, you might leave this field blank. **Note:** Blogger will not create directories on your server, so this path must already exist. If it doesn't, be sure to create it with your FTP program before publishing with Blogger.

Blog Filename | index.html

TIP

Some FTP servers have additional folders in their internal paths that aren't reflected in the URL; for instance, your blog folder might be in a path that's something like /public_html/weblog/, as opposed to how it appears in your URL, where it might just be http://www.yoursite.com/weblog/. If that's the case, make sure you enter the correct path, including the hidden directories, in the FTP Path entry box.

■ **Blog*Spot**   If you choose Blog*Spot, things are a little easier. You'll simply be asked to choose a machine name for your Blog*Spot URL. As long as you choose one that isn't already in use, your site will be created and you'll be ready to start blogging.

CREATE A BLOG   Page 3 of 4

Choose an address for your blog and indicate acceptance of the BlogSpot terms of service. The address you choose will be the URL of your new site. No spaces, apostrophes, colons, or slashes allowed.

http:// kingeddie   **.blogspot.com/**

☑ **I agree to the** BlogSpot Terms of Service.

[<< back]   [next >>]

The final step for either type of blog is to choose a format; simply click the radio button next to one of the templates that's shown on the page. (Templates can be changed at any time once you're editing your site.) When you click Finish, your site is created and you're shown the main Blogger editing page. You're now ready to add to your site.

NOTE

If you leave the Blogger editing page and need to get back to it, you can do so by going to http://www.blogger.com and signing in with your username and password.

Add Entries

If you're looking at the interface to your Blogger site, you're likely viewing the Edit page. If not, you can click the Edit button on the toolbar that appears at the top of your page. (It's actually integrated into the browser's toolbar if you're using Internet Explorer for Windows, but in other browsers it appears above the rest of the page, along with Settings, Template, Archive, and so on.) On the Edit page, adding an entry is just as easy as typing. You'll notice that the web browser window is divided into different panes that are designed to help you manage your entries. The top pane is where you type an entry. You can type text and/or HTML for emphasis or to create links.

Edit this Post

Welcome to my new site. I've decided to create a blog to cover some of the daily happenings here in the big castle. While everyone seems to think that castle life is the best, you may be surprised by the day-to-day life of a king. So, stop by regularly and I'll fill you in. Should be fun|

view web page | enter safe mode

TIP   *If you're using Blog*Spot, you can't host images on their servers. You can, however, add images to your blog entries using the <img /> element, as discussed in Chapter 3, but the URL to the image must be for a server other than Blogspot.com. If you have your own server space, you can place an image there and reference it using an element such as <imgsrc="http://www.myisp.net/~username/images/image1.gif" alt="image 1" />, and the image will appear on your Blogger page.*

When you're done entering the text and HTML of your entry, you can click the Post to Weblog button. This adds the entry to the listing of entries at the bottom of the interface and puts it in a queue for your website. You can now proceed to add additional entries, if desired. If you read over the posted entry and realize you've made a typo or you want to change something you've said, click the Edit link.

best, you may be surprised by
I'll fill you in. Should be fun.
[edit]

When you've done all the writing and editing you're going to do for this entry, you're ready to publish the entries to your site. Locate and click the Publish button, which should be near the Last Published message on the right side of the window. When you click Publish, you should see a message that says your publish request has been received. After a moment or two, your entry will be published and will appear on your website. Click the View Web Page link in the Blogger interface to see your site, or you can launch the site's URL in any browser window (see Figure 4-1).

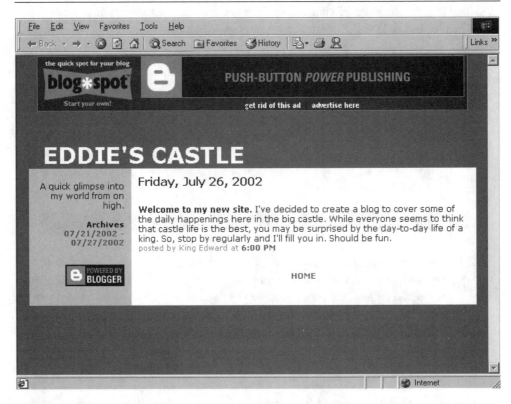

EDDIE'S CASTLE

A quick glimpse into my world from on high.

Archives
07/21/2002 –
07/27/2002

POWERED BY BLOGGER

Friday, July 26, 2002

Welcome to my new site. I've decided to create a blog to cover some of the daily happenings here in the big castle. While everyone seems to think that castle life is the best, you may be surprised by the day-to-day life of a king. So, stop by regularly and I'll fill you in. Should be fun.
posted by King Edward at **6:00 PM**

HOME

FIGURE 4-1   Success! Here's the first entry of what may prove to be a long career with Blogger.

NOTE   *Even though a story has been published, you can still return to the Blogger interface and edit an entry again by clicking the Edit link below the story post in the bottom pane.*

Once you've gotten a fair number of posts entered into Blogger, you'll start to find the calendar tool handy. You can click a date to go directly to posts that were made on that day. You can also look for particular previous posts using the Search entry box; select its radio button and then enter a keyword to use for the search. Entries that match the search keyword will appear in the Posts pane. Again, you can click Edit if you'd like to alter the post.

Let More Users Play

Want to add people who can update your Blogger site? In the Blogger toolbar, click the Team button. On the Team page, click Add Team Member(s). On the Add Team Members page, you can enter a first name, last name, and e-mail address in the New User section. Then click the New button to add that person to your team. (They'll receive an e-mail with instructions; you can use the Message entry box for any additional text you want to send them.) Do this for everyone you want to add to your team; then, when you're done, click Send Invites. Once that's accomplished, any one of those people will be able to create their own a Blogger account (if they haven't already) and log in to your site, where they can add and edit their own entries. If desired, you can also make them administrators via the main Team page, giving them the rights to add other users as well as manage, edit, and delete any entry.

NOTE   *You can get back to the editing interface by clicking the Posts button that appears under the toolbar in your web browser. (As mentioned, in IE for Windows, it actually appears in the toolbar; in other browsers, the Posts button is at the top of the page, just under the toolbar.)*

Change the Look

Although you never really have to touch the HTML in order to publish with Blogger, that doesn't mean you won't want to. Blogger gives you access to the current template used to publish your site so that you can customize the HTML as desired. You can also, at any time, choose a new template from among Blogger's built-in options, making it easy to quickly change the look of your blog. Let's begin with the easier changes, first.

Choose a New Template

Click the Template button (in the button bar if you have Windows-based Internet Explorer or in the menu links at the top of the page in other browsers) and you'll be shown the template for your blog. It's here that you can dig in and change things, as we'll discuss in the next section. But before changing the template, you might want to make sure the general look and feel of your blog is satisfactory. If not, you can pick a different theme.

NOTE

It's important to be happy with your basic Blogger template before you dig in and change its HTML. If you alter your template and then change to a new one, Blogger will replace the old with the new—including your changes. You can get around that by copying the text of your theme and saving your changes in a text document on your computer, but this introduces another step that can be a little annoying.

To pick a different template, click the Choose a New Template link that appears on the template page. As I write this, it appears at the top of the page, but of course that could change.

When you click that link, you'll see a new page, filled with different choices you can make for your site's appearance (see Figure 4-2). Scroll through them and find the one you like. (You can click the template's image to see a larger image and get a better sense of its look.) Consider it carefully, because although you can certainly change your mind later, it can get tougher and tougher as time wears on, particularly if you end up customizing your template. So, if you want to spend a few days thinking about it or experimenting with one look or another, go for it.

Once you've made your choice (click the Use This button next to the design you like), you should see a success message that leads you back to the editing page or to the Edit Template HTML page. (Note that you'll need to republish your site before you'll see the template change using the Publish button in the Edit interface.)

NOTE

If you're using Blogger to update a site via FTP, you may be told that you need to install special image files on the server with certain templates; click the Transfer These Files button if you'd like Blogger to do this for you automatically.

Edit Template HTML

Again, by clicking the Template button, you reach the Edit Template HTML page, where you can dig into the actual HTML document that is used as a template to publish your Blogger page. If you scroll through it, you'll see the special tags Blogger uses as placeholders in the template for your actual blog entries. (These tags, also

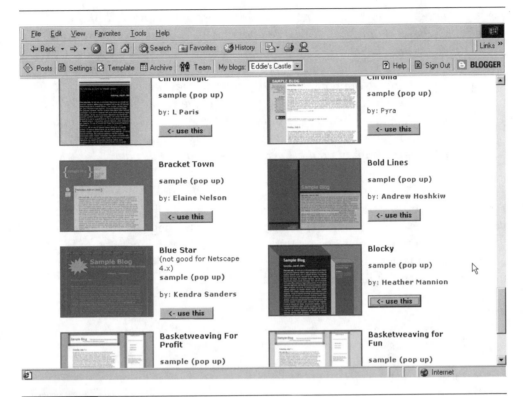

FIGURE 4-2   Choose a look for your site.

sometimes known as *variables*, are items you'll see in all blogging software. In a template, the tags stand in for items that will be added from the database, such as the headlines and body text of your blog entries.) For instance, you can scroll through and see tags such as the following:

```
<$BlogItemAuthor$>
<$BlogItemBody$>
```

These are the placeholders Blogger uses to place elements from your entries on the page. Whenever you choose to publish your site, Blogger digs into your database of entries and then uses the template to build a page that includes a certain number of entries, along with the overall look of the site. This means that, with a little HTML knowledge, you can open the template and change the way your site looks.

What if you mess something up while editing the template? If you want the default settings for that same template, you can simply reselect the theme using the instructions in the previous section. If you want to revert to changes you've made in the past, you need to make a habit of backing the template up. Simply select all the template text in the window and then use the copy and paste command to paste the template into a text editor application, thus creating a text file that you save on your local hard disk. If you ever get into trouble, you can copy the template data out of your backup text file and into the Template text area on this page.

If you read Chapter 3 (or even skimmed it) or if you already have knowledge of basic HTML, you'll find it easy to dig into the template and, at the very least, alter your personal set of hyperlinked sites that appears on the page. If you have links you want to add to your page, scroll through the template and look for an HTML comment string that suggests you're in the right place for adding links. Although the templates vary, you'll often see something like this:

```
<tr align=center>
<th bgcolor="#000033">[::...recommended...::]</th></tr>
<!-- edit the code below with your own links -->
<tr bgcolor="#777777" align=center>
<td><a href="http://www.plastic.com">plastic</a></td>
</tr>
```

In this example, from an actual template called Sandbox at Night (by Eliza Wee, according to the Blogger site), you're looking at an area that the template author recommends for your personal links. In this case, links are added in table rows (between the <tr> and </tr> elements), with each row having a single data element (between <td> and </td>). A sample link, to the popular blog Plastic.com, is included as an example. To add your own links, you would simply cut and paste a new table row into the listing, as shown here:

```
<tr align=center>
<th bgcolor="#000033">[::...recommended...::]</th></tr>
<!-- edit the code below with your own links -->
<tr bgcolor="#777777" align=center>
<td><a href="http://www.plastic.com">plastic</a></td>
</tr>
<tr bgcolor="#777777" align=center>
<td><a href="http://www.wilwheaton.net/">WilWheaton.net</a></td>
</tr>
```

```
<tr bgcolor="#777777" align=center>
<td><a href="http://www.macblog.com/">MacBlog</a></td>
</tr>
```

Here, I've added some additional links. I could also edit the Plastic.com link, if desired, or add a bunch more links following the same procedure. Here's how they look in the final product:

TIP *Remember, you need to click the Publish button on your main Edit interface screen in order to see the template changes.*

If there's a caveat, it's that the templates for Blogger are written by enthusiasts—few of them are standardized by the folks at Pyra, Inc., who maintain Blogger. So, you'll find that different strategies are used to create and document the templates. In some cases, you'll add your links using paragraph elements or line breaks; in others, you'll use tables or even bulleted lists. Here's another example from a basic template design that I like a lot (Sports Cut, by Bjoern Staerk):

```
<!--
    <p>
    <a href="">link 1</a>
    <br><a href="">link 2</a>
    <br>etc.
      -->
```

In this case, the suggested format for links has been laid out for you, albeit between HTML comment tags (<!-- and -->), which you'll need to delete before you edit the tags. Otherwise, you can see how these would be fairly easy to alter and add to (the <br> line break tag is used to put each link on a new line):

```
<p>
    <a href="www.wilwheaton.net">WilWheaton.net</a>
    <br><a href="www.plastic.com">Plastic</a>
    <br><a href="www.macblog.com">MacBlog</a>
</p>
```

Although this may not be simple to you, you'll get used to it if you decide to dig into HTML a bit. Refer back to Chapter 3 for a quick review or look to Chapter 8 for more on CSS (style sheet definitions for changing fonts and colors) and some of the more complicated items that tend to appear in these templates.

TIP   *Need more help? One place to look is http://archives.blogspot.com/, which includes discussions about working with Blogger's template code, its bugs, and inconsistencies. You'll also find great tips on adding comments, integrating JavaScript, and much more. If you're interested in templates beyond those supplied in Blogger, try http://www.blogskins.com/, where people post and trade some pretty impressive Blogger templates. You'll need to create a user account, but once you do, the site can be used to automatically update your Blogger site with a new template—no cutting and pasting required.*

Manage Archives

Items that no longer appear on your main Blogger index page (as determined by the Settings page, discussed in the next section) are placed in the archives. To manage the archives, click the Archives button at the top of your Edit page. Now you'll see the Archives page. On this page, the most basic tasks you can perform are removing from your index page a particular link to an archived week and republishing an archive. You need to republish an archive whenever you change the design of your site; you only need to remove a link if you want to.

Choose the Archive Settings link and you can determine how archives are grouped together. If you post very frequently, you may want to have an archive page created for each individual week; if you don't update that often, you might consider having archives created once per month. Make your choice in the menu and click the Enter button.

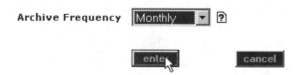

Finally, you can select the Archive Template link to change the way each individual archive template (the page that determines the standard appearance of the archive page) will look. By default, the archive page(s) will look exactly like your index page, but you can alter it here, as described in the section "Edit Template HTML" earlier in this chapter.

NOTE *When you change templates, you need to republish your archives if you want them recast with the new template style. You don't have to do that, though. You can also leave archive pages as they were originally styled, if you like. Just know that clicking the Publish button in the main Blogger interface only affects your index page and current stories, not the archives.*

Change Settings

Aside from the archive controls, Blogger offers some other settings that govern the way your blog behaves. In the toolbar, click the Settings button. On the Settings page, you can revisit some of the items you entered when you first created your blog (such as the title, description, and whether your blog should be a public blog and therefore publicized on Blogger.com). You can also use this page to change from hosting the site on BlogSpot.com to hosting the site on another web service (via FTP).

In the Formatting section, you can make a variety of choices about how your blog will appear. In particular, you should consider how posts should appear on your index page—whether you want a certain number of posts or a certain number of days' worth of posts. The number, by default, is 7, but you can choose any number you like.

In this section you can also format the date and time as well as set your time zone so that Blogger correctly updates the timestamp for your posts. You can also pick a language if you prefer something other than English, and you can decide whether Blogger will convert line breaks in your entries. In other words, if you type RETURN, do you want Blogger to interpret that as a new line, or ignore it, as HTML does? (In most cases you'll want Blogger to recognize line feeds.)

In the Archiving section you may only find one option—the frequency. As mentioned in the previous section of this chapter, you can choose the type of archive pages Blogger creates—whether they show a week's worth of entries or a month's worth of entries at a time.

The Browser Shortcuts section includes one or more interesting tools, depending on your browser version. In most browsers you'll see a Bookmarklet link—you can add this link to your favorites or bookmarks to create a *bookmarklet*. (Note that, with Internet Explorer, the bookmarklet will only work if it's stored in the Toolbar Favorites because it uses JavaScript and the scripts don't activate when stored as a regular Favorite.)

A bookmarklet is a link to a quick-entry page for your blog; instead of launching Blogger.com and logging in, you simply click the bookmarklet link, sign in (if necessary), and begin a new entry. The entry will already have a link to the page you were viewing when you invoked the bookmarklet. You'll likely find this very convenient, particularly for blogging while surfing (see Figure 4-3).

If you're using Internet Explorer for Windows, you may see an option that enables you to add the Blog This! right-click menu to Internet Explorer. This enables you to quickly open a Blogger editing window by right-clicking a web page that you're viewing in Internet Explorer—the window will appear, complete with a link to that page. Now you can blog about it quickly.

FIGURE 4-3   Using the bookmarklet link, you can quickly add a blog entry without the hassle of using the full Blogger interface.

Here's how to install the right-click menu:

1. Click the Install Blog-This link in the Browser Shortcuts section.

2. Read the message in the dialog box that appears and click OK.

3. You'll need to choose Open This File From Its Current Location and then click OK.

4. Once it's downloaded, you'll be asked whether you want to add the information to the Registry. Click Yes.

Restart Internet Explorer and you can now access the Blog This! window; simply right-click an interesting page and choose the Blog This! menu item.

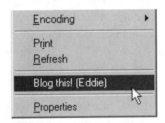

The Blog This! window will appear (the same window as the bookmarklet, shown in Figure 4-3), and you'll be able to enter an entry and quickly post and publish it.

TIP   *The Blogger API is public, meaning developers can write applications that are able to mimic the Blogger editing application but work from your desktop. That means you don't ever have to log in to the Blogger site or even use the bookmarklet to edit entries; you can actually just launch a desktop application and edit your blog from there. Some popular options include BlogBuddy (http://blogbuddy.sourceforge.net) and w.Bloggar (http://www.wbloggar.com/) for Windows, iBlog (http://iblog.soapdog.org) and BlogApp (http://www.webentourage.com/blogapp.php) for Mac OS X, Blognix (http://blognix.sourceforge.net/) for Linux, and the Java-based Jericho (http://jericho.sourceforge.net/). Because these apps can be used with many different blogging solutions, we'll take a closer look at some of them in Chapter 9.*

4

Community Living: LiveJournal

LiveJournal.com is a service that's very much like Blogger in some ways, and the antithesis of it in others (in as much as one blogging tool can be the antithesis of another blogging tool). Whereas Blogger is an open-API system designed to enable users to quickly post blogs either on Blogspot.com or on their own servers, LiveJournal is quite a bit more closed from the user's point of view. LiveJournal is a hosted service, period. You can't use its tools to update your own pages as you can with Blogger or, as you'll see, with Radio UserLand. You can forward a domain to your LiveJournal account (if you pay a nominal fee for the paid version of the service), but it must be hosted on the LiveJournal servers.

> NOTE   *I say it's closed from the user's point of view, but from the developer's point of view, LiveJournal is an open-source system, allowing programmers to download the source, change it, and start their own journaling web services (for instance, http://www.deadjournal.com/). Go to http://www.livejournal.com/ developer/ for details. You'll also find third-party tools for editing your LiveJournal, as discussed later in the section "Use a Client Application."*

Those may sound like negatives, but LiveJournal has some serious positives, too. LiveJournal is very much focused on community tools, so, unlike Blogger, the capability for visitors to comment on your site is built right in. In fact, the commenting tools are akin to discussion forum tools, making it easy to create a blog that's not just a personal journal or news site but something along the lines of a community site. In fact, LiveJournal blogs are cataloged by region, interest, and online community affiliation, making it fairly easy to link your blog into a greater community of bloggers. All in all, it's pretty cool, particularly if you're looking for discussion-driven blogging.

Create a LiveJournal

LiveJournal has an interesting sign-up policy. Before you can get a blog, you need an activation code. You can get that code one of two ways: You can get a code from an existing user of LiveJournal (someone who already has a blog) or you can pay a fee (using the PayPal.com service) and get a paid account. (Prices start at $5 for two months, with discounts for long-term subscriptions.) The idea is to keep people from creating blogs that quickly fall into disuse—they seem to figure that if you know a LiveJournal user well enough to get a code from them or if you pay a few bucks then you'll be committed to using the service. Once you have that entry code, you're ready to begin setup. Here's how:

1. Head to LiveJournal.com and click the Create a Journal entry (or go straight to http://www.livejournal.com/create.bml).

2. Enter your activation code (again, you may have to pay for it; follow the instructions on the screen to do so).

3. If your code is accepted, you'll be asked to create a username, which you'll use to log in, and to provide your full name (or a chosen nickname) and a password, along with an e-mail address and your age. When you're done, click Proceed.

4. If you succeed, you'll see a message saying so, along with the link to your site. You'll also receive an e-mail message with the verification information.

Also on the confirmation page you'll see a link to personal information; click it to head to the page where you enter information about yourself (a lot of it is optional) as well as some settings for your site. Some of the settings are particularly important, such as the following:

- **Text messaging**   If you've paid for LiveJournal service, you can enable some or all visitors to send text-message pages to your cell phone or wireless pager.

- **Interests**   This entry box is used by the system to assign you to different topic categories so that users who share your interests can find your blog.

- **Contact information**   In this section you can choose which e-mail addresses to make public (your Livejournal.com address, included with paid accounts, is automatically forwarded to your regular e-mail account), if any. You can also turn on e-mail mangling so that it's harder for "spam bots" to add your e-mail address to junk-mail lists.

- **Message boards**   Aside from the e-mail and other settings, check out the option Enable Message Boards and the related options below it. These enable you to add a commenting mechanism for visitors and decide what level of visitor can add comments.

When you're done with these settings, click Save Changes.

Before you're completely done with the startup process, you need to validate your site—this is done to ensure you've given LiveJournal a legitimate e-mail account. When you receive the Welcome to LiveJournal e-mail message, click the verification link shown in that e-mail (if your e-mail program doesn't automatically make links clickable, you can copy and paste the URL into your web browser). Once you're verified, that's it—you're ready to post and participate.

> NOTE
>
> *In the future, you can return to this setup page by logging into the LiveJournal site with your username and password and then accessing the page http://www.livejournal.com/editinfo.bml. You can change your personal information, information about your site, and whether or not message boards are enabled, IP addresses are logged (so that you know the exact Internet address of those who comment on your entries), and so forth. There are other interesting settings on this page to consider, such as the spam-blocking and robot-blocking options to keep e-mail addresses from being picked up for spam purposes and to keep your blog from being searchable via search engines. (Note that this blocks most, but not all, search engine robots.)*

Edit Your LiveJournal

LiveJournal encourages you to a use a desktop application to edit your entries. As discussed later in this section, you can also use a web-based interface; it just isn't as central to the experience as with many other blogging tools. To get your application, head to http://www.livejournal.com/download/ and download a client application designed for your computing platform.

Use a Client Application

Once you've got your tool installed and launched, you'll likely be asked to log in to LiveJournal. Do that using your username and password. Next, what you'll see is based on the application you've chosen to download. The iJournal client for Mac OS X, for instance, is shown in Figure 4-4. Not only are Mac, Windows, and Linux covered, but there are clients for all flavors of Unix and even many popular handheld operating systems, such as Palm OS, Windows CE, and even WAP-compatible (Web Accessible Phone) mobile phones.

You'll be able to perform a few standard tasks from your LiveJournal client, regardless of the version or platform. All of them, obviously, will enable you to add an entry. In the clients I've played with, you get an entry window where you type your entry's text and add a title to the entry (perhaps via a menu command). In most cases, you can use HTML within the text of your entry, although, by default, your client application will format line breaks for you (by adding a <br /> element whenever you type RETURN). You can also use HTML to create links within your

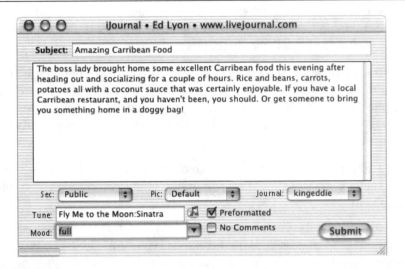

FIGURE 4-4   Here's iJournal, a Mac OS X application used to update LiveJournal.

entry (use the <a> anchor element discussed in Chapter 3) and to add images from other web servers (using the <img /> element, also discussed in Chapter 3).

Before you post your entry, you'll encounter a few standard options in most every LiveJournal client you use. These options are accessible either in the main editing window or via an Options button:

■ **Format**   You'll see an option to auto-format the entry. If you decide to auto-format, returns are turned into <br /> elements and spaces are honored. Otherwise, all the HTML is up to you. (In one client I've used, the option is called Preformatted. If it's turned on, the client will rely on you to supply all the HTML for the entry.)

■ **Picture**   You can upload pictures to LiveJournal and use them on your site. These are generally "user pictures" used to reflect your thoughts or moods, not necessarily news-related pictures. (See the section "Add Images" later in this chapter.)

NOTE   *To add pictures within your entries, you need to store the images on another web server and link to them using the <img /> HTML element.*

- **Mood**   Each LiveJournal entry can have a mood associated with it—a little emoticon (an *emotion icon*, such as the famous smiley ☺) that reflects how you're feeling as you blog.

- **Current Music**   Another standard entry in a LiveJournal blog is the music you're currently listening to. Just type in a title or band. If your client application supports it and you're playing the music on your computer, you can probably click a button to update your entry with the currently playing song or CD.

- **No Comments**   If you want to turn off the comment feature for this particular post, you should find an option in the client application that will disable it.

- **Security**   Finally, you can set the security (really, the *visibility*) of the post. You can post an entry that is public (can be seen by anyone), that can only be seen by people you've listed as friends, or that can only be seen by certain groups. You can also make a message visible only to yourself, which is good for messages that you're not finished with. (See the sidebar "Friends and Groups" for more on these security issues.)

When you're done editing your entry, click the Post or Submit button and your entry is sent to the server.

Friends and Groups

As mentioned earlier, LiveJournal is very community focused. Not only can people comment on your posts, but the point with LiveJournal, at least for many users, is to spend time reading and responding to other people's posts, both in their own blogs and within community blogs. To learn more about the LiveJournal community, check out the pages at http://www.livejournal.com/community/ to get a sense of how things work.

Once you've gotten to know some people, you can add them to your Friends list; you do that by first logging in to the LiveJournal site and then heading to your Friends page (it links from your main page). Click the Add Friends link and you can add the username of a person whom you'd like to track as a friend. (You can also add someone as a friend by clicking the Add Friend button when viewing that person's User Info.) Now, on your Friends page, the most recent posts by your friends will show up—it's a convenient way to quickly see what people have written recently without going to each of their blogs individually.

4

You can see where this list can be handy for private posts. If you create an entry that you'd like to keep just between friends, you can do that using the Security option during entry editing. Select Friends from the Security menu (it may be labeled differently if you're using a client application) and, once your entry is posted, it will only be visible to your friends.

So what's a group? It's a group of friends. Perhaps you want *certain* friends to be able to see one post, but not others. That's what groups are for. You can create a group, add certain friends to it, and then use that group to post private entries and for other reasons. Things can get complicated in a hurry, so see http://www.livejournal.com/support/faqbrowse.bml?faqid=102 for more on the "groups" concept.

Update Via the Web

If you'd like to use the LiveJournal website to update your blog, you can. This is particularly helpful if you're on the road and can't access your client application. What's more, if you're really not into a client application, you can update via the Web all the time. Here's how:

1. Go to http://www.livejournal.com/update.bml or click the Update Journal link from the LiveJournal.com home page.

2. On the Update page, enter your username and password. You should also check the date and time for accuracy.

NOTE   *Skip this step if you're already logged in to LiveJournal.com.*

3. Enter a subject for your entry, if desired, on the Subject line. Then type your entry in the Event text box. You can use HTML to format your message, although, by default, returns will be formatted as <br /> elements.

4. If you'd like to check your spelling, click the Spell Check Entry Before Posting check box.

5. Click Update Journal. If you've chosen to spell-check, you'll see an interim page if any mistakes or questionably spelled words were found. (The problem word or words will appear in red, and suggestions will appear below each

entry. You can reedit and click Update Journal again.) If not, you'll move on to a page that reports success or lets you know why the posting failed (for instance, your username or password is wrong). If you have any trouble, you can generally click the Back button in your browser and try again.

TIP *Want more options? There's a link toward the bottom of the Update page that lets you access a more advanced page that includes the options discussed in the previous section, such as Mood, Security, and Current Music.*

Edit and Delete Prior Entries

Here's a problem: Unlike Blogger and some other tools, LiveJournal doesn't make it terribly easy to view prior entries and edit or delete them. It is possible, but you'll need to get there through the Previous and History functions.

In one of the LiveJournal desktop client applications discussed in the earlier section "Use a Client Application," look for a View Previous command if you're interested in editing or deleting the most recent entry. You'll see the screen for that entry appear again, including a delete option of some kind—probably a check box or a button. Select that option and choose Post or Submit, and the entry should be deleted. If it's a Delete button, just click it to delete the entry.

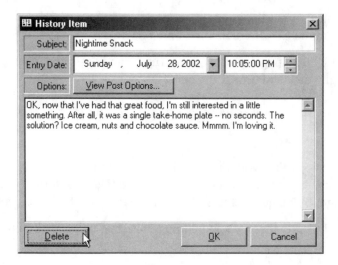

If you need to access an earlier entry, use the View History command. Now you'll see a list of entries that you can access individually for editing or deleting in the same way that you can edit or delete the most recent entry.

Editing and deleting on the Web is possible, too. Go to the Comments page of the entry you want to alter—just click its Comments link for that particular story while viewing your home page on the Web. If you're logged in to LiveJournal, you'll see a small pencil icon in the toolbar at the top-center area of the page.

Click the pencil to edit the entry. On the Edit page, you can make any changes you want. If you want to delete the entry, simply select all the text in the entry box and delete it. Then click Save Journal Entry. (You don't have to delete the date or time.)

> **TIP**   *While viewing your comment page, you'll see a small X icon next to the comment's entry information. Click it to delete the comment.*

Customize Your LiveJournal

You can do a few things to your LiveJournal to personalize its look, although there aren't as many options as with some other blogging solutions. LiveJournal has a fairly fixed number of styles and options, although, within them, you can generate some different-looking (and attractive) blogs. A number of these setting are accomplished by modifying your journal, although we'll also cover adding user images.

Modify Your Journal

Visit http://www.livejournal.com/modify.bml on the Web, either by selecting the Modify Journal link on the LiveJournal page or by using a similar command from within your editing application. You'll be asked to log in if you haven't already. Then, click the Proceed button. On the Modify page, you'll see a series of options that you can choose from to change the appearance of your page. Here's a quick look at them:

- **Available Styles**   Choose from these different options to change the way the actual entries are laid out on the page. You'll need to experiment with the different settings to see how they look. Some, such as Disjointed, Generator, and Magazine, create individual boxes for each entry on the page; others, such as the default, Notepad, and Punquin Elegant, put the day's entries in one larger box, separated by times and headlines. Note that the different pages (Journal, Friends, and Calendar) can have their own styles.

Refried Paper is a clever rip-off of Moveable Type, giving a sophisticated blogging flair to your page.

■ **Color These**   You can choose a preset color, or you can change the colors used for a variety of different elements on your page. The colors are set using the three hex numbers used when picking web-editing colors, where each hexadecimal number (from 00 to FF) represents red, green, or blue. (In hexadecimal, two numerals or letters can be used to represent numbers from 0 to 255.)

If you have a drawing, painting, or similar application (or, perhaps, a web editor), you may find a hexadecimal color tool to play with. Visit http://hotwired.lycos.com/webmonkey/reference/color_codes/ on the Web to see the codes that correspond to certain colors. See Chapter 8 for a little more discussion of hexadecimal colors.

■ **Mood icons**   If you don't like the standard smilies, you can choose others from the pull-down menu. (Note the Preview link so that you can see what the different types look like.) Also, if you want to see these same smilies on your Friends page, turn on the Force This Mood Theme option.

■ **Friends view**   These options let you dictate a little more how things look when you're viewing your Friends page.

■ **Domain Aliasing**   If you have registered a domain name for this site, you enter that domain name in this entry box; then you arrange with the service that registered your domain name to have it point at LiveJournal's servers. (See the FAQ on the topic at http://www.livejournal.com/support/faqbrowse.bml?faqid=129 for the exact addresses and steps to take.)

When you're done, click Save Changes. Now, load your site to see the changes that have been made; you can return to http://www.livejournal.com/modify.bml to make more alterations.

LiveJournal has a special area where paid members can create their own styles using special tools. Visit http://www.livejournal.com/styles/create.bml to create your style, which essentially means you're able to edit the template codes that are used to display entries as well as the HTML and style templates used to create the pages themselves.

4

Add Images

As mentioned earlier, you can add any image to your site using an <img /> element; LiveJournal also supports the addition of "user pictures," which can be used to represent you in a variety of settings, including in the message boards on your page or on other users' sites. The pictures should be at most 100 pixels by 100 pixels and 40KB in file size.

To upload your pictures, go to http://www.livejournal.com/uploadpic.bml and log in if necessary. If the image you want to add is a file on your hard disk, select From File and click Browse to locate it in an Open dialog box.

If you're using a picture that's already on the Web, choose From URL and then enter the URL to the image. Select the check box if you want that image to be your default and then click Proceed.

Once you've uploaded a few images, you can define keywords for them at http://www.livejournal.com/editpics.bml, where you can also change the default image or delete an image. With the keywords defined, you can choose an image when you post a new entry or whenever you're adding a comment at another person's LiveJournal blog; the images are simply to help identify you.

A Business-Like Presence: Radio UserLand

How does Radio UserLand fit in the mix of hosted solutions? It's similar to Blogger in that it can be used as a hosted service or as a way to update your own server space. It's also similar to Blogger in that it doesn't really support or promote community the way LiveJournal does, although Radio does offer a comments feature, depending on the template that you choose. Radio creates a weblog with a clean, standardized look to its pages, as does LiveJournal. To my thinking, it's an interesting choice for a professional or political site—one where you want to blog about news, opinions, education, or professional development. Not that you couldn't do a personal site with Radio UserLand—you could, and it would work well. But the focus seems to be a more business-like presence.

Actually, if there's any one word to describe Radio UserLand, it's *geeky*. There's quite a bit of stuff to master. But it's geeky in a good way—particularly if you plan to use Radio as a stump for your own personal online commentary site. Radio's most unique feature gives you a special page for aggregating news and then linking to it and commenting on it. There are also tools for writing longer articles (stories) and uploading and hosting images. If that sounds a little like what you'd like to accomplish, then Radio's worth a look.

NOTE

Exactly how Radio works can be confusing at first, particularly if you don't fully grasp its unique approach. Although Radio launches a desktop application (which you can access in a window on a Mac or PC, the same way you would a word processing application or similar app), it's not a weblog-editing program like BlogBuddy or BlogApp. The Radio application is actually a local web server that mimics the official, online Radio web servers. This enables you to edit your site in a web browser on the local server and then, at some point, synchronize it with your online server space. Although you can mess around with the Radio application to get a sense of how it works (see the section "The Radio Application"), you don't have to—you can leave it alone and focus on the browser-based tools for editing your site.

Get Started with Radio

Radio UserLand is a product you have to pay for. For $39.95 (currently) you get the tool and web hosting service (currently 40MB) for one year. Although you don't have to use the hosting space (and the number-based URL scheme may encourage you to seek out your own space with a more intuitive address), you still have the pay the price. (You have to pay again after a year to keep the server space, although you can keep using the software with your own site for free after the initial payment.) Fortunately, there's a free trial period if you're interested in testing the tool.

To start, you can download the free trial tool. Visit http://radio.userland.com/ and click the Download link. Then, locate and download the version that works for your platform. Once it's downloaded, install the application. When you launch it for the first time, you should see a web browser window appear with the message "It worked!" and some instructions (see Figure 4-5). You simply need to fill out the entry boxes to get started with Radio. Note that the Name entry will be used for the title of your blog (as in "Dan Smiley's Weblog"), although you can change this later. Also, remember your password!

TIP

If you're a fan of the online news site Salon.com, you can host your Radio blog on their servers, too. Visit http://www.salon.com/blogs/ to download their version of the software that hooks you up with the Salon servers. The two tools are similar, but you must download from Salon if you want to host your weblog on Salon's servers.

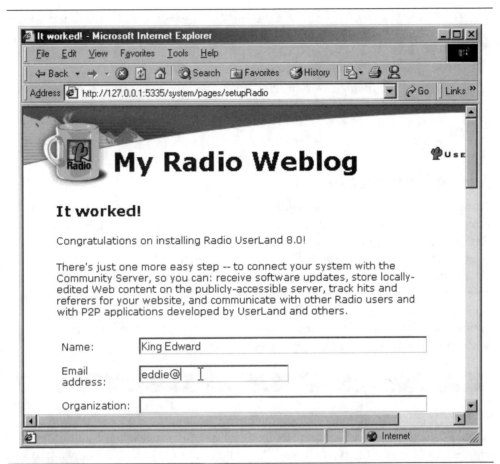

FIGURE 4-5   Here's the initial setup page. If you ever reinstall Radio, you'll scroll down to see instructions for doing that.

When you submit the page, you'll see another success page telling you what your user number is and, hence, where your page will be located on the Web. (The default URL for a Radio weblog is http://radio.weblogs.com/*usernum*/, as in http://radio.weblogs.com/0111281/.)

You'll also see a Continue button. Click it to move on to what Radio calls your *desktop website*, which is the version you'll be editing.

NOTE
This is one strike against Radio. Unlike Blogspot, LiveJournal, and others, Radio doesn't make your username part of the URL, and there's no option to register a domain name for your Radio server space. The best you can do is forward *a domain name to your Radio site via your ISP's domain forwarding feature, so that typing the domain name directs the reader to your Radio server URL. Most any domain registration service (see Appendix A for a short list) can help you forward a domain name that you've registered with the service.*

Add to Your Weblog

As mentioned, the Radio application is actually a miniature web server that's designed to serve you an editable copy of your own website. When you launch the Radio UserLand application (after the initial setup), what appears in your web browser is your *desktop* website. This is a local version of your website, saved on your hard disk. Using the browser window, you'll add blog entries, edit them, and delete them. You can also make changes from within the web browser, including altering the theme, changing preferences, and so on. You'll access most of these controls via the menu of links that appears at the top of the web browser window when you're viewing your desktop website.

Radio 8.0.8: Home | News | Stories | Shortcuts | Folder | Events | Themes | Tools | Prefs | Help

What's more, Radio makes it possible to edit your entries (on a Windows-based PC using Internet Explorer) using a WYSIWYG interface for editing your entries. And the editing itself couldn't be easier. Simply type what you want to say, adding the markup by highlighting text and clicking the items in the window or selecting them from the formatting lists. Note, in particular, the Hyperlinks button, which you can use to open a dialog box and add a hyperlink to highlighted text (see Figure 4-6).

If you don't want to use the WYSIWYG tools, you don't have to—in browsers that offer the choice, click the Source option at the bottom of the entry box and you'll be able to edit the HTML source directly.

In other Windows browsers and on the Macintosh, you'll see a slightly different window; in this one, you can enter your text and mark it up with HTML, although the returns and spaces are automatically converted.

> It seems that more than once a stray baseball has left a professional ballpark and ended up at least three states away. See the stories <a href="http://weirdsportsnewscom.net/stories/0104/today.html">here</a> and <a href="http://rogerdofterwritings.org/news/sports/0456.shtml">here</a>. <i>Strange</i>, isn't it?

Post to Weblog

When you're done with your entry in either case, click the Post to Weblog button. The entry is posted and made available on your website. What's more, if you haven't turned off the option, you'll even find that a site called Weblogs.com has been *pinged* and has posted a message saying that your weblog has been updated.

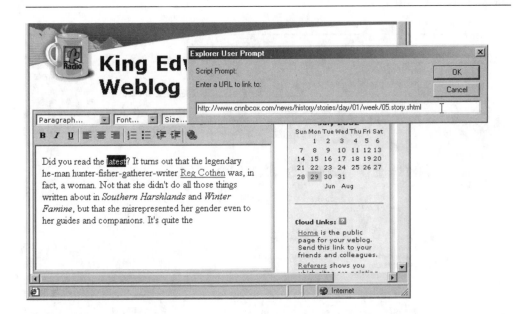

FIGURE 4-6   Editing with Radio, at least in certain browsers, is a little like using a word processor.

The blog entry you were just working on will no longer appear in the text entry area, but that doesn't mean it is gone forever. Instead, it appears in the "Previous 10 Posts" list under a now-blank editing box. If you've got something else to say, enter that blurb in the box and click Post to Weblog again.

> **TIP** *For more on using Weblogs.com to publicize your site (it doesn't require Radio UserLand), see Chapter 10.*

Want to see how your site is looking? From the home page of your desktop website, look for Cloud Links along the right side. Click the Home link and you'll be taken to your site on the Web. As you'll see, the site is similar to your desktop website, except that all the links to alter and manage the site are gone. Each entry appears on the page and, in most cases, will include links for adding comments to the page (see Figure 4-7).

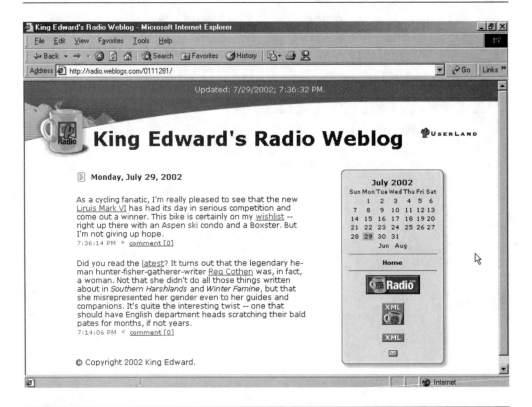

FIGURE 4-7   Here's what the Radio page looks like to the outside world.

NOTE *Because of the way Radio UserLand works, it can take up to ten minutes for your website to be updated. If you're on a modem connection that's generally set to log off after a certain amount of activity, realize that Radio checks the Web frequently, so it may keep your connection active instead of allowing it to time out. You can opt to work "offline" by right-clicking Radio in the Window status bar and choosing Offline or by choosing File | Offline in the Macintosh version of Radio. (In Mac OS X you can also right-click or control-click the Radio tile in the Dock and select Offline from the menu that appears.)*

The other Cloud Links may also prove interesting as you're getting to know your site and Radio. Click the links to see information about who is visiting your site (Referers), the most popular Radio sites (Rankings), and links to recent updates (Updates), which shows you other Radio weblogs that have been updated recently. Check your Referers to see who is linking to you—you can then link back to them, if you like their blog, to create a little more of a community feel for your site. (See the section "Set Preferences," later in this chapter, for more on adding links to your blog.)

Edit and Delete Entries

Editing and deleting entries is also accomplished from the home page of your desktop website. In the Previous 10 Posts list, you can click the Edit button that appears next to an entry to return that entry to the editing box, where you can have at it with the tools once more.   9:00 PM   **EDIT**

To delete entries, click the check box that appears next to each entry in the list that you'd like to delete; then click the Delete button that appears at the bottom of the list.

NOTE   *The ease with which you can post and then edit an entry in Radio is the basis of a satirical phrase in the blogging world: "Doing a Dave" (see http://blogicon.blogrolling.com/#D). This is when you edit a piece repeatedly, causing it to appear on your weblog in a constantly mutating form over the course of a day or longer. The phrase pays homage to Dave Winer, founder of UserLand and weblog luminary at Scripting.com, who is said to occasionally tweak his posts after they've been published.*

Write a Story

The hosted blogging tools we've looked at thus far pretty much work from the assumption that you want to display each entire entry on the index page of your site so that visitors can read those entries straight through. As you'll see in the subsequent chapters about the server-side tools, the more complex offerings tend to give you a choice of displaying the entire entry on the index or "blurbing" your story on the index and then offering a link to the complete story on a separate page. This is particularly good if you're known for the occasional long treatise.

Radio offers an interesting solution to this. Using the Radio tool, you can create *stories*, which are entries that you intend as longer, "full-page" items. You create a story and then link to it from a weblog entry. If the story is something you'd like to have stick around on your index page for a while, you can create a more permanent link to it.

To create a story, click the Stories link in the menu of links at the top of the browser window. You'll see a page introducing the stories concept; click the Create link to create a new story. Now you'll see an entry box for a title and an editing entry box that's similar to the main weblog-editing interface. Enter your entire story; when you're done, click Create New Story (see Figure 4-8).

When the story is created, you'll see it displayed in the browser window. You can click the Edit This Page button at the bottom of the page if you need to dig back into it. Otherwise, you can copy the URL from the address bar in your web browser (or you can click the Link icon that appears next to the story in the Stories list) and then head back to the home page of your desktop website (click the Home link in the menu) and create a new blog entry, adding the URL you copied. (Note that you may need to edit the link so that the machine name is http://radio.weblogs.com/*usernumber*/ instead of http://127.0.0.1:5335/. I've noticed this is true in the Windows version of Radio; the Mac version has a link button that you can use to view the online version of the story.)

```
Here's a little piece I wrote recently concerning the possibility of a hint of a
whiff of a notion that perhaps Sun and Apple should partner up and take on
the juggernaut.

<a href="http://radio.weblogs.com/0111156/stories/2002/07/29/
sunApple.html">Check it out</a>
```

Post to Weblog ?

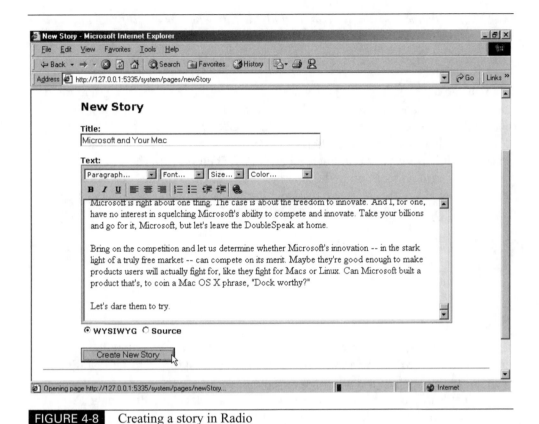

FIGURE 4-8 Creating a story in Radio

You can also opt to add the link to your Navigator links, discussed later in the section "Set Preferences."

Change Your Theme

Click the Themes link at the top of the Radio window and you'll be taken to a page that enables you to change the look of your site using one of the (very few) prebuilt Radio UserLand themes. All these themes are pretty business-like, and they all have a distinctive look that tells the trained eye you're seeing a Radio website (or one made using Manila, another UserLand product). However, once a theme is applied to your site, you can edit the HTML to change it more to your liking, as mentioned in the next section "Set Preferences."

On the Themes page, you can click the name of a theme to see an example. When you find one you like, click its radio button. Then, click the Apply Theme button at the bottom of the page. After a moment, the new theme is applied to your site.

NOTE   *The theme you choose can actually dictate whether or not your index page displays a link to user comments. See "Set Preferences" below for more on comments.*

You can also add a theme pretty easily if you find one on the Web that you'd like to use. (For starters, see http://themes.userland.com/ for a few ideas.) You'll need a theme file created specifically for Radio UserLand; once you've found it, download it and place it in the Themes folder that's inside your main Radio UserLand folder on your computer's hard disk. Then head to the Themes page in your desktop weblog (click the Themes link at the top of the browser window), and you should see the new theme appear in the list. (It won't necessarily be at the bottom of that list.) Click its radio button and then click the Apply Themes button.

TIP   *Experimenting with themes? You can turn off upstreaming, as described in the next section, to keep your Radio weblog from updating online, if desired. That way you can experiment without showing the world.*

Set Preferences

Radio gives you a lot of preferences to wade through when you click the Prefs link at the top of the browser window when viewing your desktop website. I won't cover them all in this section, because many of them are fully explained. If you want to set (or just learn about) a preference item, click its link on the Prefs page. You'll then make settings and click the Submit button to register your changes.

TIP   *Throughout the Radio interface you'll see small question mark icons that you can click to get additional help or documentation. These can be particularly handy in the Prefs section, where items can get a little more advanced and potentially confusing.*

Here are some of the preferences:

- **User Identity**   Here's where you can change your name, e-mail, and organization. Changing the name doesn't change the name of your weblog.

- **Outgoing Mail Server**   If you use any mailing features from Radio, the desktop server needs to know your SMTP server (the one you use to send e-mail over your Internet connection).

- **Upstreaming**   You can turn off upstreaming (sending items to your public web space) if you'd like to keep your public blog from being updated. (You'll need to turn it back on again before you can successfully change your online website.) This screen also gives you the option of only upstreaming when you opt to publish the whole site.

- **FTP Option**   If you'd like to use Radio UserLand to update your own site instead of the numbered site provided by UserLand, you need to dig into this preference setting.

- **Title and Description**   Change the name and short description of your site that appear at the top of the pages.

- **Days on the Home Page**   Decide how many days' worth of posts will appear on your blog's home page.

- **Enable WYSIWYG**   You can turn off the WYSIWYG tool for editing blog entries if you don't like it.

- **Categories**   You can create different categories for your blog entries, effectively giving you more than one weblog.

- **Navigator Links**   This preference provides the easy way to add links to your weblog page so that visitors can see the hyperlinks to sites you find interesting or worthy. The way you create the links is a little different from standard HTML, but it follows the example shown in the entry box. The links are done this way (using XML) so that they can be reconfigured successfully by different themes; if, instead, you edited the templates directly to add links, those manual links would be overwritten if you ever changed the theme. The Navigator Links, by contrast, would be added automatically to the new theme.

```
<navigator>
<item name="My Pictures" pagename="http://www.mysite.com/pictures/index.html" />
<item name="Plastic.com" pagename="http://www.plastic.com" />
<item name="Weblogs.com" pagename="http://www.weblogs.com" />
<item name="Wil Wheaton" pagename="http://www.wilwheaton.net" />
</navigator>
```

- **RSS configuration**   Here you can configure RSS (Rich Site Summary) headline sharing if you need to change from the default settings. (See Chapter 11 for more on RSS and headline syndication.)

- **Comments**   Turn on and off the comment feature and, if desired, change the server that's used to host the comments. (Note the link to the Item Template preferences; you may need to alter the Item Template to display your comments if you are using a template other than the default one for your Radio weblog.)

- **Item-level Title and Link**   Should each blog entry get its own title, and should the title be a link to a permanent version of the entry?

- **Templates**   Using these options, you can directly edit the templates for your pages, including the CSS style sheet definitions and, if desired, hard-coded HTML. The Main Template is the template used for most pages on your site, whereas the Home Page template is for your blog's index page. The Item template can be used to change the appearance of individual blog entries on the page. (See Chapter 8 for help with CSS and template editing.)

The other entries move on to more complex issues, such as customizing Internet and server settings as well as managing passwords and file/folder issues. You can page through them to get a sense of what they do. You'll also find links to preferences for the News Aggregator, which we'll discuss in the next section.

Aggregate News

Radio UserLand's calling-card feature is the News Aggregator. You can view this feature by clicking the News link that appears at the top of the browser window when you're viewing your desktop website. The page that results is a series of headlines from news and blog sources all over the Internet. Figure 4-9 shows the aggregator in action. Radio enables you to view these headlines and then click through to the original story if necessary. You can also click the Post button in each entry's row to post the text and link of the item in a blog entry of your own. That makes it quick and easy to post a link or quote and then start blogging about it!

You'll likely want to customize the newsfeed. Click the Subscribed link in the text under the News Aggregator heading. This gives you an opportunity to delete any of the sites listed (place a checkmark next to the doomed feed and then click the Delete button) or subscribe to any website—whether it's a commercial news site or a weblog—that allows its headlines to be syndicated. You need to enter in

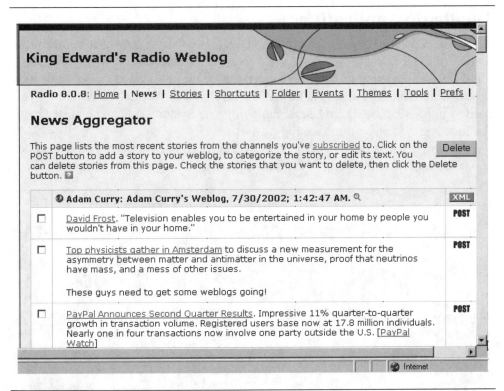

FIGURE 4-9   The News Aggregator brings in headlines from sites around the Web.

the URL entry box a valid address for an XML newsfeed. These are very common on weblogs. Although they're not always as easy to find on commercial sites, many do offer them.

> **TIP**   *See Chapter 10 for more on syndicating other sites' headlines; if you're looking for headlines to add to the News Aggregator, visit http://blogspace.com/rss/writers for starters.*

Once you have the subscriptions set the way you want them, you can use the News page to quickly move through the current stories so that you can get a sense of what's relevant to your blog. When you find something interesting, you can click the Post button and quickly start blogging. It's a great way to stay on top of the headlines at your favorite places without quite so much web surfing.

The Radio Application

Before we finish our discussion of Radio UserLand, there's one other interesting portion of the tool you might want to explore—the Radio UserLand application itself. If you're working on a Macintosh, you'll see the application's floating window appear whenever you launch Radio UserLand; if you're working in Windows, you need to right-click the Radio UserLand item in the System Tray and choose Open Radio to see the application (see Figure 4-10).

Viewing the application isn't necessary, but it can occasionally be useful. The application offers menu commands that enable you to dig a little deeper into the

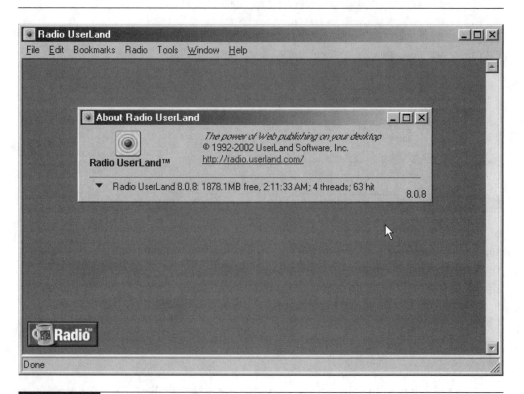

FIGURE 4-10   The Radio UserLand application

tool, particularly if you're the type who likes to tinker. This list includes a few items of interest:

- **Notepad**   Need to jot some notes or an entry you're not yet ready to post? Choose Edit | Open Notepad to view the Notepad window, where you can type your notes. Choose File | Save to save the file for later use.

- **Radio | Local Pages**   Use this menu item to move quickly to a page on your desktop website; the options in the Local Pages menu mostly duplicate the menu that you see in the browser window when you're editing your Radio site.

- **Radio | Cloud Pages**   Links to your home page, Referers, and ranking pages.

- **Radio | Templates**   Select a template in this window to edit it directly in a text editor window instead of a browser.

- **Radio | Publish**   Choose items in this menu to publish them (or republish them) to your website. This is particularly useful if you've set upstreaming to only occur when you publish new pages.

Radio has many more features that can't be touched on in this quick overview, including the ability to manage static pages along with your blog and special tools for other interesting tasks, such as Whois lookups (to see who owns a particular domain name). One that is worth mentioning is the myPictures folder, found inside the www folder inside the Radio UserLand folder. Image files that you place in myPictures are automatically uploaded (or upstreamed) to the server, where they can be accessed easily in your blog entries using an URL such as this:

```
<img src="/mypictures/image1.gif" />
```

NOTE

You may need to enable the My Pictures feature first; you can do that by clicking the My Pictures link that appears in the Status Center on your main editing page, or by choosing Tools and then clicking My Pictures.

So, that's Radio UserLand. See http://radiodocs.userland.com for more information and theory as well as the philosophy of the tool. I think it's a great way to blog, particularly if you find the News Aggregator interesting. The user number-based URLs are a bit of a tough break, though, and I've seen many folks either move their Radio site to their own server or move on to a server-side tool, such as those discussed in the next chapters, after trying Radio.

More...

In Chapter 5, we'll explore using the server-side solution Greymatter, followed by Movable Type and pMachine in the subsequent chapters. If you're already hooked on one of the hosted or desktop tools discussed in this chapter, however, there isn't too much reason to read the next three chapters. Skip to Chapter 8 and beyond, where you'll learn to tweak and augment your blog.

M	T	W	T	F	S		S	M	T	W	T	F	S		S	M	T	W	T	F	S		S	M	T	W	T	F	S
		1	2	3	4				1	2	3	4				1	2	3	4				1	2	3	4
6	7	8	9	10	11		5	6	7	8	9	10	11		5	6	7	8	9	10	11		5	6	7	8	9	10	11
13	14	15	16	17	18		12	13	14	15	16	17	18		12	13	14	15	16	17	18		12	13	14	15	16	17	18
20	21	22	23	24	25		19	20	21	22	23	24	25		19	20	21	22	23	24	25		19	20	21	22	23	24	25
27	28	29	30	31			26	27	28	29	30	31			26	27	28	29	30	31			26	27	28	29	30	31	

Chapter 5

Setting Up and Using Greymatter

In this chapter:

- Features and requirements
- Downloading and installing Greymatter
- Configuring the server
- Posting and editing entries
- Managing authors
- Administering the weblog
- Editing the templates
- Adding static pages
- Troubleshooting

Created by Noah Grey, Greymatter calls itself the "original open-source weblogging and journaling software."

Although something like weblogging was going on well before Greymatter came on the scene, it has certainly been instrumental in bringing the idea of blogging to the masses and has been at the heart of the phenomenon as blogging has become more familiar and mainstream. Although Noah himself no longer supports Greymatter, the software has continued to be popular thanks to an active support community as well as programmers who continue to work on "mods" (modifications) to enhance the usefulness of the software.

The Greymatter Decision: Features and Requirements

Greymatter hits the high points for the server-side weblog—it offers a clean design, supports user comments, and is customizable via HTML-based templates. It compares favorably to the other two server-side solutions discussed in the coming chapters—Movable Type and pMachine—with the exception that the software itself is not as actively updated. It also offers a cost advantage—Greymatter is free under all circumstances, whereas the other two charge for corporate licenses (Movable Type), and for "Pro"-level features (pMachine).

NOTE   *Greymatter is actually "donate-ware," meaning you're encouraged to donate money if you find it useful. For a minimum $10 donation, your site is listed on the Greymatter website.*

Greymatter pioneered the blogging category as I've defined it, so it isn't surprising that its feature set represents the norm of what you'd expect in blogging software. These features include the following:

- **Comments**   Users can post comments that are attached to the bottom of the article page (see Figure 5-1). Users can also offer "Karma votes" for each entry, which is a simple way to express approval or disapproval by adding to or subtracting from the Karma number.

- **Archiving**   Greymatter is based on a database, so it makes it easy to create effective archives that are easily accessible to your visitors.

- **Images**   Greymatter handles images well, enabling you to add them to entries or have them pop up in windows of their own when clicked.

- **Multiple authors**   You can register additional people as editors for your site, enabling them to post their own stories.

- **Censoring and IP banning**   Because others are allowed to post on your site (in the form of comments), you can opt to "curse-word censor" those posts automatically, and you have the option of banning a particular IP address if you find that a particular user (or users from a particular computer) is abusive or annoying.

- **Template and variable-based sites**   Your site's appearance is based on HTML templates, so you can edit them to alter the overall look and feel of the site. Likewise, Greymatter offers special variables that you use within those templates in order to place dynamic content, and you can alter those variables to get slightly different results on your pages.

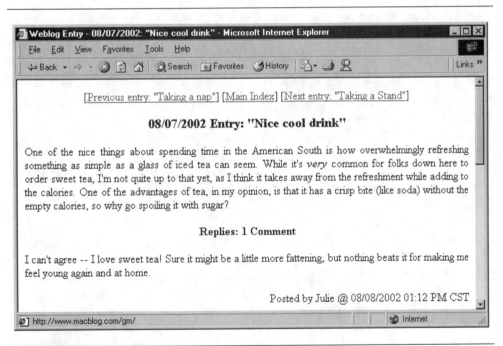

FIGURE 5-1   Comments add to the discussion in Greymatter.

Greymatter's server requirements are fairly simple. You need to have the ability to run your own CGI scripts written in Perl 5, and you need to be able to access your web server via an FTP client (if it's a remote web server) in order to upload the files and change the permissions settings so that certain files can be written to. In most cases, this means you can use *any* web server space that you pay for—some freebie sites won't let you install this type of script.

Get Started

Before you can begin working with Greymatter you'll need to first obtain it and then go through the installation and configuration process. This definitely isn't

Who Is Greymatter For?

The big question, of course, is whether or not Greymatter is right for your site. The easy answer is that Greymatter is a great choice for a personal blog, particularly one that links to many other sites, offers the occasional photo or digital image, and invites users to comment on the entries. Greymatter has been tested and used by some fairly famous bloggers, and it has come through with flying colors.

It has its limits, though. The Greymatter "world" doesn't offer many third-party options, and GM's initial design is quite basic, making it great for tinkerers but not as "install and go" as some other options. Greymatter also doesn't offer the automated linking and syndication tools of Movable Type or the community-focused options—forums, membership, newsletter tools—offered by pMachine. And creating multiple weblogs with Greymatter requires multiple installations of the software, whereas this is much easier to do in Movable Type and pMachine. If you're looking to create a "big" site with many authors and participants, Greymatter works, but it may not be the best choice in all circumstances.

The final consideration is the fact that the author of Greymatter, Noah Grey, is no longer actively involved in its development. (A fact he confirmed for this book.) Therefore, although the product is open source and has the support of a devoted community, it doesn't offer a single source in terms of a programmer or team of programmers the way that both Movable Type and pMachine do currently. In other words, you're a little less likely to get a new requested feature in Greymatter than you are in the others, and Greymatter could begin to fall gradually behind in terms of relative feature sets as the other tools advance and improve. That said, it should be a useful alternative for a long time to come.

hard (Greymatter has, arguably, the easiest installation process of the server-side tools discussed in this book), but it can be frustrating if you miss a step and end up confronted with an error message. Therefore, be sure to read the steps outlined in this section (and Greymatter's own instructions) closely.

CAUTION

Greymatter is not particularly easy to install on a Windows NT–based server—so much so that even the volunteers at the Greymatter support boards often seem to toss up their hands (virtually) in defeat. I would simply recommend using a Unix-based server or trying a different blogging solution if changing the server platform isn't an option.

Download and Install Greymatter

To begin with Greymatter you'll need to download it. Visit http://www.noahgrey.com/greysoft/ and look for the links to the mirror sites, which make Greymatter available for download. Select one of the mirror sites and click to download the Greymatter software. In most cases, Greymatter is distributed in one of two types of archives—either a Windows-oriented ZIP archive or a Unix-flavored gzip archive (this works for Mac OS X, too). Download one of them to your computer and then expand the archive.

NOTE

Mac users in particular may be used to the term folder, *which is referred to on Windows and Unix systems as a* directory. *I'll use the latter term in this section (and elsewhere in the book), but they're the same basic concept.*

Once you have Greymatter expanded into a directory, open that directory and locate the file Install.html. In most operating systems you should be able to double-click that file to view it in a web browser. If not, use the web browser's Open File command to navigate to and open Install.html. You should read the document to learn the steps and pitfalls of installing Greymatter. I'll also summarize them here a bit more briefly:

1. Most of the time you won't need to worry about this step if you're installing on a Unix-based server, but it's here for the record. Four of the CGI scripts that make up Greymatter *may* need to be edited, because they need to know the location of Perl on your web server computer. (For nearly all Unix servers, the default location is correct.) Each of these files includes a path statement for the standard location, but yours may differ (you'll need to ask your systems administrator if you don't know). The files are gm.cgi,

gm-karma.cgi, gm-comments.cgi, and gm-upload.cgi. Open these in a text editor and edit the first line of each one, which will look like this:

```
#!/usr/bin/perl
```

This is the standard location on Unix-based servers (see Figure 5-2). If your web server's version of Perl is in a different location, change that path statement here (keep the #! at the beginning) and then save the file, making sure it's still a plain-text file.

NOTE   *Your FTP application likely has binary mode and ASCII mode options for uploading files to the server. With Greymatter, all files should be uploaded as ASCII (plain text), except for the file gm-icon.gif, which should be uploaded in binary mode. If your FTP application doesn't handle this automatically, you'll want to specify the modes.*

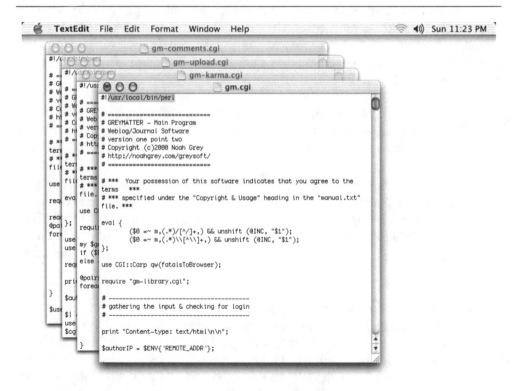

FIGURE 5-2   Editing the CGI scripts to include the proper Perl path

2. Rename the file index.htm if you'd like your blog's index page to be named something different (such as weblog.html).

3. Launch your FTP application and upload the files to your web server computer. The CGI files should go in your designated CGI directory—often that's cgi-bin, but it may be called something else on your web host. The other files can go in the directory that you've decided to use for the index level of your blog—if that's the root directory of your web server space, that's great. You can also create and use a subdirectory, such as *gm* or *blog,* if you'd like your blog to be accessible at an URL such as http://www.mywebaddress.com/blog/index.htm or http://www.ourwebaddress.com/tommy/weblog.html. The most important files are index.htm (or whatever you've named it) and gm-icon.gif, which should be uploaded in binary mode.

CAUTION *It's important that you do not store Greymatter's CGI scripts in a regularly accessible public HTML directory, even if your host makes that an option. (With many hosting accounts, CGI scripts stored right next to regular HTML documents can still be executed as scripts.) With Greymatter, putting the CGI scripts in a regular directory could be a security risk, because it would allow anyone to read the file gm-authors.cgi, where information about the author accounts is stored. Stick to your designated cgi-bin directory for Greymatter's CGI scripts and you'll be fine.*

4. Using the FTP application (or a command-line interface, if you have one available for accessing your web server), you'll need to change the permissions of your CGI files so that all of them are readable and writeable. (At the Unix command line, you can use the command chmod 666 *.cgi). Also, the four CGI scripts mentioned previously—gm.cgi, gm-karma.cgi, gm-comments.cgi, and gm-upload.cgi—need to be readable, writeable, and executable for the owner, and readable and executable by others (that's chmod 755 gm.cgi, and so on). Figure 5-3 shows the changes.

NOTE *In Unix-style convention, permissions are expressed as three numbers representing the read/write privileges that individuals have to a file based on the group an individual falls into—the file's owner, the file's group, or "the world." A number such as 755 means that the owner has read, write, and execute privileges while the other two types of individuals have only read and execute privileges. If you aren't setting permissions at a Unix command line, however, you'll likely use check boxes, in which case you'll need to make the selections manually.*

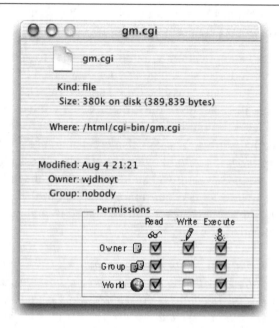

FIGURE 5-3   Here's an example of an FTP application changing the permissions on a
CGI script (shown is "755" permissions for the gm.cgi script).

5. Using your FTP program, create a directory for your site's archives. The
   easiest thing to do is to simply create a subdirectory in your main blog
   directory called "archives," although technically it can be anywhere that's
   publicly accessible and it can be called anything.

6. The final step in the installation process is to launch Greymatter in your web
   browser program and see if it works. Enter **http://www.*yourserver*.com/
   cgi-bin/gm.cgi** in your browser's Address entry box and access the page.
   (If your URL is in the form http://www.*yourisp*.com/~*yourname*/ or something
   similar, you would access the program at http://www.*yourisp*.com/
   ~*yourname*/cgi-bin/gm.cgi. In rare instances the cgi-bin directory may be
   accessed via a different name in the URL, such as /cgi-exe/ or similar.)

If you've succeeded, you should be seeing a Greymatter login prompt. For the first login after installation, the username and password are always the same—the username is **Alice** and the password is **wonderland**. (If you have trouble, note the case of the username and password and enter them as shown.) Type these, click the ENTER button, and then move on to the next section.

If you don't see the login prompt, one of a few possible problems has occurred:

- Make sure you're entered the correct URL. If you get an error message saying "404 File Not Found" or something similar, it may mean that you entered the URL to the file gm.cgi incorrectly.

- If you can access the file gm.cgi but you see a file listing, you may have failed to store the file in its proper CGI scripts folder. Check your ISP's instructions for the proper place to put CGI scripts.

NOTE *As mentioned earlier, for security reasons you should only place CGI scripts in the designated cgi-bin directory.*

- If you get a Server Error message or a permission-related error, it's possible that you haven't set permissions correctly. See step 4 in the previous list. You might also have luck uploading the files again, making sure their type (ASCII mode for all files except gm-icon.gif, which requires binary mode) is set correctly.

NOTE *Still having trouble getting up and running? Aside from the HTML-based manual that's included with Greymatter, check the Greymatter discussion boards at http://foshdawg.net/forums/index.php or the Greymatter Installation for Dummies website (not the "official" book series) at http://wiccked.com/gmfd/.*

Configure Greymatter

Once you've logged in to Greymatter successfully, your first step should be to configure it. Greymatter has a fairly extensive number of options, found by clicking the Configuration button in the main interface.

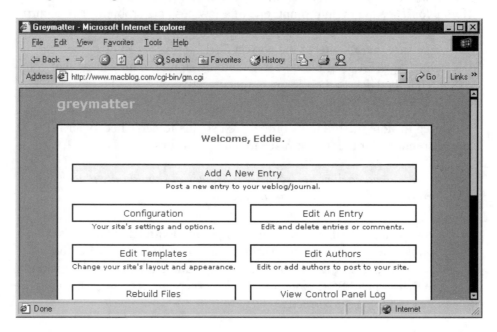

Set Up Directories

On the Configuration page, the first step is to set up your directories so that Greymatter knows where things are stored. If you've used a standard installation and followed the recommendations (your index is named index.htm and you created a subdirectory called archives in the main directory of your blog), then these settings *may* already be correct. In most cases, though, you'll need to change them slightly. In my experience they tend to point to the cgi-bin directory, which is incorrect—many of them need to point to the main weblog directory, where the file index.html (or whatever you've named it) is stored.

Here's a quick look at each entry (note that *local* paths are from the perspective of the web server computer, whereas *website* paths are the URLs to those items as they would be accessed over the Web):

■ **Local Log Path**   Enter the path to the main directory of your weblog; in many cases this will be almost correct, although it may point to the cgi-bin directory instead of the directory where you've uploaded the index.htm file.

■ **Local Entries/Archives Path**   This is the path to the directory you created for archives.

■ **Local CGI Path**   This is the path to the cgi-bin directory where the gm.cgi file (along with others) is located. In most cases, this entry will be correct.

NOTE   *The way these local paths work may be confusing at first. The idea is that they represent the path to a particular file as if you were using your server computer's keyboard. For instance, the path to your main HTML directory might be something like /virtualhosts/mysite.com/www/myblog/, which is the same path you'd use if you had access to your server computer and you were trying to alter files in that directory. Greymatter often gets these path statements close, so usually you just have to worry about getting the last directory or two correct (for example, /virtualhosts/mysite.com/cgi-bin/ vs. /virtualhosts/mysite.com/www/myblog/).*

■ **Website Log Path**   This is the URL to the directory where the file index.htm is located.

■ **Website Entries Path**   This is the URL to the archives folder you created.

■ **Website CGI Path**   This is the URL to the cgi-bin directory on your web host.

If you've changed the name of the index.htm document, you'll need to change that in the Index & Archives option; likewise, if you'd like to use a filename extension other than .htm with your files, you'll want to change that as well. (You may simply prefer .html, for instance, or you may have reason to use .shtml, .php, or whatever.)

NOTE   *Why use these different extensions? Usually because you want to use special commands or scripting in your web pages. The .shtml extension is used for web pages that include server-side includes, whereas .php is used for web pages that include PHP scripting. Each extension is a signal to the web server computer that it may need to look in the document and process a script or command before it can send the page to the reader's web browser.*

Once you've set these up, you can either move on to the additional configuration options or, if you'd like to skip ahead with the default settings and get started on your blog, scroll to the bottom of the page and click Save Configuration. Then, move on to the section "Diagnostics & Repair."

Other Configuration Options

On the Configuration screen you'll see a number of entries beyond the directories you've set up. The options cover how Greymatter behaves, the extent to which users can comment on entries, how many entries appear on the screen, and so forth. Here's a quick overview of the options (I'll touch on the highlights and may skip an option or two that are well explained on the Configuration page itself):

- **Index & Archives**   In these options you can specify the name of the index file and the suffix used for filenames, as discussed in the previous section. You can also choose the number of days' worth of entries to show on the main page and whether or not individual pages should be generated for each entry (if not, you can't use the comments feature). You can opt to keep a master index (creating an index.htm file that's stored in the archives folder that shows a master list of archived stories) and to keep archives in a monthly or weekly format, depending on the status of the Archive Monthly or Weekly option.

- **E-Mail Options**   Enter the path to Sendmail, if you know it, or ask your ISP. (Sendmail is the Unix e-mail program that's generally used on web servers; if your server has another program that should be used, you can enter that instead.) Then, enter an e-mail address and turn on the level of notifications you'd like to receive. You can use this feature to get an e-mail whenever someone comments or votes on an entry.

- **Karma And Comments Options**   Greymatter offers your readers two different community features. They can comment on your entries, and they can give them a "Karma" vote, which is sort of a rating system. The other options dictate how comments and voting work and whether they work in the archives. The instructions on the page are very good, so I've little to add to them except that you *might* want to limit the HTML that readers are able to use in their comments, because it will keep them from linking to images or attempting to embed complex HTML in their responses. (Of course, you might not think that's a bad thing, but it can be a slight security risk and/or you might find people embedding ads, large images, or other content in their responses.) The option to limit HTML to linking and emphasis is one interesting solution.

- **Date & Time Options**   Use these to enter an offset between your local time and your server's time, because your server may be in a different part of the country (assuming you want your site to reflect your local time). You can also enter a time zone (if the current one is incorrect), which can be included in posts.

- **File Uploading Options**   If you enter filename types in the entry box, then only those types can be uploaded; otherwise, any type can be uploaded. (Of course, only you and authorized authors can upload them, so this might not be an issue.) You can also specify a maximum size for uploaded files.

- **Censoring Options**   You can turn on censoring for entries, comments, or both; when you do, censored words are replaced with asterisks. You enter the words that you want to censor in the Censor List. Note the instructions for using brackets so that censored words that match portions of other words don't end up asterisked.

- **Advanced Options**   These options are used to include additional files in your Greymatter blog—generally static pages that you'd like to have the same "look and feel" as your blog. More on these in the section "Add Static Pages," later in this chapter.

- **Miscellaneous Options**   Here you'll find the catch-all category, including options that allow you to choose whether to place cookies on your (and your authors') machines to remember them for future logins, whether a log of control panel activity should be kept, and whether to allow a special "easy formatting" approach for entries and/or comments. You can also choose a default view for the Edit An Entry list (see the section "Post and Edit Entries," later in this chapter, for more information). We'll touch on some of these other options in other parts of the chapter as well.

Whenever you're done changing options, you should head down to the bottom of the screen and click the Save Configuration button. You're taken to the main control panel screen, where you can move on to other tasks.

Diagnostics and Repair

One other option on the Configuration screen is worth discussing before we move on to the day-to-day items of your site. At the bottom of the screen is the Diagnostics

& Repair button. It's a good idea to click this button soon after installing Greymatter and making configuration choices, because it checks Greymatter's ability to work with all the files and folders as you've configured them (and it makes sure they exist). On the Diagnostics & Repair screen, read the introductory text and click the Perform Diagnostics & Repair button. Depending on your number of entries, it can take a while to complete. Once completed, you'll see whether the operating was successful and what, if anything, you need to fix.

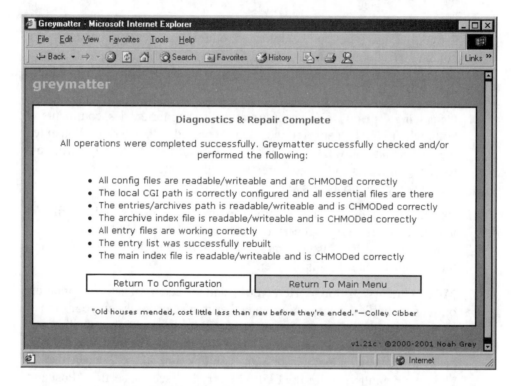

Once you've soaked up the message, click the Return To Configuration button to change any configuration that needs to be changed or click Return To Main Menu to move on. (You may actually need to launch your FTP application and change permissions or other settings if that's the report you get from the Diagnostics & Repair tool.)

You can return to this tool at any time, by the way, particularly after you've changed files and folders on the server, after you've made changes on the Configuration screen, or whenever you seem to be encountering some trouble.

Manage Authors

I know, you're dying to start posting. First things first, though. You need to change your current author account; otherwise, you're going to post as Alice, your password will still be wonderland, and someone may come along and figure out how to poke holes in your Greymatter setup.

Edit an Author

From the main menu of the control panel, click the Edit Authors button. This loads the Author Panel screen. Now, select the radio button next to Alice and click the Edit Selected Author button. You'll see another full page of configuration options. To begin, change the name in the Name entry box to the name you'd like to appear on your posts; in the Password box, enter a new password. (Try for one that's at least eight characters long and includes nonsense words with numbers.) Enter your e-mail address and home page as well and then move on to all the various options.

NOTE   *If you include an e-mail address without a home page, your name at the bottom of your entries (by default) will include a link to your e-mail address. If you do include a home page, your name will link to that home page. That's just something to consider if you'd prefer not to have your e-mail address listed on your site. (E-mail harvester programs can grab e-mail addresses stored in this way on web pages, adding them to junk mail lists.)*

The rest of the author-related options basically enable you to set up different levels of access for *other* authors; presumably you can trust yourself. Once you do add other authors, assuming you ever do, you can use the configuration options to limit those authors in their power over the blog. For example, you can enable them to edit only their own entries, and you can disable their ability to configure the blog and/or upload files. The power is in your hands.

When you're done editing the author, click Save Changes To This Author. The changes are saved and the main Author panel reappears.

Add an Author

If you decide to add an author, you can do that from the main Author panel. In the Register A New Author section, enter a name and password for the author; the e-mail and home page are optional, but again they follow the rule discussed earlier in which the author's name becomes a link to the home page if one is listed, the e-mail address is used if there isn't a home page, and the author's name appears as regular text if neither a home page or an e-mail address is entered. Choose the author's default access—All Access, No Access, or Post & Edit Their Own Entries Only—then click the Create New Author button. Once created, the author is added to the list at the top of the page; select that author's radio button and click the Edit Selected Author button to see the full configuration page for that author.

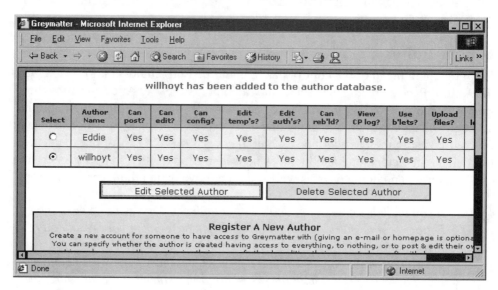

To delete an author, select the radio button next to the name in the author list at the top of the Author panel; then click Delete Selected Author. The author is deleted without warning.

 For future logins, it's worth noting that Greymatter is case sensitive, so you'll need to use the same capitalization for your username as you do when creating the author. Otherwise, you may have trouble logging in.

Post and Edit Entries

The whole reason to install this software, of course, is to make it a little easier to post and edit entries that appear, in journal format, on the front page of your site. So let's cover how to post and edit entries in this section.

Post an Entry

From the main menu of the control panel, you'll add a new entry by clicking the Add A New Entry button. (If only everything in life were this well labeled.) This brings up, as one might guess, the Add A New Entry page (see Figure 5-4).

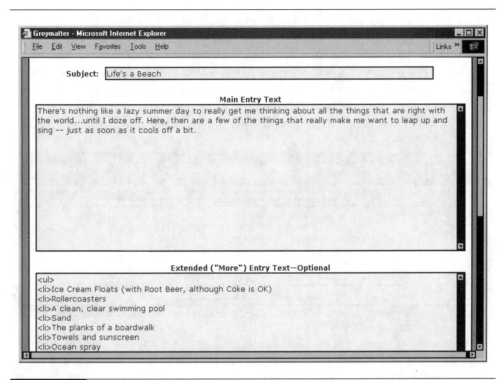

FIGURE 5-4   The Add A New Entry page is where you'll spend a fair amount of time.

The Add A New Entry page has three different boxes—Subject, Main Entry Text, and Extended ("More") Entry Text. Begin by entering a subject for your entry; it won't actually appear on your blog's index page (by default), but it will appear in the list of stories that you can later edit. Next, you type your entry.

If you'd like your entry to appear exclusively on the index page (or, later, on the archives page) without "jumping" to its own page, you should type the entire thing in the Main Entry Text box. As you type, note that spaces and returns (when you press ENTER or RETURN) will be displayed when the final version is posted. Also, you can use HTML codes to mark up the text, adding emphasis, hyperlinks, and so on. (Remember that this is actually based on a setting in the configuration options, so if you've turned off HTML you many not be able to use it.)

If you'd like your story to jump to another page, you should type part of it (the part that will appear on the main page) in the Main Entry Text box and then type the rest of it in the Extended ("More") Entry Text box. The portion of the entry that's in the More box will only appear on the jump page that's created. (A link in the original entry on your index page will lead to the entry's own page, which will include both the Main Entry text and the More text on that same page.)

When you're done entering text, you have some options at the bottom of the page; scroll down and you'll see the option to turn off karma voting and/or comments if you don't want this particular entry to offer these features. You can also turn on the Keep This Entry at the Top of the Main Log option if you'd like this to be a "cover story" of sorts that doesn't scroll down the list when new stories are added.

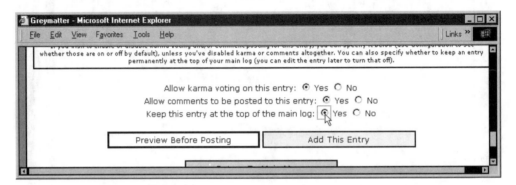

After making your choices, click Add This Entry and it will be added to your blog and you'll be returned to the main menu. Alternatively, you can click the Preview Before Posting button to see a preview of your entry; on the preview page you can click Re-Edit This Entry if you see a mistake, or you can click Add This Entry to add it to the blog.

Want to check out your page? In the main menu, the bottom button is the Visit Your Site button; click it to launch your blog in a new browser window and see your handiwork.

Edit or Close an Entry

Once you've gotten some entries into your blog, you can edit them by clicking the Edit An Entry button in the main menu. When you do so, you'll see the Entry Selection screen, shown in Figure 5-5, where a list of your most recent entries is available. Note that you can change which entries are listed by selecting one of the entries in the List menu and clicking Change View. You can also use the Sort By radio buttons to change the order of the list.

To edit an entry, select it in the list and click Edit Selected Entry. The actual editing should be familiar—you'll see a page that's nearly identical to the one you used to create the entry. Make any necessary edits and then make changes to the

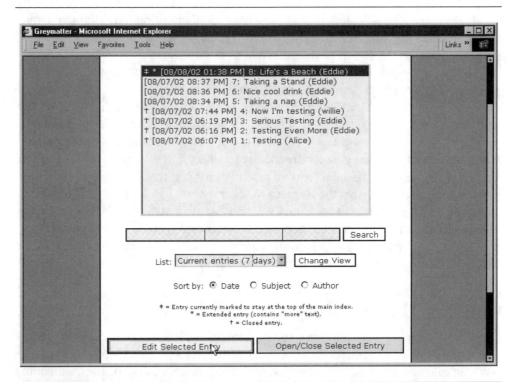

FIGURE 5-5 The Entry Selection screen enables you to select and edit your entries (note the coded markings next to each message that show their status).

entry's karma and comment options, if desired. Finally, click the Save Changes to This Entry button if you made changes worth saving, or you can click the Undo Changes Since Last Save if you've made some mistakes or otherwise want to start again with the entry as it was before you began editing it. If you have no desire to save the changes for this entry, click the Select Another Entry or the Return to Main Menu button.

NOTE *Wondering why you might want to uncheck the option Automatically Rebuild Main Index Page and This Entry's Page After Saving? Because you might want to edit more than one entry in this session and then rebuild them all at once. (You rebuild in Greymatter so that any changes you make can be reflected in all the pertinent files—the index, the archive, the entry page, and so on. This is discussed in more detail in the section "Administer the Weblog.") Doing so will save you time if you have a number of changes you need to make in one sitting.*

Back on the Entry Selection page, you have another option. Highlight an entry and choose Open/Close Selected Entry, and you can toggle its status. An "open" story is posted on the site or in the archives; a "closed" story is effectively deleted in that it won't appear in the blog. It remains here, however, so that you can reinstate it by opening it sometime in the future, if desired.

Finally, the Search And Replace button can be clicked if you'd like Greymatter to perform the special tasks of replacing *every* instance of a particular word in all your entries. You won't use this much, but it can be really handy for changing a word, phrase, or link that you use frequently (such as if you've put your own site's URL in a number of entries but you've recently changed that URL) or for deleting a word or phrase (just leave the Replace With entry box blank and the Search For item will be deleted). It's also a handy way to rewrite history—replace your old significant other's name with the new one's and, presto, you've always loved that person (at least, according to your blog's archives, and, er, assuming you didn't describe the original significant other too carefully).

Administer the Weblog

There isn't too much administration to Greymatter, particularly because your readers don't really log in or maintain user accounts as they do with some blogging software. You can manage a few things, however, including the rebuilding of files, uploading files and banning users by IP address.

Rebuild Files

Unlike some blogging software, Greymatter doesn't build pages "on the fly" when they're requested by a visitor's web browser. Instead, Greymatter is really just a database-driven tool for building "static" web pages. So, whenever you make a change in the software, your files need to be rebuilt to reflect that change on the index page, on the entry page, in the archives, and so on. That's what the Rebuild Files command is for—it's basically the equivalent of the "publish" or "publish all" commands in other tools.

If you've opted to turn off the automatic rebuilding of files while you've been editing entries, you can rebuild them all at once easily. Click the Rebuild Files button in the main menu. On the Rebuild Files screen, you'll have a number of options. Most of them are fairly self-explanatory, and many of them won't really need to be performed unless you've changed the underlying template for your indexes or individual pages. (Greymatter, like most weblog software, builds the published pages based on HTML templates.)

If you've recently added entries and you want your site to reflect them, you can choose Rebuild Last Entry Only or Rebuild Main Index File; if you've made extensive changes, though, you might just want to use Rebuild All Entry Pages (every page that has an entry on it) or, simply, Rebuild Everything. (This can take a while, though, once you have hundreds of entries.)

Upload Files

If you want to add images to your entries or link to files that your users can download from a link in your blog, you can do that from within the Greymatter control panel. (You could also ftp them separately and simply use the <img /> element to add an image or the <a> anchor to link to a file on your server.) From the main menu, click the Upload Files button. On the Upload Files page you'll see an entry box for the filename and path; if you don't know it, click the Browse button to browse for the file you want to upload.

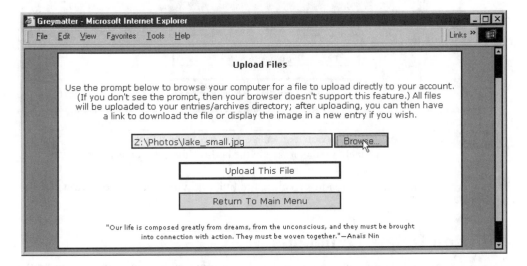

After you click the Upload This File button, if your file is a picture, you'll see it in the browser window and you'll be shown the proper HTML code to use to link to the image in an entry (see Figure 5-6). In fact, you can click the Include This Image In A New Entry button or the Include In Entry As A Popup Window to cause the Add A New Entry screen to appear, complete with the appropriate link for the file already in the Main Text Entry box.

If you've uploaded a file, you'll see the Include This Link In A New Entry button, which enables you to link to the document or file that you've uploaded via

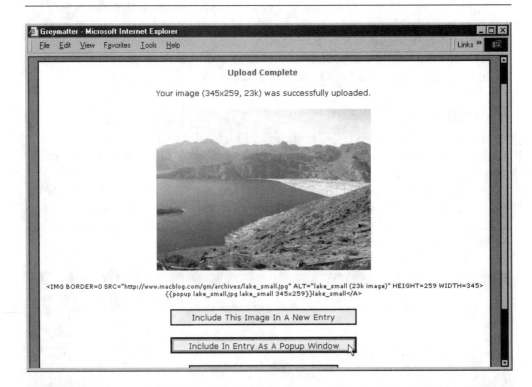

FIGURE 5-6   When you're uploading an image, you have the opportunity to create a new entry that includes that image in the body of the entry or as a pop-up window.

a blog entry. This will allow readers to click the link and view the image or download the file.

Edit and Delete Comments

If you've enabled comments to your entries, you may occasionally get a comment that is either distasteful or offensive or otherwise inappropriate—particularly given that Greymatter doesn't require any sort of membership or e-mail address confirmation, which will sometimes deter people who have something untoward to say on the Internet from saying it in *your* blog. In any case, you have the option of editing or deleting comments (including your own) that are added to your blog entries. Here's how:

1. From the main menu, click Edit An Entry.

2. In the Entry Selection list, choose the entry with the comment you want to edit or delete and then click the Edit Selected Entry button.

3. In the Editing Entry window, scroll down until you see the comment.

4. Select the radio button next to the comment in question and then click Edit Selected Comment or Delete Selected Comment.

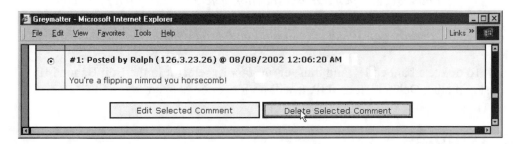

If you choose Delete Selected Comment, it's gone immediately. If you choose Edit Selected Comment, you'll see a new page that lets you edit the author's name, e-mail address, home page, and comment. Click Save Changes To This Comment when you're done with it.

Ban IPs

Greymatter gives you the option of banning a certain IP address (or a range of IP addresses) from being able to comment on stories or, if you've enabled the feature, from "karma voting" on entries. If you have someone who is posting items that you don't think are appropriate, that you find offensive, or that just annoy you, you can ban that person's IP address. (An IP address is a particular computer's unique numerical address on the Internet. Realize that a particular user's IP address can vary if she uses a dial-up or otherwise dynamic Internet connection or service, so banning isn't always effective.)

Of course, before you can ban an IP address, you first you need to figure out what IP address to ban. You can do this by viewing the Editing Entry window and scrolling down to see the comment and its author—next to the author's name will be the IP address that Greymatter logged for that comment.

To ban an IP, click the Edit Banned IP List button in the main menu. In the New IP To Ban entry box, enter the IP number you just located. You can also enter the person's name, if desired. (It's only for use in this list.) Then, click the Add New IP Address button.

Don't ban your own IP address. You won't be able to access the Greymatter control panel. (I found this out the hard way while writing this chapter.) If you do, you'll need to access the control panel from another IP address (either change yours, which you can sometimes do by resetting your modem or broadband connection, or use a different computer) and delete the banned IP. Alternatively, you can use FTP to download the file gm-banlist.cgi, open it in a text editor, delete your IP from it, and then save it and re-upload it using FTP. Once it's returned, you may need to set the permissions for the file to read and write (chmod 666) again.

To delete a banned IP (and thus, er, *un-ban* it) select it in the Edit Banned IP List and click Delete Selected IP. It will no longer be banned.

Edit Templates

You may have noticed something about the basic Greymatter site layout if you've previewed it after adding some entries—it's kinda dull (see Figure 5-7). There is very little design, the title of the site is "My Weblog," and some very basic fonts are used. To change things, you'll want to dig into the templates.

Download Templates

The easiest way to change the look of your site in a hurry is to find some prebuilt templates, many of which are available for Greymatter. In many cases, you can simply copy the prebuilt templates from a website and then paste them into the editable templates that Greymatter provides access to via the control panel. For Greymatter-specific templates, see GM Templates (http://foshdawg.net/gm/templates/), where you can grab one of four very popular looks and paste them directly into the individual template pages available via the control panel.

NOTE　*You can also use a variety of other prebuilt templates for your site, but they'll require some customization. See Chapter 8 for hints and details.*

Edit Templates Yourself

The more grueling, but personalized and flexible, way to change the look of your Greymatter blog is to dig into the templates yourself and make changes. To see the templates, click the Edit Templates button in the main menu. On the Edit Templates screen you'll see buttons that lead to the various templates used as the foundation

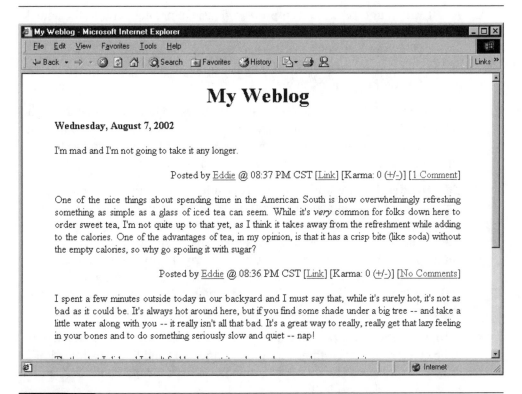

FIGURE 5-7   The site that Greymatter generates by default is fairly bare and boring.

of your site. To edit them, you'll open each one individually. Here's a quick look at what each template button leads to:

- **Edit Main Index-Related Templates**   Here is where you'll edit the template used for your site's main index page, as well as the way that individual entries are formatted on that page. You can individually change the way the Date header looks on your blog, and you can add a special separator between each entry. Finally, you can format the "Stay at Top" entry if you elect to use one.

- **Edit Archive-Related Templates**   These are basically the sample templates mentioned previously, but they're for the archives portion of your site, not the main pages. With these templates you're free to make things a little different in your archives so that visitors can immediately know that they're digging into the past.

■ **Edit Entry Page-Related Templates**   These templates refer to the actual full-page presentation of an entry, whether it's a page that has "more" text or not. (These are the pages that are reached by clicking the Link, Comments, or More hyperlink in an entry.) Likewise, you can alter the full-page templates for the archives as well.

■ **Edit Karma & Comments-Related Templates**   Here you can change the elements that appear when an entry has the karma voting and/or comments features active. If an entry does have those turned on, it will look to these templates to see how to render the related links and information.

■ **Edit Header, Footer, and Sidebar Templates**   With these templates you can define special elements that you'd like to see on every page (or most every page) of your site, whether in the header, in the footer, or along the side of the page—all common places to put fixed elements such as the name of the site, special links, controls, copyright information, and so on. You define an item in these templates (for instance, a header) and then you add simple variables to your other pages (such as {{header}}) to add this markup easily to those pages.

■ **Edit Miscellaneous Templates**   You can you change a variety of smaller templates used for everything from formatting Next and Previous hyperlinks to how various lists should appear, how the Search form should look, and how the calendar will look.

Some of these templates get a little complicated and specific, but they're meant to be—the idea is to provide as much control as possible over the way the site looks and behaves. That means offering up tons of little templates to enable you to make changes and tweaks.

The broader strokes, however, are a bit easier. If you'd like to change the title of your blog, open Main Index-Related Templates and locate the following code:

```
<FONT SIZE=6><B>My Weblog</B></FONT>
```

Change it to whatever you like. Here's an example:

```
<FONT SIZE=6><B>Eddie's Castle</B></FONT>
```

Actually, Greymatter's templates leave something to be desired for an XHTML purist, because they adhere to a slightly older standard and use some elements that aren't recommended. Instead of the preceding, you could replace the entry

```
<P ALIGN=CENTER>
<FONT SIZE=6><B>My Weblog</B></FONT>
</P>
```

with something like this:

```
<h1 align="center" style="font: arial, Helvetica;
font-variant: small-caps">Eddie's Castle</h1>
<hr align="center" width="35%">
```

This produces a fairly pleasing result, as you can see (I'm using some CSS style sheet code here, which will be discussed in more detail in Chapter 8):

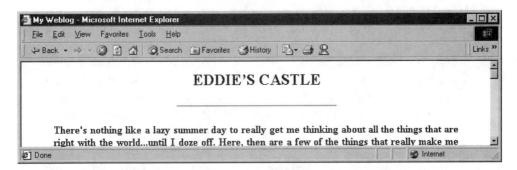

Even better, of course, would be to create an attractive image to go at the top of the page and then include it using an <img /> element. In fact, you could include that image at the top of every page using the header feature. Choose the Edit Header, Footer, and Sidebar button on the Edit Templates page and then add the following in the header section:

```
<div align="center">
<img src="http://www.myowngreatwebsite.com/images/topflag.gif"
alt="Eddie's Castle" />
</div>
```

You'd need to upload the image to the proper location, as specified in the src portion of the <img /> element. With this header created (scroll to the bottom of the page and click the Save Template Changes button), you could return to Main Index-Related Templates and simply delete

```
<P ALIGN=CENTER>
<FONT SIZE=6><B>My Weblog</B></FONT>
</P>
```

because the {{header}} variable right above it will be used to render the new header:

```
<P ALIGN=CENTER>
{{header}}
</P>
```

This would cause the header to appear on this page and on any page that uses this one as a template. You could then add the {{header}} variable to any template (such as the Archive-Related and Full-Page Entry-Related Templates) that represents a page where you want that particular header to appear. In fact, you'll find that many of them already have the {{header}} variable, meaning all you need to do is delete any text that you no longer want on the page. The same is true of the {{footer}} variable and the {{sidebar}} template, which is particularly useful if you'd like the same links, personal images, bio, and so on to appear on each of your pages.

NOTE *Most of the template pages have a check box at the bottom that you can uncheck if you don't want your site (or portions of it) rebuilt before you click the Save Template Changes button. Otherwise, you may wait for the entire site to be rebuilt when you're making even minor changes that don't yet warrant a rebuild.*

As you dig further into the templates, you'll come across Greymatter's own template variables. *Template variables* are the item names that are stand-ins for the database content that Greymatter will pour into the template, such as the body of the entries, their authors, datelines, and so forth, whenever you rebuild the pages.

Back on the Main Index-Related Templates page you can scroll down to the templates that govern the standard entries, for instance, and rearrange items as desired. For a quick and simple change, you could alter the Date Grouping Template, for instance, by changing

```
<P ALIGN=LEFT>
<B>{{weekday}}, {{monthword}} {{day}}, {{yearyear}}</B>
</P>
```

to something like this:

```
<h2>{{monthword}} {{day}}, {{yearyear}} ({{weekday}})</h2>
```

Using Greymatter's date-specific variables, you can rearrange the timestamp so that it looks a little different, as shown here:

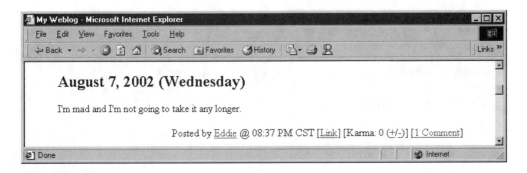

That's how the templates and variables work. Again, to get serious about changing the overall look of your site, you'll need to know some HTML. But if you spend a little time with the templates, they'll become more familiar and you'll get a sense of how they work together to make your Greymatter site look the way it does. (The Greymatter HTML manual, included with the software and available at http://www.noahgrey.com/greysoft/manual.shtml offers a complete look at the Greymatter template variables and how they can be used.)

Add Static Pages

Although most of what you want to do is accomplished in the blogging software itself, you'll occasionally find that you want to add static pages to the site—for example, your bio, your resume, a list of your favorite albums, and a page of links to your favorite sites. This is easily done with a combination of the {{header}}, {{footer}}, and {{sidebar}} variables, which can be used to add the markup from those templates (discussed in the previous section) in your static pages.

Here's how it works:

1. Build the static page in HTML. You can create a simple page or a complex one. If you plan to include the {{header}}, {{footer}}, and {{sidebar}} variables, make the body of the page look reasonably simple and similar to your other Greymatter pages.

2. Add the {{header}}, {{footer}}, and {{sidebar}} variables to the page where appropriate (see Figure 5-8).

3. Upload the page to your server, preferably to the root folder that you're using for your Greymatter files (not the cgi-bin folder, but the public HTML folder).

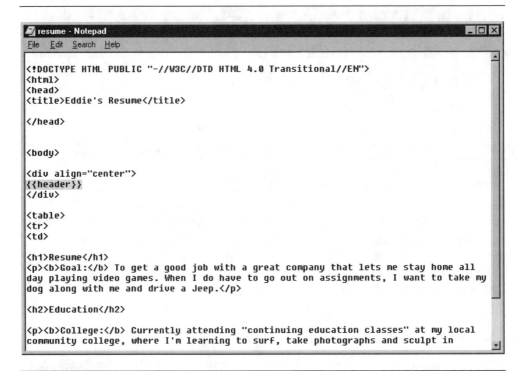

FIGURE 5-8   Creating a static page and adding template variables

4. Using your FTP application, you need to give the static file different permissions (**chmod 666 filename.html**, if you happen to be at the command line or have access to a similar tool via your FTP app), which correspond to read and write permissions for all users.

5. Now you'll "connect" the file. From the main menu in the control panel, click Configuration. On the Configuration Options page, scroll to the Connect Other Files section. In the Filename List, add the filename and virtual path to that file. (Because gm.cgi is stored in the cgi-bin directory, you'll need to create a virtual path to the new file you're creating.) See the Filename List instructions for details on a virtual path.

6. Turn on the Update Them When Adding Entries option so that connected files are updated along with others. Scroll down and click Save Configuration.

Troubleshooting and Backup

You shouldn't experience too much trouble with Greymatter, but it's always a good idea to keep a backup of important files, such as gm.cgi and others. The easiest way to do that is to simply use your FTP application to copy items from your server to your hard disk at fairly regular intervals. In particular, you should back up the four CGI files that store important data—gm.cgi, gm-karma.cgi, gm-comments.cgi, and gm-upload.cgi—and the entire folder that you use on the HTML or Public_HTML side of things (the folder that I called gm way back during the installation), including the archives subfolder, if it's in there. Of course, having said all that, it's probably just easiest to back up your entire CGI directory and your entire Greymatter directory, if you can.

If you run into trouble, remember the Diagnostics & Repair tool that's available on the Configuration page; many problems that crop up will have to do with permissions. Occasionally, you may accidentally overwrite a file when you're ftping. A combination of a good backup and the Diagnostics & Repair tool should help with the majority of problems.

The biggest warning that Greymatter provides in its manual is to avoid interrupting long rebuild tasks—particularly when you choose to rebuild your entire site. The Greymatter server software is essentially rewriting every HTML document on your site; if you interrupt that, you'll end up with files that are half-written, corrupt, or mismatched. Your first line of defense will be to rerun the rebuild task and let it do its thing; if that doesn't work, you may need to reinstall from your backups.

That's it—this static file is now connected. You can add markup and HTML as you please, but the real trick is that you can use Greymatter variables in the document, such as {{header}} and/or {{sidebar}}, and Greymatter will process those as if this page were part of the blog.

More...

Greymatter is a good choice for a basic server-side blog that doesn't require a high-end server or particularly daunting scripting capabilities, but it still gives you the freedom and flexibility of a server solution.

In the next chapter, we'll move on to Movable Type—a step beyond Greymatter, perhaps, and arguably the most popular server-side tool for blogging. If you're already hooked on Greymatter, you can skip to Chapter 8 and start with the suggestions for tweaking your blog.

T	W	T	F	S		S	M	T	W	T	F	S		S	M	T	W	T	F	S		S	M	T	W	T	F	S
	1	2	3	4				1	2	3	4					1	2	3	4					1	2	3	4
7	8	9	10	11		5	6	7	8	9	10	11		5	6	7	8	9	10	11		5	6	7	8	9	10	11
14	15	16	17	18		12	13	14	15	16	17	18		12	13	14	15	16	17	18		12	13	14	15	16	17	18
21	22	23	24	25		19	20	21	22	23	24	25		19	20	21	22	23	24	25		19	20	21	22	23	24	25
28	29	30	31			26	27	28	29	30	31			26	27	28	29	30	31			26	27	28	29	30	31

Chapter 6

Setting Up and Using Movable Type

In this chapter:

- ■ Features and requirements
- ■ Download and install Movable Type
- ■ Configure the server
- ■ Post and edit entries
- ■ Manage authors
- ■ Administer the weblog
- ■ Edit the templates
- ■ Change the look

Easily among the most popular server-side blogging solutions today is Movable Type, a great way to manage one or more blogs on your own web server account(s). Movable Type is a very elegant solution, offering an attractive default design, a number of third-party templates, and a familiar interface for many of your readers. It's a great option for a personal site, and a good one for a commercial or organizational site, particularly if you'd like to be up and running with a slick look very quickly.

The Movable Type Decision: Features and Requirements

Movable Type (MT) calls itself "a decentralized, web-based personal publishing system designed to ease maintenance of regularly updated news or journal sites, like weblogs." I'm particularly fond of the "personal publishing system" phrasing, because that's a great way to put what Movable Type does. Not unlike Greymatter, Movable Type is a tool designed to help you create an interesting site with timestamped posts and comments from readers. Movable Type's special features, though, are designed to make MT work in an ecosystem of sorts. In particular, it's good at communicating between your blog and other MT-based blogs.

Written by Benjamin Trott and Mena G. Trott, Movable Type is actively developed and has a strong user community. It offers tools for working with important data from other blogging software, support for Blogger-API editing tools, and support for plug-ins (code that third-parties write to extend the capabilities of Movable Type). Perhaps the most obvious difference between Movable Type and other blogging solutions is the look of its pages, which many Movable Type sites maintain. You'll find that it's a common look when you start surfing blogs (see Figure 6-1).

Here's a quick rundown of some of Movable Type's features:

- **Comments**   Like Greymatter, Movable Type supports commenting by readers. Movable Type makes it easy to have comments appear on either the same full pages as stories or in pop-up windows, which can be a handy way to allow your readers to comment on stories without opening a new page. You can also ban commenting users by IP address, and you can be notified by e-mail when a new comment has been added.

- **Flexible storage**   Movable Type can be used with the Berkeley DB, a database that's installed on most web servers that have Perl installation (another requirement). You can also use MySQL, if desired, which may improve performance somewhat.

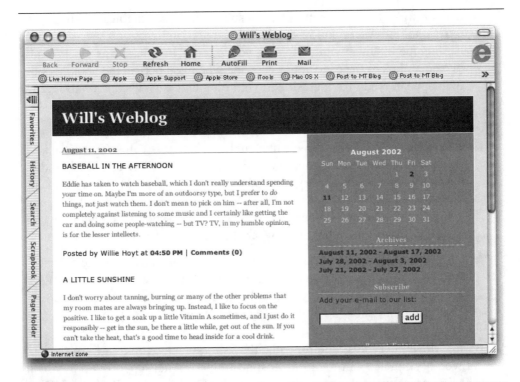

FIGURE 6-1   Here's the basic MT look when you first install and create your blog.

- **Data import**   Movable Type can import data from other blogging software, such as Blogger and Greymatter. If you've been using a different blog technology and want to switch to Movable Type, it's reasonably simple to do.

- **Multiple authors**   You can have more than one author signed up, with varying levels of authority over the blog and its entries.

- **Multiple blogs and multiple templates**   You can manage multiple blogs from the same Movable Type installation, if desired, enabling you to have blogs on different topics or for different people on the same server. The multiple output templates can be used to output your data to different documents at the same time, such as an RSS headline syndication page, an index page, and others (for use on PDAs, for instance).

- **Categories**   Your entries can be placed in categories for your personal use or for use on the site. You can also assign more than one category to an entry, enabling them to be cross-referenced and accessed in either category.

- **Bookmarklets**   A bookmarklet is a special link that enables you to pop up a small browser window to use to comment on items you see as you're surfing the Internet, without forcing you to log in to your site as you typically would. A link to the page you're viewing when you pop up the bookmarklet will appear, ready for inclusion in your blog entry. (MT's bookmarklets are also capable of working on both Mac and Windows computers, which is an advantage over Greymatter's bookmarklet feature.)

- **TrackBack**   Movable Type's most unique feature is called TrackBack, and it essentially enables automated communication between MT-based blogs. When you see an entry on another MT blog that you'd like to comment on, you use your bookmarklet and choose a special option. When you comment on that entry, your blog will send a message to the blog on which you're commenting, letting the owner know that your entry has been posted.

- **Entry management**   You can change the date on entries, delete entries, and put them on hold or release status, thus enabling you to create drafts, approve entries written by other authors, and date entries in the future so that they don't show up in your blog until the prescribed time.

As for Movable Type's requirements, they shouldn't be too tough for the typical web-hosting account to meet. Most hosting accounts support Perl 5, which Movable Type requires, and most offer support for DB_File Perl (Berkeley DB)

Who Is Movable Type For?

As with Greymatter, the real question is whether Movable Type is the right tool for your site. Movable Type offers many, many advantages, including a large base of users and people who like to hang out in Movable Type's support discussion groups. It has many useful features if you run a site that has a large number of entries, if you have multiple authors, or if you are adept at tweaking your journal's templates and style sheets using HTML and CSS. Movable Type's strongest feature is its peer-to-peer blog-promotion tools, which include RSS headline syndication and the TrackBack feature, which can be used to turn weblogs into distributed discussion groups of sorts. A discussion can start on one blog and continue on another blog, and another, and so on. For the most part, Movable Type is a great tool to use for personal blogs—both of a personal journaling and link-heavy newshound nature—particularly if you're interested in joining the greater Movable Type "community" of sites.

or a MySQL database. (You'll specifically need the DBD::mysql module, which is a Perl module that enables access to MySQL databases.) If you're not sure whether your server meets these requirements, the Movable Type website provides a recommended e-mail you can send to your web server company's support staff. See http://www.movabletype.com/requirements.shtml for details.

> NOTE   *Movable Type is free for noncommercial use, but a license is required for commercial sites that use MT, with the current price set at $150. The authors of Movable Type appreciate donations from satisfied users—a donation of $20 or more qualifies you for a "key" that enables your blog to be part of the Recently Updated list on the Movable Type website.*

6

Get Started

Before you can start posting, you'll need to download the software and get it installed. Movable Type is fairly simple to install, although it does require a few steps, and special services and features may require additional steps. Once you have it installed, you'll want to move through a few additional steps to configure Movable Type and get ready for your first entries.

Download and Configure

You can download Movable Type from http://www.movabletype.org/download/ for a noncommercial installation. (If you're going to use Movable Type in a commercial setting, you should head to http://www.movabletype.org/commercial_download.shtml and be prepared to pay.) Once you've accepted the license agreement (in either case), you'll move on to the download page, where the archive should be downloaded automatically. It's a Unix-style gzip archive, which you'll need to expand. Mac users can use StuffIt Expander (http://www.aladdinsys.com/); Windows users can use WinZip (http://www.winzip.com/), among other utilities.

In the archive's folder, you'll find a subfolder called docs, which you can open to reveal the documentation for Movable Type in HTML format. Load the file mtinstall.html in a web browser to see the detailed instructions for installing Movable Type. The main points are to change the Perl directory for the CGI scripts, if necessary, to create the proper directories, and to upload the scripts and support files to the appropriate places on your server.

> NOTE   *If you're upgrading from a previous version of Movable Type, check this same document for instructions specific to upgrading existing Movable Type installations.*

I'll summarize the steps for a Berkeley DB (standard) installation here:

1. The first thing you need to know is the path to Perl on your server computer. You'll need to update that path, if it's different from /usr/bin/perl/. If that path is different, update its entry (the first line of each file) in all the following files: mt-add-notify.cgi, mt-check.cgi, mt-comments.cgi, mt-load.cgi, mt-send-entry.cgi, and mt-tb.cgi. Each of these is a Perl script that will run as a CGI script once uploaded to your web host. Edit the files using a text editor, if necessary, and save them as plain text.

> NOTE
>
> *If you don't know the correct path to Perl on your server, you'll need to ask for your IPP's support staff, although, on Unix-based servers, the default use by MT is usually right. If you happen to have direct command-line access to your (Unix-based) server, you can use the command **whereis perl** to locate the path to Perl.*

2. You need to decide which directories you'll use for MT and which directories you may need to create.

    ■   If your host allows it, you may be able to store your CGI scripts in a directory created in your public HTML space, such as a new directory called mt or something similar. However, the more secure place is in the special cgi-bin directory that your IPP makes available to you. (If you opt to forgo the cgi-bin directory, read the instructions that MT provides for using cgiwrap or suexec for better security.)

    ■   You'll also need to create a directory called mt-static that is accessible over the Web (inside your public HTML folder), where you'll upload the images, documentation files, and style sheet for your site.

    ■   For a Berkeley DB-based installation, you'll need to create a directory for your database. If your CGI scripts are stored in the cgi-bin directory, you can create the db subdirectory within it; if your CGI scripts are stored in your public HTML space, you should create a directory outside of that space (perhaps in your home directory) so that the database files can't be accessed directly via the Web. Here's an example of a directory called "db":

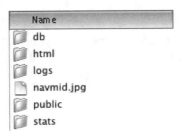

3. Finally, you'll need to create a directory, in your public HTML space, that you'd like to use for your blog. This is the directory that will be part of your URL, as in http://www.myserverspace.com/blog/. (If you'd like, you can create another publicly accessible directory that can be used for your archives, as well.)

With all these decisions made, open the file mt.cfg and edit some of the entries to configure Movable Type. Specifically, you'll need to locate and fill in the following entries:

- **CGIPath**   Locate this variable and enter the path to the directory where your Movable Type CGI scripts will be stored, as in the following example (note that the trailing slash is important):

```
CGIPath  http://www.fakeblogsite.com/cgi-bin/
```

- **DataSource**   At this variable you'll enter the full path to the directory that you're using for your database. Note that this needs to be the *full* path on the host system, as shown here:

```
DataSource  /usr/eddie/db
```

NOTE   *A path statement simply represents the series of directory names that are required to get from the root of a disk to a particular directory or file. In this case, the path might be /usr/www/e/eddie/db in order to get to the db directory created earlier. It usually needs to be the full path as if you were working directly on the web server computer. (You may have to ask your IPP.) Also, if you're on a Windows-based server, you may need to include a drive letter as part of the full path in this entry.*

■ **StaticWebPath**   Here, you enter the relative path (the portion of the URL) to the directory you're going to create for your static Movable Type items (images and so on). If that folder is at the root of your server directory, the entry would look like this (remove the # character if there's one in front of the line):

```
StaticWebPath /mt-static/
```

(Note that if you chose a different location for your static files, you need to put that here, as in StaticWebPath /myblog/mt-static/.)

You're done. Now save the file mt.cfg and prepare to upload files.

> NOTE *You'll need to take some additional steps if you plan to use MySQL as your Movable Type database. Check the installation documentation for details.*

Upload and Set Permissions

With mt.cfg configured correctly, you're ready to upload files. If you're uploading all your files into the same directory, you'll first need to create that directory and then upload everything in the MT folder to the newly created directory on your web server. If you plan to use the cgi-bin folder for your scripts, you'll take other steps:

1. Upload all files that end in .cgi or .cfg to the cgi-bin directory, as well as the lib, schemas, and tmpl folders. (Remember that scripts should be uploaded in Automatic or ASCII mode.)

2. Create the directory for static elements (mt-static) and upload the images folder, docs folder, and the styles.css file to that directory. (The images in the images folder should be uploaded in binary mode if your FTP application doesn't do that automatically.)

3. Create the directory where your blog's index page will be accessed. Also, create a separate directory for your blog's archives.

Now, in your FTP program, you'll need to set permissions for the CGI scripts and for your database folder. For each CGI script, the permissions are 755. This indicates read/write/execute permissions for the Owner, and read/execute for Group and Other. (If you copied the scripts to the cgi-bin directory, there's a good chance their permissions are already set properly.) The database directory will need to be set to 777 (read/write/execute permissions for all users). Finally, set the permissions for the main blog directory and the archives directory (if relevant) to 777. See Chapter 5 for more on setting permissions.

Configure Movable Type

Now for the moment of truth (or, at least, *a* moment of truth). Open a web browser and point to the CGI script mt-check.cgi on your server. If you've uploaded files to a particular folder, you can link directly to that folder, as shown here:

```
http://www.myserverspace.com/mt-files/mt-check.cgi
```

In this example, *myserverspace* is your domain name. If the files are stored in the cgi-bin directory, then use the following:

```
http://www.myserverspace.com/cgi-bin/mt-check.cgi
```

Figure 6-2 shows the document that results if mt-check.cgi is successful. If it doesn't execute, or if you see the text of the script instead of the script itself, then

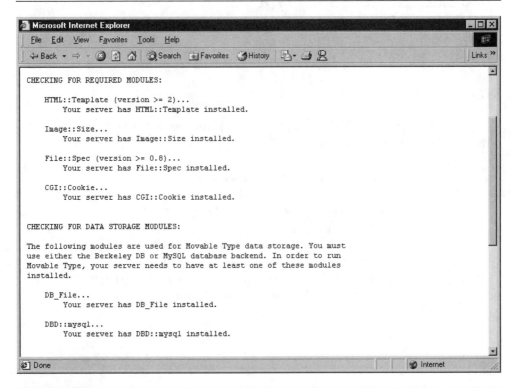

FIGURE 6-2   Results of the mt-check.cgi script

it's possible that the script's permissions aren't set correctly. If you see nothing but nonsense characters or an error message that doesn't involve permissions, then it's possible you uploaded the script as a binary file instead of as an ASCII file. You'll want to try uploading it again.

This script does more than ensure that Movable Type is working—it also checks to see whether certain important Perl modules are present on your server. If they aren't, according to mt-check.cgi, then you'll need to download and install them. In most cases you'll do this by creating a directory called exlib in the directory where you installed Moveable Type (or in the cgi-bin directory, if that's where the CGI scripts are) and install the Perl extensions in the exlib directory. You should be able to do this even on typical inexpensive hosts that offer CGI access—only some of the freebie services will likely block the extensions. See the Movable Type installation documentation (either in your distribution or at http://www.movabletype.com/docs/mtinstall.html) for more on these modules, including links for downloading them.

Load and Run Movable Type

If you pass the mt-check.cgi test, you're ready to create the databases and launch the Movable Type application. For starters, load the mt-load.cgi script, again using the correct URL for your installation type:

```
http://www.myserverspace.com/mt-files/mt-load.cgi
```

Again, *myserverspace* is your domain name. If the files are stored in the cgi-bin directory, then use the following:

```
http://www.myserverspace.com/cgi-bin/mt-load.cgi
```

The result should (hopefully) be a message that shows you successfully created a database and loaded the initial data (see Figure 6-3). If you don't see that message, it's possible you've incorrectly configured the mt.cfg document and/or you didn't create the database directory on your remote server. Check those steps again.

If you've succeeded, you should use your FTP application to delete the file mt-load.cgi. Then, get ready for the rest of your blogging life.

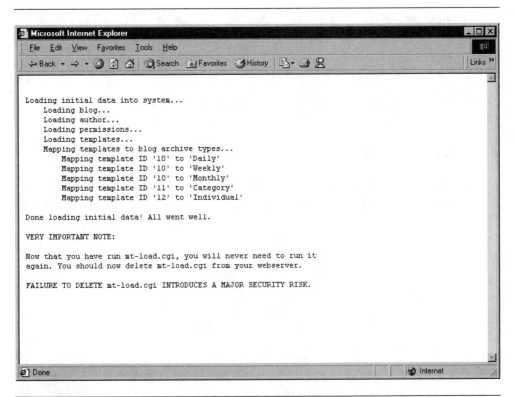

FIGURE 6-3   Movable Type has created the database, and you're ready to log in and go.

CAUTION

Movable Type warns you on this screen to delete mt-load.cgi because anyone who knows enough to be dangerous could access this file in a web browser (the same way you just did) and overwrite your databases, destroying a lot of hard work. That's also a reason to regularly back up your database, which is easy to do if you're using Berkeley DB and you've created a special db folder outside of your blog hierarchy—just download the db folder periodically and keep the copy in a safe place. (You should also consult with your IPP to see what sort of backup options they offer.)

And now for the second moment of truth. Launch the Movable Type application in your web browser using a command structured like the following:

```
http://www.myserverspace.com/mt-files/mt.cgi
```

Again, *myserverspace* is your domain name. If the files are stored in the cgi-bin directory, then use this:

```
http://www.myserverspace.com/cgi-bin/mt.cgi
```

You should see the Movable Type login window, complete with Username and Password entry boxes. Enter the defaults—Melody and Nelson—and click the Log In button.

Username:
Melody

Password:
xxxxxxx

Remember me: ☐

LOG IN

Forgot your password?

If you've logged in successfully, you'll see the main menu. Your first stop is the Edit Your Profile link, where you should give yourself a new username and nickname (unless you happen to be named Melody) as well as a new password (regardless of what your name is). You can also specify an e-mail address and your place of birth so that Movable Type can identify you if you happen to forget your password at some future date. Click Save, and your profile will be set. (Remember your password for future logins!) Now you're ready to start managing your blog and adding entries.

NOTE   *You'll use the full username for the MT login screen (not the nickname). Also, you should remember that on Unix-based servers, the name will be case sensitive, so consider that when creating the username and subsequently using it. If you find you can't get logged in at some point, check the capitalization.*

Post and Edit Entries

The main menu in Movable Type has only a few different hyperlinks that lead to different aspects of the blog that you can manage. These include Create New Blog, Add/Edit Blog Authors, Edit Your Profile, View Activity Log, and Set Up Bookmarklets.

A lot of activity will take place within the weblog itself; click the First Blog link, for instance, to see the blog's management tools. First Blog is good for your original blog—Movable Type supports the ability to manage more than one blog, each with its own templates, database entries, and so on. This enables you to allow multiple authors to have their own blogs at your site (http://www.ournonprofitorg.org/ jill_blog/, http://www.ournonprofitorg.org/roger_blog/, and so on) as well as to create more sophisticated magazine-style sites that can use multiple blogs for categories (such as Sports, Finance, World News, and so on) and blend them together on a single main index page.

For now, let's get started with a single blog and a new entry.

TIP   *Looking for help? Movable Type has handy little question marks throughout the interface that you can click to see contextual help that appears in a new window.*

Edit the Blog's Core Setup

If you've clicked the First Blog hyperlink in the main menu, you're looking at the welcome message. This message can actually change (see the link at the bottom of the page). This way, if you have additional authors in the future, you can tell them things about the blog and offer any advice or instructions. At this point, however, the first step is to ensure that your blog is configured correctly. On the left side of the window, locate and click the Blog Config button to access the Core Setup page, where you should scroll through the entries to make sure your various paths are set correctly. Here's what you'll find:

■ **Blog Name**   Here you can give your blog a name other than First Blog, if desired.

■ **Local Site Path**   The is the path, as your server computer sees it, to the location of the index page of your blog. If your blog will ultimately be at http://www.myserverspace.com/blog/ on the Web, you'll need to enter the private (or local) path to that directory on the server computer. This can sometimes be a slightly complex path statement, depending on the way your host computer is configured. For instance, the path on one of my servers looks something like this:

```
/usr/local/www/virtual/m/macblog/html/blog
```

■ **Site URL** This is the URL to the blog directory that your readers will use (the less cumbersome URL). Here's an example:

```
http://www.myseverspace.com/blog/
```

■ **Local Archive Path** Again, this is a local path, as the web server sees it, to the directory you've specified (and created) for archives. It should look something like this:

```
/usr/local/www/virtual/m/macblog/html/archive
```

■ **Archive URL** This is the URL to the archive directory.

■ **Timezone** Choose your local time zone from the menu so that entries are correctly dated.

With these changes made, click the Save button.

NOTE *In order to see changes made in this section on your public site, you need to click the Rebuild link that shows up at the top of the page after you've saved the configuration changes you made. This isn't necessary at this point if you haven't yet added any entries (because you don't yet have a blog!), but it would be an important step if you change these settings again in the future.*

We'll get back to some of the other settings in later sections. Right now, though, you're finally ready to post your first entry.

Post an Entry

While viewing any page for your blog, you can click the New Entry button (on the left side of the screen) to see the Create New Entry screen (see Figure 6-4). If you've read any of the other chapters regarding blogging tools, this page will be reasonably familiar. You can enter a title for your entry in the Title entry box and the entry text itself in the Main Entry Text entry box. If you'd like this entry to begin on your index page but then "jump" to a full page that includes additional text, enter this "More" text in the Additional Entry Text entry box. You can also enter different text in the Excerpt box if you'd prefer that a different "blurb" of text summarizes the entry. The Excerpt text is only used in certain situations, such

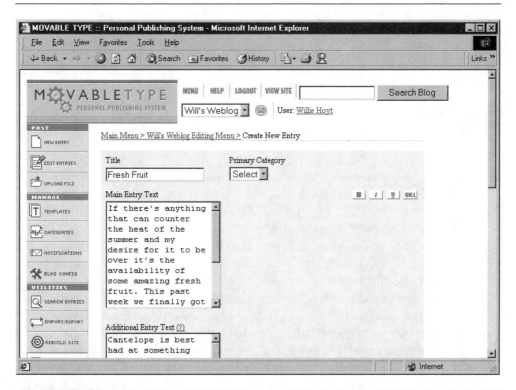

FIGURE 6-4   Adding the first entry to the blog

as when RSS headline syndication pages are generated. If you don't enter blurb text, the first 20 words of the entry will be used in place of the blurb.

By default, the items you enter in these main entry boxes will have their line breaks (when you press RETURN or ENTER) converted into paragraphs, although you can turn that off at the bottom of the entry screen if you prefer to add paragraphs using HTML <p> elements. You can use other HTML within your entries, as well, including emphasis elements, hypertext anchors, and even image elements (for images that you've manually uploaded or that appear on other web servers).

In fact, in Internet Explorer for Windows you'll see small buttons on the Create New Entry page that enable you to add bold, italic, underline, and hyperlink markup. Type something, highlight it, and then click one of the buttons.

Toward the bottom of the Create New Entry screen you can choose from a few different options. The Post Status menu is used to choose whether the entry should be saved as a draft or should appear on the website when saved. If you're still working on the entry, leave the choice on Draft; if it's ready to be seen, select Publish from the menu.

NOTE *There's also an option near the title of your entry that enables you to choose a category. We haven't yet covered creating categories but will in the next section.*

To the right of the Post Status menu are three additional check box options: Allow Comments, Convert Line Breaks, and Allow Pings. If you don't want readers to be able to comment on this entry, turn off Allow Comments; if you're using full HTML for this entry (including <p> paragraph elements), turn off Convert Line Breaks. (The third option, Allow Pings, is used in conjunction with the URLs to Ping entry area, both of which are elements of the TrackBack feature, which we'll discuss later in the chapter.)

Now, you're ready to either preview the entry or save it. If you click Save, the entry is either saved as a draft or published immediately. If you click Preview, you'll see the entry in its own window. On that page you can choose the Re-Edit This Entry button to revisit the entry page, or you can click the Save This Entry button to save it. In either case, once you've saved the entry, it will either be ready for more editing (if it's a draft) or will appear on your index page. In fact, if this is your first entry, the entry page will be created and you can access it by clicking the View Site button at the bottom of the toolbar or by entering its URL in a new browser window (see Figure 6-5).

NOTE *If you have trouble publishing the page, you should make sure the directory for your blog's index page, which you specified in the Core Setup section, has been created and that it has the proper permissions set (in this case, chmod 777, although 755 will also work under some circumstances).*

Create and Edit Categories

Categories can be useful in two different ways. By default, assigning a category to an entry doesn't change the way it's displayed on your index page, and it doesn't add any ability for the reader to view categories, although that is something you can add to your templates (we'll discuss this topic later in the section "Edit the Templates"). Once you've added support for categories, they can provide a useful way for readers to navigate a site that has many entries or a blog that has many topics of interest.

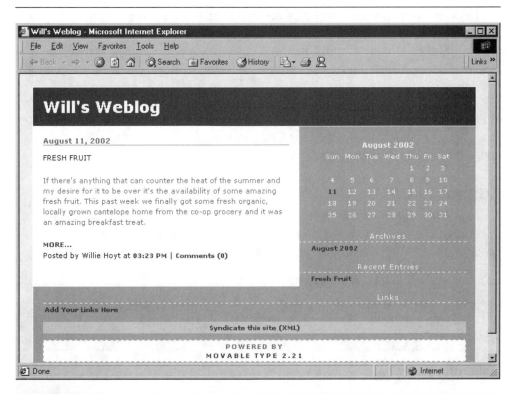

FIGURE 6-5   Success! The new story has caused an index page to be created.

The other use of categories is for your own benefit: You can assign internal categories to your entries. Then, on the Edit Entries screen discussed in the next section, you can view only entries that fit those categories. How you use the categories is up to you, but they're there for your consideration.

Click the Categories button on the left side of the screen to see the categories interface. If no categories have been created, you'll see a simple screen with five empty boxes—fill in the name of one or more categories and click the Save Changes button.

On the next screen that appears (the Edit Categories screen), you can edit or alter the categories. Edit the category's name in its entry box and click the Save Changes button at the bottom of the screen to rename a category. Click the Edit Category Attributes link in a particular category's row if you'd like to give the category a description. (You can also use the Category Attributes page to make choices regarding the TrackBack feature, which we'll discuss later in the chapter.)

To delete a category on the Edit Categories screen, shown in Figure 6-6, click the Delete check box next to one or more categories; then scroll down and click the Delete Checked button. A confirmation window will appear. When you delete categories, the corresponding entries *aren't* deleted, but their category assignment is cleared.

To add even more categories, simply type their names in the empty text boxes at the bottom of the Edit Categories screen and click the Save Changes button. After the changes are made, the new Categories page will reflect the recently added (and/or deleted) categories.

Edit an Entry

You can edit an entry at any time. On the left side of the screen, click the Edit Entries button. On the List & Edit Entries screen, a list of your entries will appear toward the bottom of the screen, including the entry name, category, date, author,

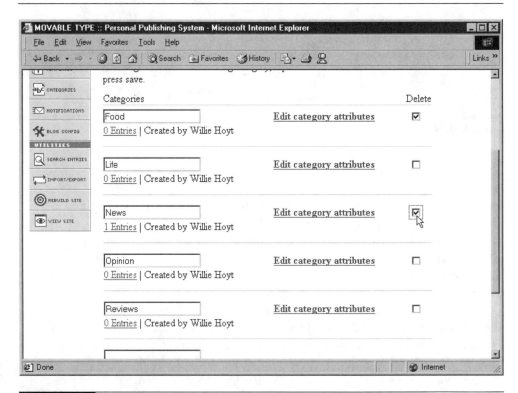

FIGURE 6-6   On the Edit Categories page you can view, rename, and delete categories as well as change their attributes.

and status. To edit an entry—including changing it from Draft to Publish status—simply click its title, which is a hyperlink. You'll be taken to the Edit Entry screen, which is similar to the Create New Entry screen, except that you'll see three buttons at the bottom of the screen: Preview, Save, and Delete Entry. That's how you can delete an entry if you've read through it and decided it's time for it to go. (When you choose Delete Entry, a confirmation box will appear; click Delete to follow through and Cancel to stop the process and return to entry editing.)

TIP *Another item you can edit is the date of an entry; MT will change the date on an entry if you edit it so that it will appear in a different order on the page, if desired. You can also postdate an entry—make it for a few hours from now—and then choose to publish it. The entry will be set to appear on the your index page, but it won't appear until the prescribed time.*

6

Actually, the Edit Entry screen has another difference or two compared to the Create New Entry screen. Scroll below the Preview and Save buttons and you'll see some advanced options (see Figure 6-7). The first option enables you to edit or delete comments that have been added by readers to this entry. Click the comment author's name to edit that comment, or click the Delete check box in the comment's row and then the Delete button below the comment listing to delete the selected comment.

NOTE *When you choose to edit a comment by clicking the author's name, you'll also see that author's IP address, which you can use for IP banning in the future, if necessary. Also, if you do edit a comment, it's good netiquette to note that the comment was edited by adding something like "Edited by admin at 12:34 7/2/03" to the message.*

The other advanced option of interest (as we're saving the TrackBack discussion for a later section in this chapter) is the Send a Notification section. This is used to enable you to send a message to your readers, letting them know that you've added an entry. Type text for the note in the Send a Notification entry box and then check one of the options (Include Excerpt or Include Entire Entry Body) and click the Send button.

NOTE *How does Movable Type know to whom it should send e-mail announcements? You enter e-mail addresses on the Edit Notification List screen. Click the Notifications button on the left side of the screen and you'll see the list. You add addresses by entering them in the Email Address entry box.*

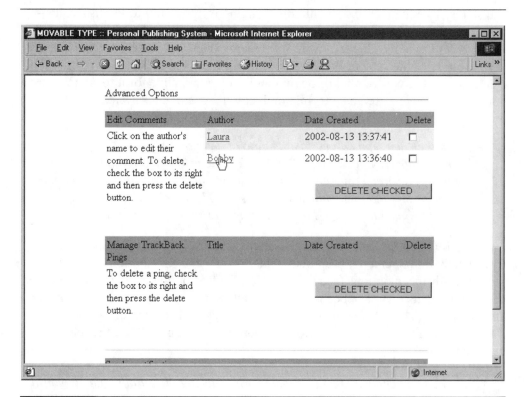

FIGURE 6-7   The advanced options appear on the Edit Entry screen.

Delete an Entry

The other way to delete an entry is to select the Delete check box next to the entry on the List & Edit Entries screen and then click the Delete button. You'll be asked to confirm your decision; click Delete to delete the entry.

Power Editing Mode

MT offers an interesting mode for editing a number of entries at once. On the List & Edit Entries screen, click Open Power Editing Mode. This displays a new window that you can use to quickly alter a number of entries at once. You can change the name of the entries, the category, date, author, or, status, or you can select them for deleting. Click the Save button when you've made your changes.

Upload Files

If you'd like to upload a file—either an image or another sort of file, perhaps one that you want to link to for downloading by your readers—you can do that in one of two ways. You can upload it directly using your FTP program, or you can upload it via Movable Type's interface. When you upload an image in this way, you get the added benefit of being able to create a thumbnail version of that image.

To upload an image via MT, click the Upload File button on the left side of the Weblog Editing Menu. A window will appear, as shown in Figure 6-8. At the top of that window, you can click the Browse button to use an Open dialog box to locate the file you want to upload. Once you've done that and you're back in the Choose a File window, you can choose the destination for the file toward the bottom of the

6

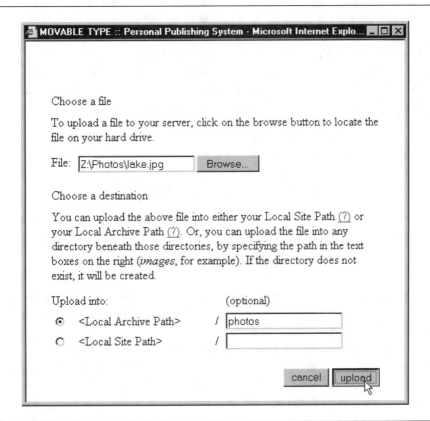

FIGURE 6-8 Uploading a file or image

window. (You can choose whether to upload it to the main folder for your site or to the archives folder.) Note that you can also add to the path, if necessary, by typing a folder name in the entry box. When you're done, click the Upload button.

> **TIP**
> *You can actually create a folder from this window, if you need to. For instance, if you're uploading an image and you want it to appear in the folder yourblog/images, then simply type **images** in the < Local Site Path> entry box.*

After the image or file is uploaded, you'll see a new window. If you've uploaded a non-image, you'll be given the option of creating a new entry that includes a link to the file, or you can just be shown the HTML that you can use to link to that file.

If you've uploaded an image, you'll have some additional options, particularly if your server has the special Image::Magick Perl extension installed. If that's the case, you'll see a window that asks, as with other files, whether you'd like to create a new entry using the file or if you'd like to see the HTML for the file. You can also choose to create a *thumbnail* of the image, which simply means a smaller version. You can determine what size the thumbnail should be either by selecting particular dimensions in pixels or by choosing a percentage, as shown here:

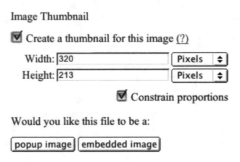

When the reader clicks the thumbnail, the main image will either be loaded in the browser window or will appear in a new pop-up window, depending on the button you choose in this window.

If you've chosen to create a new entry with this file, you'll be taken to the Create New Entry screen, with the HTML required for the link already in the Main Entry Text area. You can then finish your entry and click the Save button to save your entry and post it to your site, complete with the image (if the file was an image file) or the link (if it was some other type of file).

Administer the Weblog

Once you've built up a few weeks' worth of entries—or even before that—you may find that you need to dig into the administrative side of Movable Type. Fortunately, the administrative tools are very straightforward.

Manage Authors

If you'd like additional authors to be able to post entries to your blog, you'll need to add them. You do that from the Main Menu screen (not the Weblog Editing Menu). On that page, where you also find the Create New Blog and Edit Your Profile links, you can click the Add/Edit Blog Authors link to add some cooks for your soup.

To add a new author, scroll down in the Add/Edit Blog Authors window until you get to the Add an Author section. Here, enter a username, e-mail address, and password as well as a confirmation of the password. You should also select a blog with which to associate the user (see Figure 6-9).

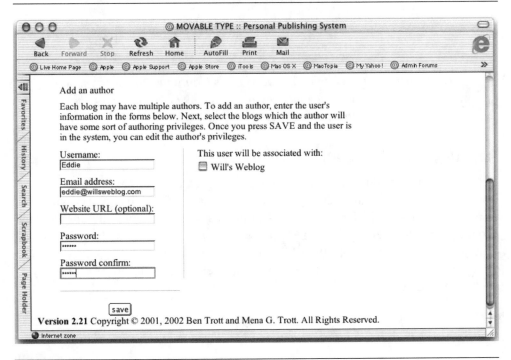

FIGURE 6-9   Adding an author to your blog

Once you've created the author, you may want to edit that author's permissions. Editing permissions gives you control over what that author can do within Movable Type, including whether the author can edit posts, upload files, rebuild the weblog, and so on. If you'd like to limit the author's abilities to performing important configuration tasks, for instance, you can do that in this section by unchecking the appropriate box. You can also add the author to another blog, if desired, from the Add User to An Additional Blog menu.

General Permissions
☐ User can create new blogs
☐ User can view activity log

Weblog: Will's Weblog

☑ Post   ☐ Configure Blog
☑ Upload File   ☐ Rebuild Files
☐ Edit All Posts   ☑ Send Notifications
☐ Edit Templates   ☑ Edit Categories
☐ Edit Authors & Permissions   ☐ Edit Address Book

[SAVE]

> **TIP** *On the Preferences screen of each blog's Configuration section, you'll find an option to input a welcome message, which will be viewed by the authors when they visit a particular blog's editing page.*

Ban IPs

Got a problem with someone entering comments that aren't helpful or appreciated? If necessary, you can ban users by IP address. You'll need to ban a user who's associated with a particular blog—you can't ban a user from your all your weblogs at once. From the Weblog Editing Menu, select the Blog Config button. On the Configuration screen, choose the IP Banning link. In the IP Banning section, you can enter an IP address that you want to ban in the IP Address entry box. Finally, click Add to List.

> **TIP** *You can learn a user's IP address by editing an entry that has comments attached to it. With each comment, you'll see the user's IP address.*

If you'd like to delete a banned IP address (so that it's no longer banned), you can select the Delete check box next to the entry in the IP Ban list and then click the Delete button. You'll be asked to confirm this action; when you do, that IP address is no longer banned.

NOTE   *If you ban the IP address of someone who uses a dial-up or dynamically assigned account, then it's likely you won't effectively ban that person, because you'll only be banning one of a pool of potential IP addresses offered by the user's ISP. So, in some cases, don't be shocked if IP banning isn't an effective solution to a problematic visitor.*

6

Use a Bookmarklet

If you read Chapter 5, you're familiar with the bookmarklet concept—it's a quick bookmark or *Favorite* (as Internet Explorer calls it) that you can use while surfing the Web. Whenever you read or see something you need to blog about, click the bookmarklet, and a pop-up window will appear, complete with an abbreviated interface to your weblog. You can then blog quickly on the topic of whatever you're reading—in fact, a link to that topic will appear in the Bookmarklet window (see Figure 6-10).

To use a bookmarklet, you'll need to set one up. Begin from the main menu and click the Set Up Bookmarklets tab. On the Bookmarklets screen, place a checkmark next to each element you'd like to see in the bookmarklet window you're creating. If you add all the options, you'll end up with a screen that looks quite a bit like the standard Create New Entry screen, but you're free to leave off features, if desired. Click the Create button, and your bookmarklet will be created—it will be a link in the window. You can now drag the link to your browser's Favorites or Bookmarks toolbar, or you can access the page and right-click (or CONTROL-click on a Mac) the link and choose to add the link as a Favorite or bookmark.

Now, when you need to blog, just click the Favorite or bookmark in the toolbar, and a window similar to Figure 6-10 will appear.

Use the TrackBack Feature

The TrackBack feature in Movable Type enables you to use multiple blogs—yours and other people's—as sort of a wide area discussion forum. When you have something to say about an entry in another person's MT weblog, you can create

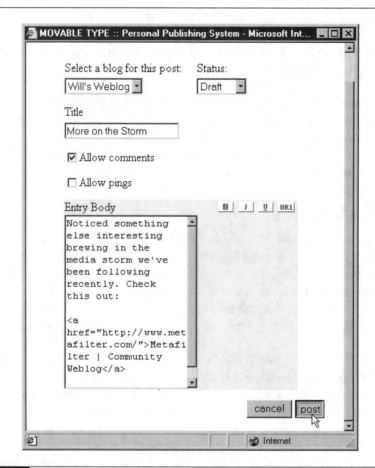

FIGURE 6-10   Using a bookmarklet to blog in Movable Type

an entry about it and then *ping* that weblog with a TrackBack message, sending the URL for that entry to their site so that the site owner can link to it, if desired.

> **NOTE**   *The term* ping *is used to suggest that you're alerting another computer to your presence. The term is based on a program called Ping that's used to test network connections by sending out a simple data packet and waiting for an "I got it" response from a remote server.*

The TrackBack feature can also be used in the reverse—someone can visit your site, blog about something you've written, and then ping your site with the URL.

To work with the TrackBack feature (assuming you've installed a new version of Movable Type since the early summer of 2002), all you need to do is create a bookmarklet and make sure you enable the TrackBack Items field. Now, when you go to blog about an entry that's part of a Movable Type blog, you may see an option at the top of your bookmarklet window that reads Select a TrackBack Entry to Ping. You can then choose the entry that you're writing about.

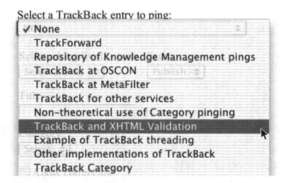

Now, edit your post and publish it. When it's published, the TrackBack ping will be sent to the other Movable Type blog. Then, when a user clicks the TrackBack link that appears under that blog entry, the user will be able to see a link to your associated entry in order to continue on to your blog to read more.

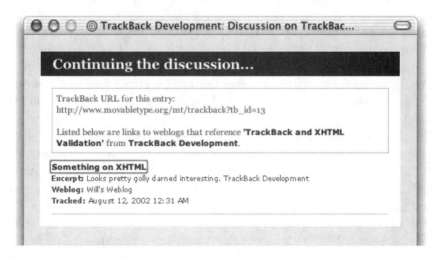

NOTE

The TrackBack feature can get even more involved because you can use categories in different weblogs to create TrackBack pings—whenever you write an entry in a particular category (say, archery), your blog can ping other blogs (presumably those that want to know what you think about archery) and post a link to your new story. That, too, will work in reverse (that is, you can receive pings from another MT blog regarding a particular category.) It's a method of targeted headline syndication, as discussed later in this chapter and in Chapter 10. TrackBack is an evolving feature, so check the Movable Type website's TrackBack development page (http://www.movabletype.org/trackback/) and the documentation for more details.

Manage Your Archives

Movable Type will automatically archive your posts as you continue to maintain your blog. How exactly it goes about that is determined by a number of different configuration settings. The first steps you've already accomplished—you created an archives directory (if desired) and set up the path to that directory in the Core Setup section of the Blog Config screens. Archiving can get a bit more involved, however, so you may want to click Blog Config again at some point and check the others settings.

On the Preferences screen of Blog Config (click the Preferences link near the top of the page), you have just two preferences regarding archiving. First, you can choose the default archive type in the Preferred Archive Type window. This is the method used to permanently link to archived entries. Each archive link can either be to an individual full-page version of the entry (which is preferable for longer entries) or to a monthly archive on a single page, using a special link that jumps straight to that entry within the month's full listing (best for smaller entries). As you'll see in a moment, you can create multiple archive types, so here you're choosing the default.

The other option on the Preferences screen allows you to choose the filename extension for the archives. In most cases this will be .html, which is standard for pages on the Web. You might opt for a different extension, however, if your archive templates have any scripting or code that needs to be preprocessed by the server— common filename extensions in that case include .shtml, .php, and so on.

To set up your overall archiving scheme, click the Archiving link at the top of Configuration page. The result will be the Archiving screen shown Figure 6-11. Movable Type is very flexible in its archiving options. By default, it archives entries in two ways: It creates an individual page for each entry, and it create a monthly

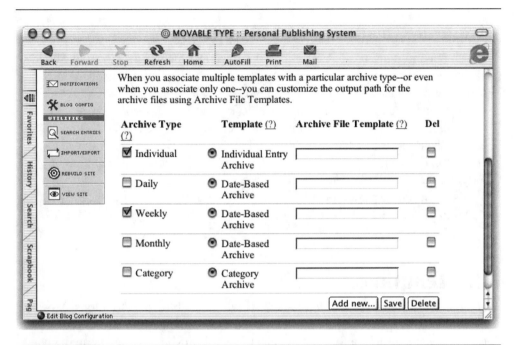

FIGURE 6-11   Choose the type(s) of archiving you'd like to do.

archive, on which every entry in a given month is stored. You can change that on the Archiving screen by turning off the Individual option, for instance, opting to have entries archived only on daily, weekly, or monthly pages.

> **TIP**   *You can also use a different naming convention (entered in the Archive File Template entry box) for your files by using special variables. Click the small question mark (?) next to the Archive File Template header to learn how this works.*

One thing worth noting, however, is that if you do change your approach to archiving, you'll also need to change the special tags used in your templates. By default, the index page of your MT blog has the monthly variable built in, allowing it to automatically display each month on the index page. If you switch to weekly or daily, you'll need to change the variable on the index page's template as well (see the section "Understand MT's Tags," later in this chapter, for details).

Syndicate Headlines and Ping Others

The final item to discuss in this section is Movable Type's ability to syndicate the headlines of your entries and ping some "recently added" sites. Syndication is built in and standard, so there's nothing you really have to do to make it work. You can set some options for how Movable Type promotes itself, however. On the Blog Config page, click the link to the Preferences screen and then click the link on the Preferences screen to the Publicity section. Once there, you can turn on the option Notify Weblogs.com of Updates. Also, if you've donated money for your version of MT, you can enter a recently updated key, which causes your blog's entries to be posted on the Movable Type home page in the Recently Updated section. See Chapter 10 for more on these technologies and websites.

Edit the Templates

Want to change the way your blog looks? As with most blogging solutions, Movable Type relies on templates to help it create the pages you and your readers see on the Web. The templates offer a form into which the words in your blog are poured, giving it the overall design. The templates have both static portions and variables that are used to hold the place of the entries that will be added from the database.

To edit the templates, click the Templates button on the left side of the screen. On the List Templates screen, you'll see a long page of links to the different templates that are used to put together your blog. The first set of templates, the index templates, are the main templates you'll likely work with to begin—in particular, you will likely find yourself editing the main index and master archive index, for starters, and then digging into the others, perhaps over time.

TIP *A great place to look into all sorts of customization for your Movable Type blog is http://www.thegirliematters.com/tips/, where you'll find links to all sorts of Movable Type topics, including working with templates, redesigning your archive pages, and so on. Also, if you ever mess up your templates beyond recognition, the Movable Type folks have posted the default template at http://www.movabletype.org/default_templates.shtml, where you can copy and paste them back into your blog.*

When you click a link, you'll see a page that enables you to edit that template's text and markup in the Template Body entry box. You'll also see some other interesting options:

- **Name**   You can rename the template if desired.

- **Output file**   You can change the name of the output file, if desired, although this generally isn't recommended unless you have a strong sense of what you're doing.

- **Link This Template to a File**   This option is interesting because it enables you to accomplish one or two important tasks. When you link to a file (it needn't exist, although if it does, it will be overwritten), the current template markup is written to that file. Now, you can edit that file in a different text editor (if desired) and then upload it again via FTP. It will be synchronized when the site is rebuilt. Likewise, you can use that file to back up your current template(s) which is always a good idea, just so your blog is easier to restore should problems crop up with your host.

- **Save**   Click this to save your changes, regardless of whether you want to rebuild the page (or site) and see your changes immediately.

- **Rebuild**   Click this button only after having saved changes to the template; otherwise, they won't be used when the site is rebuilt. Clicking this button or the Rebuild link results in a new, small window where you can choose what, exactly, should be rebuilt.

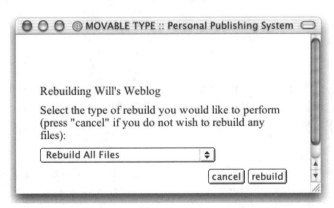

Using Downloadable Templates

Movable Type's popularity means a lot of people are using it, and a lot of them have come up with creative designs for the templates. If you'd like a different-looking blog, but you're not much of a web designer (or, not yet), you can download templates from sites on the Web. Try BlogStyles (http://blogstyles.com/mt/) for a few different looks—they're simple, but easily worked with and altered, at least in terms of their colors. Loveproductions.com (http://www.love-productions.com/graphics/setlist.html) has some great-looking templates that you can download specifically for Movable Type, as does Elegant Inspirations (http://elegantinspirations.com/index.php), where they charge for their templates, depending on whether you're using them for personal or commercial use and whether or not you want an exclusive design (which you buy and no one else can use). We'll look more closely at third-party templates in Chapter 8.

Add Your Own Links

One of the first things you'll likely want to do is dig into your index page and add some links—if only to get that text on your home page that reads "Add Your Links Here" to say something else. To edit that text, open the main index (click it in the Index Templates list on the List Templates page) and in the Template Body entry box, look for the following:

```
<div class="side">
<a href="">Add Your Links Here</a><br />
</div>
```

Replace the fake anchor line with the links you want to add to your site—you're favorite news sites, fellow bloggers, static pages on your site, famous blogs, and so on. Eventually you'll have something like this:

```
<div class="side">
<a href="http://www.metafilter.com/">MetaFilter</a><br />
<a href="http://www.wilwheaton.net/">Wilwheaton.net</a><br />
<a href="http://www.plastic.com/">Plastic</a><br />
<a href="http://www.macblog.com/">MacBlog.com</a><br />
</div>
```

As you're editing, you can feel free to change other things around a little bit. The different visual aspects of the interface are governed by style sheet definitions, assigned using the <div> element and the class attribute. So, you could take an existing entry such as

```
<div class="sidetitle">
Links
</div>

<div class="side">
...your links here...
</div>
```

and add to it with an additional area for links, so as to break them into categories, along the lines of this:

```
<div class="sidetitle">
News Sites
</div>

<div class="side">
<a href="http://www.cnn.com/">CNN.com</a><br />
<a href="http://www.msnbc.com/">MSNBC.com</a><br />
<a href="http://www.bbc.com/">BBC.com</a><br />
<a href="http://www.salon.com/">Salon</a><br />
</div>

<div class="sidetitle">
Links
</div>

<div class="side">
<a href="http://www.metafilter.com/">MetaFilter</a><br />
<a href="http://www.wilwheaton.net/">Wilwheaton.net</a><br />
<a href="http://www.plastic.com/">Plastic</a><br />
<a href="http://www.macblog.com/">MacBlog.com</a><br />
</div>
```

When you're done making the changes, click the Save button. Next, click the Rebuild button to rebuild your index page to reflect the changes. A window will appear in which you can choose what files to rebuild. Then click the Rebuild button.

6

The following image shows the difference that adding these links can make to personalize your site once the index page is rebuilt.

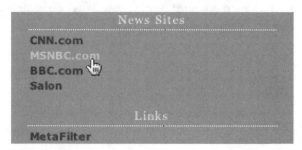

Add Notifications Entry

Earlier in this chapter we discussed sending notifications to readers when you post a new blog entry. Movable Type includes a special CGI script that can add people automatically, but you have to paste the code into your blog's index page (or wherever you'd like the code to appear) first. The code appears at http://www.movabletype.org/docs/mtmanual_notifications.html. Copy it from that page into your index page's template (if desired, mark it up with some of the other elements on the page to make it fit into the design):

```
<div class="sidetitle">
Subscribe
</div>

<div class="side">
Add your e-mail to our list:
<form method="post" action="<$MTCGIPath$>mt-add-notify.cgi">
```

```
<input type="hidden" name="blog_id" value="<$MTBlogID$>" />
<input type="hidden" name="_redirect" value="<$MTBlogURL$>" />
<input name="email" size="20" />
<input type="submit" value="add" />
</form>
</div>
```

This code integrates the form into the site's design, as you can see here:

Understand MT's Tags

As you've seen in the previous example and in the templates themselves, Movable Type uses special tags as placeholders for the items that are added automatically to the template by the MT software, thus building the final page. Once you get to know the tags, you can start to move items around on your page, if desired. You can also change the way some tags behave, and you can substitute one tag for another under certain circumstances.

Take, for instance, the possibility that you'd like to have weekly archives instead of monthly archives for your site. As was discussed earlier, you can change the

Archiving setting on the Configuration page to weekly, but it won't show on your blog's index page until you've change the archive tag on that page. Here is the default tag and surrounding markup:

```
<div class="sidetitle">
Archives
</div>
<div class="side">
<MTArchiveList archive_type="Monthly">
<a href="<$MTArchiveLink$>"><$MTArchiveTitle$></a><br />
</MTArchiveList>
</div>
```

Should be pretty straightforward, right? Change archive_type to "Weekly" and we should be set:

```
<MTArchiveList archive_type="Weekly">
```

Save the template and rebuild it. Then, assuming the archiving preferences are indeed set for weekly, you should now see weekly archives listed on the page:

The Movable Type documentation includes a thorough explanation of the tags used in your templates in /docs/mtmanual_tags.html or online at http://www.movabletype.org/docs/mtmanual_tags.html. For more explanation of the theory behind Movable Type's tags (which have similarities both to Blogger and to Greymatter's variables), see http://www.movabletype.org/docs/mttags.html on the Web.

Categories and Template Tags

As another example of the template tags, let's look again at how to add categories to your blog's index page. If you defined categories in the earlier discussion, you're ahead of the game—it also helps to have actually used those categories as you were creating entries. Now, all you have to do to add a list of categories to your blog's index page is to turn on category archiving and then add the template tags.

In order to link to pages where one can view your blog entries by category, you need to ensure those pages exist. You can make MT create them automatically by turning on category archiving. Click the Blog Config button and then click the Archiving link at the top of the options. Scroll down to the bottom of the archive type and click the check box next to Category. Click Save and then click the Rebuild link, if desired. Now MT is set up to create category pages.

The next step is to edit your index page's template and add the category code. Here's an interesting place to note how MT handles template tags. There are two types of MT template tags: container tags and empty tags. Using them together, you can create blocks of variables that are repeated on the page, as necessary. For instance, the container for displaying the categories on your index page looks like this:

```
<MTCategories>
  <a href="<$MTCategoryArchiveLink$>"><$MTCategoryLabel$></a><br>
  <MTEntries>
  <$MTEntryTitle$> 
  </MTEntries>
  <br /><br />
</MTCategories>
```

The <MTCategories> tag is a container tag in which you define the appearance of a single category line. The way it's designed right now, each category's name (<$MTCategoryyLabel$>) in your blog will be a link to that category's archive page (<$MTCategoryArchiveLink$>) so that clicking the News link, for instance, will take you to the page of blog entries that are in the News category. Then, after that, the names of the entries in that category will appear, thanks to the following:

```
<MTEntries>
<$MTEntryTitle$> 
</MTEntries>
```

As you can see, once again a container tag (<MTEntries>) is used to contain a mini template that will be used for each of the entries. The empty tag (<$MTEntryTitle$>) is just a variable that will be replaced by each entry's title until there aren't any more.

You can add this code to the index template of your document, much the same way you added the archives links. However, I'd like to change it up a bit so that only the category names appear, not their associated entries. Therefore, I'll trim up the final product, as shown here:

```
<div class="sidetitle">
Archives
</div>
<div class="side">
<MTCategories>
  <a href="<$MTCategoryArchiveLink$>"><$MTCategoryLabel$></a><br>
</MTCategories>
</div>
```

By adding this to my template, I now have links that the reader can click to see the archive page that matches only my entries on the chosen topic.

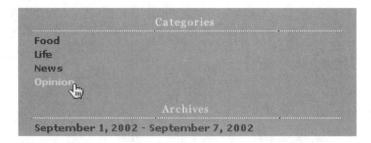

Change the Look

Like many websites designed using XHTML and CSS, Movable Type creates a blog in which the content and the design (or style) of that content are separate. This is done using style sheets—specifically, the Cascade Style Sheet (CSS) standard. We'll discuss this standard in more detail in Chapter 8.

If you'd like to edit your blog's style sheet, that's easy enough to do—it appears in the Index Templates list on the List Templates page in MT. Click the Stylesheet link and you'll be able to see (and edit) the style sheet in all its glory. You can also edit the file directly. It's called styles-site.css and is stored in the main directory of your blog (wherever your blog's index page is stored).

Editing style sheets can get a little involved, which is why we'll save some of the discussion for Chapter 8. But if you're really dying to change something about the blog, you can change the colors. In the style sheet, locate every instance of the color code #003366. Each two digits make up a *hex number* (a number in base-16), and each hex number represents the red, green, and blue levels that make up the particular color (this is a common approach for Web colors). For each instance you find (there should be four, three in the <a> section and one for the #banner definitions), change it to #660066. Now, save the template, rebuild your site (or at least the indexes), and see how things have changed—all that was blue should now be purple.

NOTE   *If you find that your changes don't seem to show up in the browser—and you're using Internet Explorer for Mac—it may be that you need to clear the cache first. IE keeps the style sheet cached once loaded, so it may not notice your changes unless you clear the cache and let it reload the page and the altered style sheet together.*

Before making too many changes to the style sheet, you might want to consult Chapter 8 and/or the CSS resources listed in Appendix A. Then, you can feel free to experiment with different CSS settings.

More...

In this chapter, you were familiarized with Movable Type, a very popular and useful server-side weblog management tool. You saw how to install and configure it as well as how to choose preferences, add your first entries, edit entries, add authors, and more. You were also introduced to the concepts of MT templates and tags, and you got a quick glimpse of how you can change the appearance of your blog through style sheets. If you've decided that Movable Type is the software for you, feel free to skip ahead to the customization discussion in Chapter 8.

If Movable Type still doesn't quite do it for you, turn to Chapter 7 and learn about pMachine, which is great software for a community-focused blog—one where you'd like to send e-mail messages to your readers, have active conversations on your entries, and even allow readers to sign up as members of the site and post their own entries or even their own blogs. pMachine is flexible, powerful, and an interesting option for building an online village of sorts.

M	T	W	T	F	S		S	M	T	W	T	F	S		S	M	T	W	T	F	S		S	M	T	W	T	F	S
	1	2	3	4					1	2	3	4					1	2	3	4					1	2	3	4
6	7	8	9	10	11		5	6	7	8	9	10	11		5	6	7	8	9	10	11		5	6	7	8	9	10	11
13	14	15	16	17	18		12	13	14	15	16	17	18		12	13	14	15	16	17	18		12	13	14	15	16	17	18
20	21	22	23	24	25		19	20	21	22	23	24	25		19	20	21	22	23	24	25		19	20	21	22	23	24	25
27	28	29	30	31			26	27	28	29	30	31			26	27	28	29	30	31			26	27	28	29	30	31	

Chapter 7

Setting Up and Using pMachine

In this chapter:

- Features and requirements

- Downloading and installation

- Configuring the server and your weblog

- Posting and editing entries

- Managing users

- Adding pBlocks

- Managing mailing lists and sending mailings

- Digging into the templates

- Extras: Using static pages, blurbs, and headlines

PMachine is one of the newest blogging solutions available, but it's already made quite a name for itself. Written by Rick Ellis (who is also the technical editor of this book), pMachine is based on work Rick originally did to automate Nancy Sinatra's website. According to Rick, the *p* in pMachine means *publishing*. It's meant as both a blogging tool and something beyond that—a platform for independent publishers. Based on a fast PHP/MySQL foundation, pMachine is very good for all sorts of publishing, offering sophisticated options that enable you to create a site that might just redefine what ends up being called a blog. It's my personal favorite blogging tool, if only because I find it to be extremely flexible and community oriented.

The pMachine Decision: Features and Requirements

pMachine is very powerful blogging software—perhaps with the strongest community-oriented features covered in this book. It allows for site-wide user registration, meaning a user can sign in to the site once and then access various features, such as the ability to write comments more quickly or to post actual entries (if you've given the user that privilege). You can also require membership for other things, such as accessing the registry of members. Members are automatically tracked on the birthday calendar. Also, when members sign up, they can elect to join your mailing list so that you can send them mass mailings to let your users know about news regarding your blog, your organization, and so on.

You can see how pMachine's personalization features make it good for developing an online community. The sign-in and user management tools make it easy for you, as the site publisher, to manage visitors as a group or as individuals—you can change the administrative level of a user, for instance, and enable him or her to edit other people's entries. pMachine Pro, in particular, is well suited to commercial online communities or for use in an organizational or corporate setting, because it also includes support for a basic message forum and allows for multiple weblogs. In fact, pMachine has quite a community of users who have found it flexible for building sites well beyond what one might consider a blog, as in Figure 7-1.

Here's a quick look at some of pMachine's features:

- **Comments**   Like other blogging software, pMachine enables you to accept comments from your readers. With pMachine, however, you can choose whether or not users must be registered (and, if desired, whether

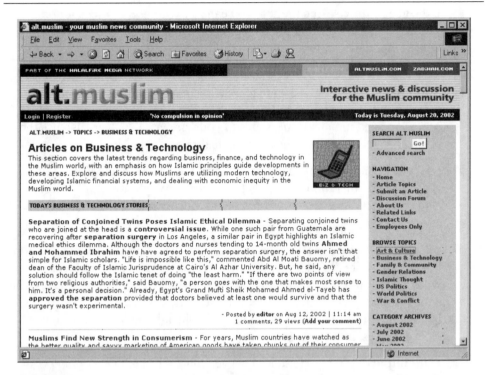

FIGURE 7-1   This site, alt.Muslim, is built using multiple weblogs and pMachine's Headlines feature to create a full-blown news portal.

users must have a confirmed e-mail address) before they can post comments.

■ **Categories**   You can assign a category to each entry as you post it to your site. Your readers can then use a menu on the index page to view only the entries that conform to a certain category, if desired. You can also customize the display of entries on your index page so that the categories are shown.

■ **Headline syndication**   pMachine lets you syndicate your headlines to others using standard RSS formatting (see Chapter 10).

■ **Collective weblogs**   You can designate your weblog as a "collective" weblog, meaning others can add entries. You can also specify that such entries are posted as "closed," by default, so that you can then moderate the entries before they appear on the site.

■ **User accounts**   As mentioned, you can ask your users to register on the site before allowing them to post comments and/or post entries. By registering, they can join your mailing list, appear on the member profile page, and be listed in your birthday calendar.

■ **Mailing list features**   Even readers who aren't members can pop their e-mail address into your mailing list. You can then use the built-in "post office" to send broadcast messages to your readers. (You can also use the post office to send messages to individual registered users.)

■ **pMcode**   These special codes can be used by your readers instead of HTML to add markup to comments or entries. Why not just allow HTML? You can—but pMcode limits what your reader can add, which is a bit more secure.

■ **pBlocks**   Another special pMachine feature is the pBlock, which is a little tough to describe. In essence, it enables you to set up special blocks (or what I'll call *snippets*) of HTML, CSS, or even JavaScript code that can be added to your page with a simple variable. The pBlock can have different behaviors—it can be randomized or it can change every time a web page is reloaded. It is, in a word, *interesting*.

■ **Data import**   The 2.1 (and higher) versions of pMachine can import from Greymatter and Movable Type, with support for other blogging tools slated for later versions.

■ **Bookmarklet**   You can create a bookmarket for quickly blogging as you surf—when you see something interesting, just click your special bookmarklet link and a window pops up, ready for you to blog.

■ **Post- and predating**   You can change the time or date of an entry to make it fit into your blog where you want it to go. If you want the entry to appear below a current story, date it just before that story; if you want it to appear automatically in the future, postdate it and then publish it. It won't show up on the home page until its time rolls around.

If pMachine has a downside, it's that its requirements are a bit steeper than those of Greymatter or Moveable Type. It's written in PHP, which must be active on the server, and you'll need to have a MySQL-based database in which to store your entries. This makes setup slightly more complicated for pMachine than others—although, in actuality, the hardest part is simply getting the correct type of web hosting account. You need a hosting account that supports PHP and

MySQL, and you'll need to know the username, password, and database name to be used to access the MySQL database. (In some cases, as you'll see, you can set that up yourself; in others, you'll need the information directly from your IPP or system administrator.)

NOTE *Another issue is that although you can get some additional great features, they'll cost you. pMachine comes in two versions: Free and Pro. pMachine Free can be downloaded immediately and features everything listed previously. pMachine Pro requires an online payment before it can be downloaded, but it offers support for multiple weblogs, a discussion forum, an XML parser (for displaying RSS-based headline feeds from other sources, such as Salon.com or other blogs), and an events calendar. The Pro version is great for building a portal-like site or for a collaborative site aimed at organizational use. Currently, the license is $45 for noncommercial and nonprofit use; $125 for commercial use.*

Get Started

To get pMachine up and running, you'll need to download the scripts and edit the configuration file and, perhaps, some others. Along the way you'll need to make decisions about your directory hierarchies, and you'll need to make sure your MySQL database is set up properly. Once pMachine is installed, you can launch the control panel and make sure everything is working well.

Download and Install

To get started with pMachine, you must first register on the pMachine website and log in. Here's how:

1. Visit http://www.pmachine.com/ in your web browser. Choose Register from the Member bar at the top of the page (at least that's where it is currently).

2. That should launch the Register page, where you need to enter your user information, make some preference choices, and click the Register button. (Take note of this page, because it's the same type of registration page you'll be offering to your users once you've got your blog set up.)

3. Once you've completed your registration, you'll receive an e-mail message that includes a link. You've got to access that link to confirm to pMachine

that you've given a valid e-mail address. (This is the e-mail-verification feature, which can be useful if you want to require that users who post on your site give you a valid e-mail address.)

4. Once you've accessed the link, you're verified. Now you need to log in. Click the Log-In link in the Member bar.

5. In the Login window, enter your username and password and then click Submit. You should see a message saying that you're logged in, and your name will appear in the Member bar.

6. Click the Download link. You should be able to click the Download pMachine Free link. You'll see a license page. Read it. If you agree with the license, click Accept. Your browser should download the file to disk.

The file that you download is a Zip archive; you'll need to unzip it if it doesn't unzip automatically. (In Windows, right-click and choose Extract All; on a Mac, drag the file to StuffIt Expander if it doesn't expand automatically.) The result is a folder that includes the scripts that make up pMachine.

To install pMachine, you may want to start by viewing, in a web browser, the file pm_installation.html, which is found in the docs folder that's inside the pMachine folder. There you can read the installation instructions more thoroughly than I'll be covering them here. Also, if your MySQL database hasn't yet been created, you'll need to do that now, and you'll need to know the username and password to use with the MySQL database. (Actually, pMachine will attempt to create a MySQL database when it's installed, but it will only succeed if your hosting account allows for database creation.) For instance, with my web hosting account, I can create a MySQL database from the built-in control panel that's accessible via a web browser (see Figure 7-2). If you have the option of creating multiple databases, create a new one for your blog and give it a simple but unique one-word name (such as blogbase or pmdata, or something along those lines).

Once you've gotten the database created, you're ready to begin the installation process. Here are the basic steps:

1. Begin by deleting the updates folder from the pm subfolder. The updates folder isn't necessary because you're installing from scratch.

2. With a text editor, open the file config.php in the pm folder. (If Notepad in Windows doesn't work well with this file, try WordPad, which can open and display the file. Just make sure you save it as plain text, not as RTF or Word format.)

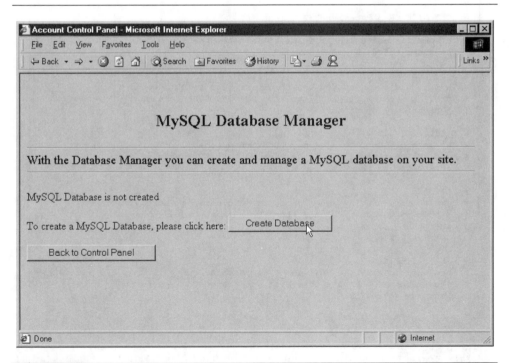

FIGURE 7-2   Creating the MySQL database. (With some ISPPs, the database is named automatically.)

3. In the config.php file, set the values for the four variables (see Figure 7-3). The values go between the blank quotation marks for each variable. The hostname is the name of the domain where your blog is located. (This should be the root level of the domain, not necessarily the full path to your blog's directory on the server.) For instance, even if the blog will eventually be at http://www.*yourservername*.com/blog/, you only need to enter **www.*yourservername*.com** for the host.

4. Save the config.php file as plain text.

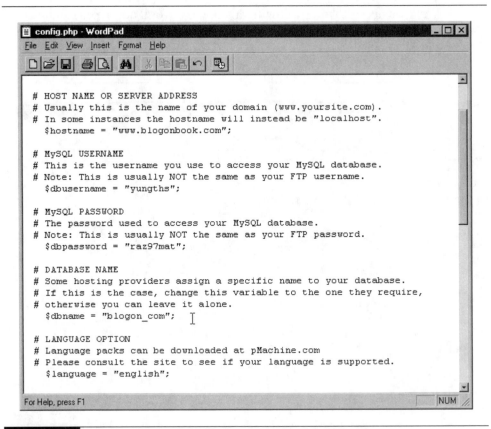

```
# HOST NAME OR SERVER ADDRESS
# Usually this is the name of your domain (www.yoursite.com).
# In some instances the hostname will instead be "localhost".
  $hostname = "www.blogonbook.com";

# MySQL USERNAME
# This is the username you use to access your MySQL database.
# Note: This is usually NOT the same as your FTP username.
  $dbusername = "yungths";

# MySQL PASSWORD
# The password used to access your MySQL database.
# Note: This is usually NOT the same as your FTP password.
  $dbpassword = "raz97mat";

# DATABASE NAME
# Some hosting providers assign a specific name to your database.
# If this is the case, change this variable to the one they require,
# otherwise you can leave it alone.
  $dbname = "blogon_com";

# LANGUAGE OPTION
# Language packs can be downloaded at pMachine.com
# Please consult the site to see if your language is supported.
  $language = "english";
```

FIGURE 7-3   Editing config.php with the appropriate MySQL values

5. If desired, you can now rename the pm folder. (This is done so that visitors to your site can't easily guess the name of the folder where scripts are stored. For instance, a person could notice that you're using pMachine and just try the pm folder on a whim to see whether they can access it.) If you do rename it, you'll need to open two files, both named pm_inc.php. One is located in the root of the pMachine folder, and the other is in the members folder. In these files, change "pm" to the new name you've given the folder. Make sure you resave the files as text files.

6. Now, upload all the files to your web server computer. If you intend to have the blog in the root folder of your site (for example, accessing http://www.*yourservername*.com/index.php will access the blog's index), then copy the *contents* of the pMachineFree folder to the server. If you want to put the blog in a subdirectory (as in http://www.*yourservername*.com/*blog*/weblog.php), you can rename the pMachineFree folder to whatever name you're giving the subdirectory of your site's blog and then upload or copy that folder to the root of your web server computer.

7. Once the entire pMachine installation is uploaded, you'll need to use your FTP program to change the permissions on two items. For the /images/ uploads directory, change the permissions to 777; in your blog's main directory, find index.xml and change its permissions to 666.

8. Now, you're ready to launch the installation script and see whether PHP is operating correctly. In your web browser, enter **http:// www.*yourservername*.com/pm/install.php**. (Note that you'll need to substitute your actual host name as well as any additional directories you created for your blog's main folder, and you'll need to substitute the proper name for the pm directory if you decided to rename it.) If things go well, you should see a page that looks like the one shown in Figure 7-4.

9. Now, walk through the steps of the installer, answering questions when necessary. In particular, take care that you enter the correct URL and path to pMachine's script directory (that is, the pm folder, which you may have renamed) and, on a later page, the absolute path to that same script directory.

10. When you've gotten past all that, you'll be asked to register as the administrator. Choose a username, enter a password twice, and then enter your e-mail address and a name to display on the entries you add to the blog. (Remember these—they're the username and password you'll use to log in and manage your blog.)

7

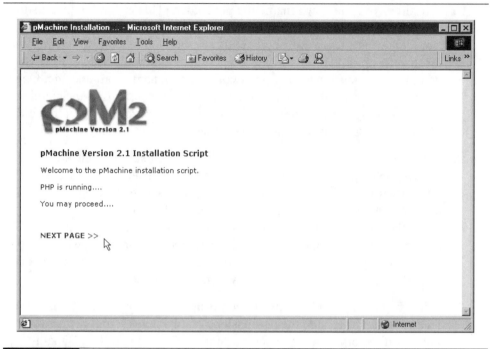

FIGURE 7-4   PHP appears to be working on my web server computer.

11. If you've succeeded in registering, you'll be told the URLs to your homepage and the URL to your blog's control panel. You'll also be told to delete the file install.php in the pm directory (or whatever this directory is now called). Do so using your FTP program; otherwise, you won't be able to access your site's control panel.

CAUTION   *Why is it important to delete this file? Because if you were to ever run it again, it would go through the same steps you just went through—including re-creating the blank database you just created. That would wipe out all the data in that database, thus deleting your entire blog!*

Configure pMachine

Ready to take a look at the control panel? In your browser, enter the URL to the pMachine control panel—it's the index.php document inside the pm folder (if you've renamed it, mentally substitute that new name whenever I refer to the pm folder). Launch that page in your web browser, and you should be asked to log in. Enter the username and password you just created for the administrator's account and then click Login. If you've entered the correct name and password, you'll see the control panel screen (see Figure 7-5).

NOTE
By default, you should be able to access the script folder (such as http://www.blogonbook.com/pm/) without including index.php, because the server should be configured to serve index.php documents by default. If it's not (if you get the index.html page instead, which will auto-refresh to index.php), you may need to consult your IPP to see whether they can turn on index.php as one of the default document names. If you're running your own web server, you may need to configure support for index.php; it's a setting in the Apache configuration file.

7

FIGURE 7-5   The pMachine control panel opens to a screen of statistics with commands down the left side and some important options across the top.

Note a few important buttons across the top: The Main button brings you back to the main page of the control panel, the Help button launches the pMachine manual in a new browser window, and you can click the Exit button to log out of the control panel. Click the big Visit Your Site button to see a new window with your blog's index page displayed.

You don't need to do much configuration before you begin posting—pMachine is set up with its default behavior, ready for you to blog. If you'd like, however, you can dig into the main configuration page for your site just to see whether anything needs tweaking. To see general preferences, click the General Preferences link under the Admin subject header. Now you'll see a number of different options you can alter.

TIP   *Note the clickable letter* i *next to each option in General Preferences; click one to see an explanation of its corresponding option.*

Here's a quick look at the general preferences:

- **General Setup**   Check these entries to make sure they're right—you can use them to change the name of your blog, the URL, or the admin's e-mail address. In the Time Offset menu, choose the time zone difference that you are from the location of your server so that posts are dated and timestamped correctly. You can also opt to turn on the curse word–censoring features for weblogs (actual entries made by others) and/or comments.

- **Directory Paths**   These should be correct, but check them to make sure. If you change anything in the future, you'll need to change the entries here.

- **Member Preferences**   Here you can make choices about whether you require member registration in order for readers to add comments to stories and, separately, whether nonmembers can send in blog entries. You can also set who can view member profiles and change some of the formatting of the member listing.

NOTE   *Rick warns that these settings may move to the Weblog Management settings in a future version, so look for them there if you don't see them in General Preferences. Weblog Management options are discussed later in this chapter.*

- **RSS Syndication**   In this section you can turn on RSS (headline) syndication and set your preferences for it, including the number of entries, weblog title, description, and an image's URL, if you'd like to include one.

- **Username and Password Preferences**   Set the maximum and minimum sizes for usernames and passwords.

- **Image Display Preferences**   Set the formatting options for images that are uploaded via pMachine.

> **NOTE**   *In version 2.2 and higher, you'll set all image options when you are actually uploading the image.*

- **Search Preferences**   Set the search results page and some basic options for how the results will look.

- **Hit Counter Preferences**   Choose the number to start with and the type of hit counter, along with other basic options.

Configure Your Weblog

You'll find additional choices you can make that specifically govern the default weblog that was created when you installed pMachine. (Remember, pMachine Pro can manage multiple weblogs, which is why they have separate preference pages.) Under the Admin heading in the command list, click Weblog Management. On the Current Weblogs page, click the Preferences link in the *weblog* row.

Now you'll gain access to a number of preference settings. At the top of the page, make sure the absolute path to your blog's root folder is correct; then edit the names of the various page types (more on these later). You can also choose a template set, if you've created more than one (this is really for pMachine Pro's multiple weblogs feature).

You can turn on the collective weblog feature, which enables other authors to add entries to your blog. (Whether or not those authors need to be registered and logged in is based on the settings in General Preferences.) If you turn on the collective weblog, you can choose whether entries are closed when submitted, meaning they won't actually be published on the site until you or another administrative user approves them.

Other options include how the index page is formatted, how many items appear on it, and how HTML and pMcode will work in this weblog. You can also enable comments for entries in this blog from this page, and you can decide the comment order (newest entry last or first). Finally, you can turn on the E-mail Notify feature (which sends an e-mail to the address listed when activity takes place), and you can enable a ping to Weblogs.com if you'd like to publicize the site in that way. When you're done making changes, click the Update Preferences button.

NOTE   *We'll be back in here throughout the course of the chapter because some important settings need to be covered in a little more depth.*

Change the Index's Name

By default, pMachine names your blog's index page weblog.php. Although this is convenient if the page is one of many weblogs (or if you're integrating it with an existing site), it's not quite as handy if you're using the pMachine Free version and your whole site is a blog. You may want to change the name to index.php, for instance, so that the weblog's index loads automatically when the blog's URL is accessed.

To do this, you'll need to make three changes:

1. In General Preferences, update the Home Page URL entry so that it points to the proper URL plus index.php, not weblog.php. Scroll to the bottom of the page and click Update Preferences.

2. Click Weblog Management and then view the preferences for the weblog. In the Main Weblogs Page box, change the name to index.php. Scroll to the bottom of the page and click Update Preferences.

3. You'll need to locate the file weblog.php in your blog's root directory and change its name to index.php. You'll need to use your FTP application because you can't use the pMachine File Browser tool (see the section "Dig into the Templates") to change the name of a file.

With these three changes made, you should be able to view the page index.php over the Internet and see it appear in your web browser window. When you do, you'll see the default appearance of pMachine, complete with one placeholder entry, as shown in Figure 7-6.

FIGURE 7-6   Here's how pMachine looks when you first install it and load its index page.

Post and Edit Entries

If you've read any of the other chapters on blogging tools, you'll find that pMachine's entry-editing page is very similar to those of the other tools. You type a title, the body of the message, and the "More" text, if desired. Then you choose a category (if applicable) and either preview or submit the entry.

Post an Entry

To post an entry, click the Create a New Entry link under the Weblog heading. You'll see the entry page (see Figure 7-7). At the very top of the window you'll see the time and date entries—you can edit these if you'd like to predate or postdate your entry. A predated entry will appear in the blog before other entries (as long as it's predated far enough in the past). A postdated entry won't appear on the blog's index page until the date and time you choose.

In the Title entry box, type the title for this blog entry; in the Body entry box, you can type the entire entry if it's short and designed to appear completely on the index page of your blog. If you'd like the story to "jump" to a full-page entry, put content in the More entry box. This content won't appear on the index page but rather only on the linked-to page or the comments page when viewed by the reader.

NOTE   *The Blurb field isn't coded into the standard templates, so it won't appear by default on the pages of your blog. However, once you get into editing the templates you may find it handy for special situations, such as when you want to have the headlines from this blog appear on another page. Ideally, the blurb content would be a quick sentence or two that describes the entry. Unlike the text in the Body entry box, the Blurb text won't be seen again when you click to view the full-page entry. It's more of a description of the entry than it is part of the entry itself.*

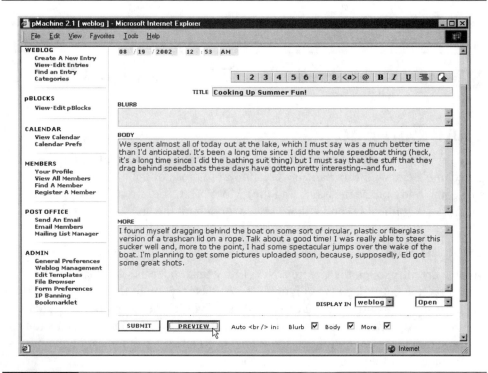

FIGURE 7-7   Adding an entry in pMachine

When you've done all your typing, you can scroll to the bottom of the window and make some choices. In the Display In menu, you can choose from among many blogs if you have more than one set up. In the menu next to it, you can choose to make the entry open or closed. A closed entry doesn't appear on the index page or in the archives; an open entry is ready to be read. If you're still working and want to save the story as a draft, set it to Closed before you submit it.

You also have the option of turning off the Auto <br /> feature, which automatically turns your carriage returns (pressing RETURN or ENTER) into the line break element. If you've been using full HTML for your entries (including block-level elements such as <p>), you might do better turning off Auto <br />. Otherwise, it's pretty standard to leave it on.

Now, if you'd like to see the story before it's posted, click the Preview button. You'll visit a page that lets you read through the story. If you see a problem or typo and want to return to editing (or otherwise change something), click the Continue Editing button.

On either screen, if you feel good about the entry, click the Submit button. The story is submitted to pMachine. If it's an open story and its time has come to be posted, it will appear on the index page.

Add an Image

If you'd like to add an image to your blog entry, you can do it in one of two ways. If you've uploaded the image without using the pMachine control panel—or if the image is already on the Internet—you can reference the image in your blog entry using a standard <img /> element. (This assumes you've allowed HTML in your entries, which is an option—called HTML Display Option in Weblog—you can turn off in the weblog's preferences accessed via the Weblog Management link.)

If you'd like to upload the image specifically for this story, you can do that. While editing the entry, click the Upload Image button that appears in the toolbar at the top of the page.

The Upload an Image window will appear, where you can select the image file you'd like to upload. Enter the name of the file (and path) if you know it, or you can click the Browse button to bring up an Open dialog box so that you can locate the file. It will need to be web-compatible (JPEG, GIF, or PNG format) and, ideally, shouldn't be too big (about 250 to 300 pixels wide is usually ideal for a blog entry). Once you've found the image and clicked Open in the Open dialog box, you'll be back in the Upload an Image window, where you can choose whether to apply the image formatting. You can also click the Upload button to transfer the image to your blog.

In pMachine 2.2 and higher you'll see a bigger image window with additional options. In the Upload Destination menu, you can choose a different folder for the image. (You set the possible folders by clicking Preferences, lower in the window.) Select the Image Browser, and you can review images that have already been uploaded to your server, just in case you want to use an image that you've uploaded previously or one that you've added via FTP.

With the image uploaded, you'll see the window change, asking whether you'd like the image's code added to the Blurb, Body, or More field. Make your choice and click Add Image to Your Entry. The image is added to your entry field, using the code that's specified for images in General Preferences. By default, the image is added using an HTML table that's designed to give it a certain amount of padding and a crisp presentation. You can use the Cut and Paste commands to move the code around, if desired, so that it shows up in the right place in your entry.

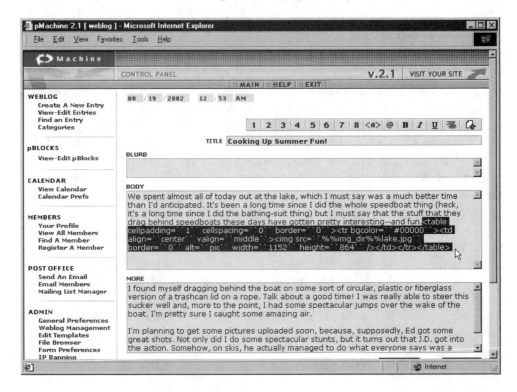

TIP

You should edit the alt text to something more meaningful so that anyone without a graphical browser can tell what the image is supposed to represent.

If you don't like all that table code, you can open General Preferences and change it (see Tip below). Alternatively, you can opt not to include the image with formatting; then you can add an image element like this to your entry:

```
<img src="%%image_dir%%name.jpg" alt="alt description"/>
```

You'll need to change *name*.jpg to the name (and proper extension) for the image as well as enter your own alternative description. The variable %%image_dir%% will cause pMachine to automatically substitute the correct path to your uploaded images directory. (By default, in pMachine 2.1 this is the /images/uploads directory for which you set special permissions during the installation process. If you have pMachine 2.2, you can have multiple image paths, so you'll need to enter the correct variable, as in %%imagedir[1]%% for the default image directory or %%imagedir[2]%%.)

NOTE

Having trouble uploading images? If you encounter an error, it's probably because you didn't properly set the permissions for the image directory you're trying to use. See the section "Download and Install," earlier in the chapter, for details.

You can also use other attributes with the <img> element, such as the align=left or align=right attribute to change the image to a floating image that allows text to wrap around it.

TIP

If you want the automatic formatting to create a simpler image element, just delete the entries in the General Preferences under the headings Image Pre-formatting and Image Post-formatting. You can then customize the Image Properties entry (adding an align="right" attribute, for instance). Now, when you select the formatted image option, you'll get a regular <img> element with the specified attributes. (Again, in version 2.2 and higher, you'll access these by clicking the Preferences link in the image pop-up window instead of in General Preferences.)

7

Once an image has been uploaded, you can use it again in another entry, if you like, using the same <img/> element you used in the original entry. The image will still be there and accessible in the default images directory, assuming you haven't deleted it using your FTP program.

Edit an Entry

Once you've gotten a few entries entered, you may find you need to edit them or the comments that readers have written in response to those entries, if relevant. To do either, click the View-Edit Entries link under Weblog in the command listing. On the Weblog Entries page, you'll see a listing of all the entries you've added to your blog thus far.

Create A New Entry View-Edit Entries Find an Entry Categories	WEBLOG ENTRIES						View all - newest first ▾
	TITLE	**AUTHOR**	**DATE**	**EDIT**	**COMMENTS**	**STATUS**	**DISPLAY IN**
	Cooking Up Summer Fun!	willhoyt	08/19/02	Edit	(0) Comments	Open	weblog
pBLOCKS View-Edit pBlocks	Welcome to pMachine	willhoyt	08/18/02	Edit	(0) Comments	Open	weblog

To edit an entry, click the Edit link that appears in that entry's row. (If you click the entry's name, you'll see an intermediate screen where you can view the entry before deciding to edit it or delete it.) The Edit screen looks just like the composition screen you saw when creating a new entry. Edit the Title, Blurb, Body, and More sections of the post, as desired, and then choose whether the message should be open or closed. Then click Update to save your changes or Preview to see them before saving.

Alter or Delete an Entry

From the View-Edit Entries screen, click the title of an entry to see that entry's text and any images you may have included. Scroll to the bottom of that page and you'll see links. You can click the Edit link to bring up the editing screen, or you can click the Close link if you'd like to close the entry (meaning it will no longer be displayed on the site.)

To delete the entry, click the Delete link. You'll see a screen asking you to confirm that you want to permanently delete the entry from the blog's database, noting that comments will be deleted as well. If that's what you want to do, click the Delete button; otherwise, choose the Back command in your browser or click a different command link.

> **TIP** *Remember, you don't have to delete an entry to keep it from being visible on the blog; you can choose to close the entry, even temporarily, and it won't be visible to your site's visitors.*

Add Categories

pMachine makes good use of the categories concept—even with a single weblog, you can create categories that you assign to each individual entry. You can then make a menu available to readers on the index page so that they can choose to view only a single category of entries at a time, if desired. It's a quick way to make the site considerably more organized, and something your readers will appreciate once you've got a lot of entries posted.

You begin by defining the categories. In the Weblog section of the tool links, click Categories. You'll see the Current Weblogs listing; click the Edit Categories link for the default weblog. (Again, with pMachine Pro you can have multiple weblogs, each with its own categories, which is why this interim page is here.) Now you'll see another page where you can enter a category name. Do so and then click Add New. On the screen that appears next, you'll see a list of the categories you've created begin to build. Keep adding categories as desired:

| Category Name: | News | |

| ADD NEW |

Category	Edit	Delete
Events	Edit	Delete
Wrap Ups	Edit	Delete

When you're done, you can move on to another part of the control panel or click the Main button to return to the main control panel screen.

7

So what's next? As you're creating or editing your entries, choose a category for each from the category menu that appears at the bottom of each entry screen. When you save the entry, it's now assigned to a category.

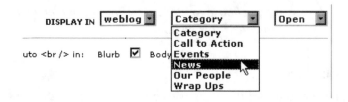

When you've created categories and assigned them, something cool happens—your index page changes to reflect the new categories. A menu will appear just above the calendar on your page, where readers will be able to click a category to see the entries that have been associated with that category.

If you like, you can change the way that categories are displayed. For example, you can use a pull-down menu to show the categories. (That's my preferred method, but be warned that it uses JavaScript, which may not work in all browsers.) To do that, you'll need to edit the index page and add the relevant function call to the page. Here's how:

1. In the control panel, click the File Browser link (under the Admin heading).

2. In the File Browser, click the link to your index page. (By default, it's weblog.php, but it may be index.php if you've changed it as I recommended earlier.)

3. Now you're viewing the HTML for that page. Locate the following:

```
<?php weblog_categories($id,"weblog","text"); ?>
```

4. Change "text" to "drop" so that the code line looks like this:

```
<?php weblog_categories($id,"weblog","drop"); ?>
```

5. Click the Save File button.

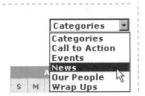

That's it. Your index file is saved. When you next access your site's index page, you should be able to see the drop-down menu for accessing categories. When the reader selects a category from the menu, the index page immediately reloads and shows only the entries that match that category.

Add pBlocks

Unique to pMachine is the pBlock, an interesting concept that can take a little getting used to, but one that becomes very powerful once you do. Essentially, a pBlock is a special container that you can use to place special content on your website. The pBlock is particularly interesting because you can give it a behavior—you can randomize it, for instance, or otherwise cause it to change.

Many pMachine publishers use a pBlock to place a randomized image on their index page—you might do the same, or you might use it to display the book you're currently reading or the CD you're listening to, or to rotate randomly through these sorts of things. You can also use a pBlock to add different types of code, including style sheet code, making it possible to, for instance, change the colors of your page randomly. And, finally, pBlocks can be static, too. On one of my sites, I use a simple pBlock for the navigation links. The advantage is that I only have to change those links in one place, and everywhere that the pBlock shows up, the changes will be made automatically.

Use a Bookmarklet

The bookmarklet concept, also discussed in Chapter 6, is one that pMachine offers as well. Essentially a bookmarklet is a link you can use to quickly open a window so that you can add an entry to your blog. When you click the bookmarklet, a link to the current page in the browser is also included in your entry, as a convenience. (If text is highlighted in the browser window when you click the link, it's added to your bookmarklet entry as well.) Using a bookmarklet is handy for blogging about items you encounter as you're surfing.

In pMachine, all you need to do to add a bookmarklet is to click the Bookmarklet entry in the Admin section of the command links. There you'll see a page, complete with the linked bookmarklet. In most browsers, you can drag that hyperlink to your Favorites or Bookmarks menu, or to the toolbar Favorites section of your browser window.

To add a pBlock, you'll need some idea of what you're going to add—it could be plain text, but most pBlocks will be HTML markup of some sort. Once you have that figured out, you can begin building the pBlock:

1. Click the View-Edit pBlocks command link. You'll see the pBlocks screen.

2. Click the Create a New pBlock link.

3. On the Create a New P-Block page, enter a name for the pBlock (note the rules—one word with no spaces) and choose a behavior from the menu (see Figure 7-8).

4. Click Submit.

Now you'll see a list of your pBlocks. What you're doing at this point is beginning to add *members* to your pBlock. Each member is simply a discreet block

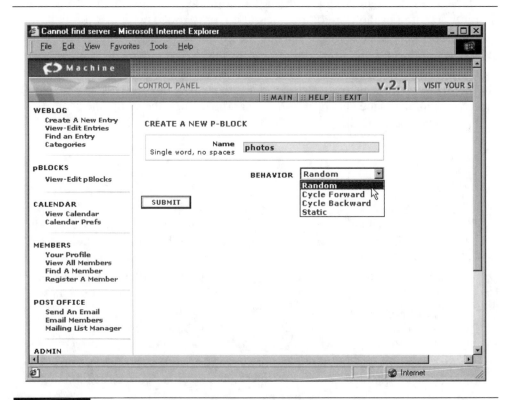

FIGURE 7-8   Naming a pBlock and choosing its behavior

of text or HTML code—a paragraph, an image link, and so on. A pBlock only needs one member, for instance, so if you're creating a static pBlock, you're likely to create only one member for the pBlock. In other cases, you're able to cycle through each member or move randomly through them every time the pBlock is loaded. Click the Add/Edit Members link to add a new member to a particular pBlock.

On the Add a Member page, enter a name for the member and then enter the code in the pBlock Data entry box. As mentioned, this can be almost any sort of HTML code, scripting, and so on. (At the time of writing, it can't be PHP code or a pMachine tag.) Realize, though, that it will need to fit into the overall page that's being created, so it needs to be written with that in mind. If you're not much of an HTML coder, you might want to stick with some simple members to start with, such as small image files.

In any case, enter the text and/or HTML markup for this member. Then decide whether you want your line breaks (where you've pressed RETURN or ENTER) to be turned into HTML line breaks (the <br /> element). If you've been entering your own markup, the answer is probably no; if you simply entered paragraph text without much (or any) block-level HTML markup, then turn on the Convert Line-Breaks option by clicking its check box. With that decision made, click the Submit button and the member is submitted.

> **NOTE** *You can upload an image via the Add a Member screen by clicking the Upload icon above the pBlock Data entry box. You can then use a series of windows to upload the image and add it to the page, as discussed in the section "Add an Image," earlier in this chapter.*

Once you've added one member, you may be ready to add more. Click the Add a Member link above the Member list to continue adding members. (Note in the list that you can edit existing members, when necessary, and that you can also delete a member from the list.)

MEMBER UPDATED...

MEMBERS OF P-BLOCK: PHOTOS		ADD A MEMBER
NAE	EDIT	DELETE
Bridge	Edit	Delete
Lake	Edit	Delete
Statute	Edit	Delete

When you're done adding to your pBlock, you're ready to add your pBlock to your site's HTML templates. You'll do that by clicking the File Browser command link and then clicking the template to which you want to add the pBlock. (It can be the index.php or weblog.php template, if you'd like to add the pBlock to your main index page. Alternatively, you can pick one of the other templates if you'd like this pBlock to appear on some other part of your blog.) In the template, find the location where you'd like the pBlock to appear. Now, just add its line. Here's an example:

```
<?php pblock("photos"); ?>
```

Substitute the actual name of the pBlock for *photos* in this example. Now, at the bottom of the file-editing screen, click Save File. That's all it takes. The next time you load a page that uses the template you just altered, your pBlock's content should appear on that page. When you reload the page, other members should appear according to the behavior you set.

For instance, I've added my pBlock to the top of the Menu Items section of the index.php (or, by default, weblog.php) template. By adding an <h4> heading (<h4>Random Image</h4>) and the pBlock code, I end up with a pBlock that cycles through the images that I add as members, while fitting in nicely with the rest of the sidebar.

```
<div class="menuitems">

<h4>RANDOM IMAGE</h4>
<?php pblock("photos"); ?>
<br />
```

The result of this code is shown in Figure 7-9.

> **TIP**   *If you do add images in this way, I recommend that they be around 200 pixels in width and basically uniform in size (the height can vary, if absolutely necessary, but not by much). That will keep the site looking very crisp and professional. And remember, because you can add most any markup in the pBlock member entry box, you can wrap an image like this in a hyperlink so that your visitors can click this "thumbnail" image to see a full-sized image that fills the browser window.*

Remember, pBlocks can be nearly any code. Experiment with adding not only visible members, such as text, markup, and other code, but also with "invisible" code, such as CSS style sheet definitions. For instance, you could create a pBlock

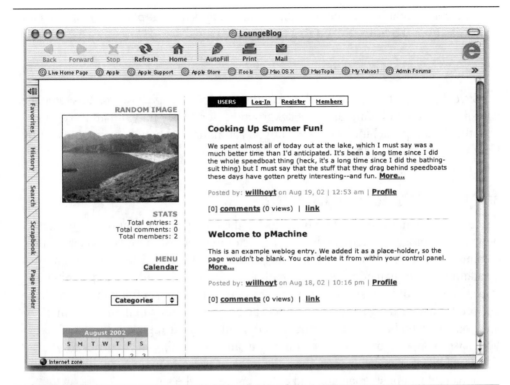

FIGURE 7-9   Via a pBlock, I've added an attractive random image display.

that changes the background color of your site randomly, using style sheet markup. Create a new pBlock called background, make it Random, and then create members that have code that looks like this:

```
<style>
body {background: blue}
</style>
```

Create a few different members and change the name of the color in each (yellow, red, white, and so on). Now, with the pBlock saved, dig into the template that you want to add this random behavior to and add the pBlock (you can add it anywhere, but right below the opening <body> tag is a great place so that you can find it easily in the future). Add this code to the page:

```
<?php pblock("background"); ?>
```

Save the template page. Now, the next time you load a page based on this template, you should get a different, random background color. (They may not all look good with the default pMachine template, but you can figure out how to overcome that by learning more about style sheets, which are discussed in Chapter 8.)

Manage Users and Mailings

Aside from the innovative nature of pBlocks, the real standout feature that pMachine brings to the blogging game is site-level registration. Part of the way you can build community with pMachine is to encourage your visitors to register—either simply by adding their e-mail address to the mailing list or by going all out and signing up to be a member of your site. Once users are signed up, you can track their birthdays and send them birthday messages, others can communicate with them via e-mail, and you can send broadcast e-mails directed only to your registered users. Plus, you have the option of limiting commenting and/or creating new entries to your registered users. You can even make a few of your users editors, if you like, enabling them to create, publish, manage, and delete entries on the site.

User Registration

Users register in pMachine by clicking the Register link in the Member bar, which by default appears at the top of most pages in pMachine. When the link is clicked, a Registration page appears, nearly identical to the User Profile page that you used to create your account when first setting up pMachine.

NOTE
In some cases, laws may affect what personal information you can legally ask for from your visitors (particularly, in the U.S., from minors and/or for commercial purposes), so you should take those laws into consideration if you decide to implement a pMachine community site. It's also a good idea to post a privacy statement of some kind to let your users know why information is being gathered and what sort of e-mail or other communication they can expect from you if they give you their e-mail address.

On the Registration page, users can enter their personal information and make a few decisions about the types of e-mail they'd like to receive.

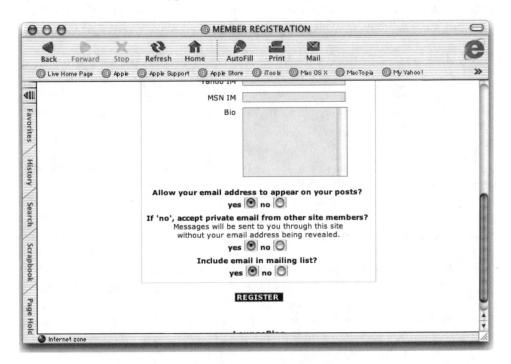

7

How pMachine reacts to users after they register depends on you. In the General Preferences area, you can set Member Preferences with the Require Account Activation option turned on; if it's turned on, users must respond to an e-mail message sent to the e-mail address they registered in pMachine. After clicking the link that appears in that e-mail message, the user's account is activated and the user is free to log in to the site. (If you don't have this option on, the user can log in immediately.)

TIP
You can also directly register your users if you don't want to make them go through the formal steps themselves. Just click the Register a Member command in the pMachine control panel. If a user does register but doesn't activate the account, you can use the status menu (discussed next) to change the account from Pending to Active.

Once logged in (by clicking the Login link in the Member bar and entering a username and password), users have access to all the items they are privileged to access. If you've limited weblog entries and/or comments to registered users, the logged-in users can now take advantage of these functions.

NOTE *Also in General Preferences is the Public Viewing of Member Profiles option. If it's set to Only Registered Members Can View, then members will need to be logged in before they can see the list of other members that appears when they click the Members link in the Member bar while viewing the blog.*

As the administrator, you can look at any user's account at any time. Choose the View All Members command link and you'll see a list of your members. Quickly, you can see a user's activity, join date, and status. To edit the user, click the user's name. On the screen that follows, you can change almost anything about the user, including username, password, e-mail, and all the other personal details.

NOTE *You cannot look up a member's password because it's stored in an encrypted format. You can, however, change the user's password if need be. A user who knows his username can also have a temporary password mailed to him if he forgets his password and can't log in. The Login pages include a Forgot Password? link that can be used to send a new password.*

You can also change the status of your registered users (called *members*), if you like, enabling them to access portions (or all) of the control panel to add entries, make editing changes, or even delete entries and manage other users.

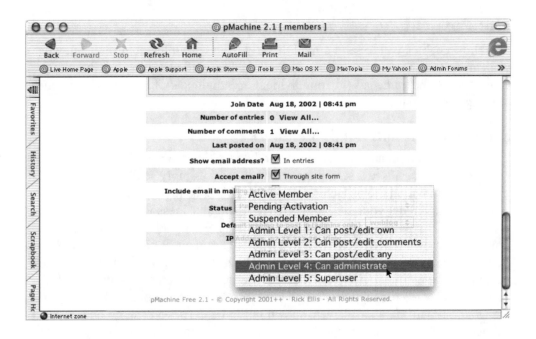

Level 3 is the typical user level, representing a user who can add entries to collective weblogs and comment on other entries (assuming you've limited those options to members). Level 4 users can actually log in to the control panel (you'll need to tell them how) and create their own entries; they can also edit their own entries and comments. Level 5 users can create their own entries but can also edit other people's comments—this is a good level for a day-to-day moderator. Level 6 users can edit any entry; Level 7 users can manage all entries and all users but can't make changes to the templates or change the site-level preferences. Only a Level 8 user, the superuser, can do everything we're discussing in this chapter. (The original user you created when setting up pMachine is a superuser.)

TIP

If you have many users, you can search for a particular user by clicking Find a Member instead of View All Members from the main control panel screen.

The Post Office

pMachine enables you to send e-mail directly from within the control panel, which you can do for a variety of reasons. In fact, the Post Office section has three commands: Send an Email (to an individual or individuals), Email Members, and Mailing List Manager.

Send an Email and Email Members

These first two commands are somewhat related. Click the Send an Email command and you'll see a screen that enables you to simply send an e-mail message from within the pMachine interface. This is handy for quickly letting someone know about your site, for conducting blog business via e-mail, or for pretty much any purpose you desired. Just enter an e-mail address in the To entry box and your own reply-to e-mail address in the From entry box. (This address can be anything; it doesn't have to relate to your blog. It will show up in the Reply To field when the recipient views the message.) Enter a subject, type your e-mail message (HTML isn't supported), and click Send to send it along.

On the Email Members screen, shown in Figure 7-10, you can go one step further. You'll see a similar interface that enables you to enter the From (reply-to) address and a subject for the message. Then, you'll notice that by default a salutation appears in the message area—this is to show you the variable <<name>>, which can be used to automatically place the member's name in the body of the message. This can be handy for some basic personalization of the e-mail. Now, type the rest of your e-mail message.

When you're done, you can select the members to whom you would like to send this message in the Group menu. Pull it down and you'll see different options—you can send the message to active members (to tell them the latest news), pending members (to encourage them to activate their membership), or just to administrators (to let them in on some insider site news).

Outside of the Group menu, you can use the Send To option either to send the message to all the members that fit the group criteria you've chosen or to send to a range of those recipients.

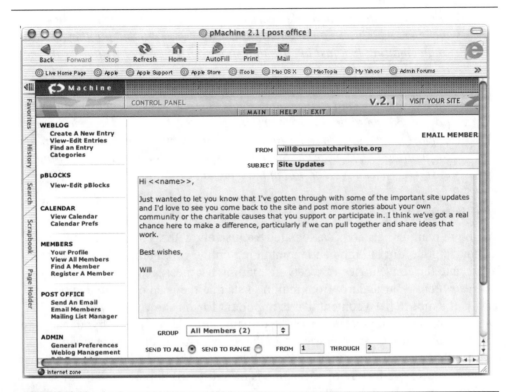

FIGURE 7-10   The Email Members screen lets you send bulk messages to your site's registered members.

NOTE   *If you have trouble getting your e-mails to reach all your members, you may have better luck if you restrict each sending session to a range of about 50 people at a time—you should do this if it appears your e-mail messages aren't being sent successfully. Send to one range of about 50 (1 through 49) and then paste your message in and send to the next range (50 to 99), and so on.*

Finally, you have the option Exclude Members Who Are Also in the Mailing List. This is a good idea, because it keeps you from sending messages to the same user twice if you're using both the member list and the mailing list to send the same message.

TIP

You can use the Exclude Members option to send messages to those members who aren't on the mailing list—to remind them that they aren't on the mailing list, just in case they may want to be. For instance, on one of my sites, my desire is to only send the regular, weekly updates to the mailing list members who opt in. However, people may join the site from time to time and not realize they're missing out on the regular mailings by having chosen to not be on the mailing list. So, I can send a periodic (once a quarter or year) reminder to those members just so they can sign up for the mailing list, if desired. Registered users can sign up for the mailing list easily by checking an option in their member profile.

Mailing Lists

Although mailing lists aren't associated exclusively with weblogs, they can be an amazing tool for building and maintaining online community. People tend to appreciate the convenience of receiving mailing list messages *with content that interests them*—particularly from mailing lists that they can opt in to and out of easily. It's nice to have content that is important to you show up in your e-mail. Most people don't appreciate unsolicited spam (or junk mail), but if you take care to make sure you're keeping away from that category, you can be reasonably assured that maintaining a mailing list will help your blog maintain its reader base.

One impressive feature of pMachine is its ability to support a mailing list separate from the member list. This makes it possible for members to participate without receiving your mailing list messages. It also makes it possible for people to sign up for your mailing list without going through the registration process. And, whenever a reader receives a mailing list message from you, it includes an automated option for unsubscribing from the list.

Therefore, I think you can feel confident about implementing a mailing list, if it seems appropriate for your site. Some bloggers send a message to their list that gives the headlines or brief blurbs of the latest posts, with links back to them. Others send the entire text of their most recent blog entries. Still others send a mailing list message that has different content from the blog component—perhaps special alerts or "breaking news" items.

As mentioned, readers can sign up for your mailing list when registering by turning on the option Include Email in Mailing List. If a reader isn't registering, she can still join the mailing list by entering her e-mail address in the Mailing List entry box that appears, by default, on your site's index page.

MAILING LIST

`me@ourco` **SEND**

Once you have some members in your mailing list, you can send the list a message. Click the Mailing List Manager and you'll see the Send to Mailing List screen. Enter the From address that you'd like to use, a subject for the message, and then the text of the message in the main entry box. To send the message, select either Send to All or Send to Range; if you choose Send to Range, enter numbers in the range boxes. Then, click the Send button to send your mailing list message.

NOTE   *As with sending messages to users, you may encounter problems sending your mailing list message to more than about 50 members at one time, depending on the way PHP is configured on your server computer. (pMachine tries to compensate for the problem, but it can't override the settings for a PHP implementation that's running in Safe Mode.)*

7

From the Send to Mailing List screen you can also view and manage the members of your mailing list. At the top of the screen is the Total Email Addresses in Mailing List entry. Click the View link to see that mailing list. On the next screen, you can choose how to view the list from the View radio buttons and the

Sort List menu. Do so, and then click View. A list of the e-mail addresses in the mailing list will appear; you can click one of the addresses to open an e-mail message (in your default e-mail program) to that person. To delete addresses from the mailing list, click the check box next to one or more of the addresses and then click the Delete button.

Dig into the Templates

pMachine really has two different sets of "templates" that work together to determine the way your weblog will look to the reader. The first templates are the HTML documents you've already done some work with—index.php, weblog.php, and so on. As you've seen, you can change those via the File Browser tool in the pMachine control panel. (You can also change them using a text editor and FTP program, just as you might any other HTML document.) The second type of template is the template that governs the way pMachine formats its auto-generated output—the entries and information that come out of the central database. We'll look at those in more depth in this section.

How the Templates Work

Throughout the chapter you've seen that some features—pBlocks and the Category menu, for instance—are added to your pages by opening up an HTML template file (such as index.php or weblog.php) and adding a special PHP tag, such as the following:

```
<?php pblock("background"); ?>
```

This is essentially only half of the way in which you can change the look of your site. You're free to edit the HTML document index.php or weblog.php to change the index page of your site, and you can alter the HTML documents comments.php, more.php, search.php, calendar.php, and archives.php in order to add static images, reformat the page, and so on. Use your HTML skills to the fullest in these pages to design them; then use the PHP tags to cause database content to appear on those pages when the reader visits them. For instance, all that's needed to display all the entries that appear on the typical pMachine index page is the following tag:

```
<?php weblog_entries($id,"weblog"); ?>
```

This tag tells pMachine to place the predetermined (by the Weblog Management preferences) number of entries on the page, using the weblog named "weblog." In fact, your index.php or weblog.php document could be little more than this one tag (inside the <body> element of a well-formed HTML document), and you'd see a page remarkably like the default index page that pMachine creates. (The difference would be that there are no formatting constraints on the width of the entries and no column of controls, calendars, and archive links.) All the other markup, including pBlocks and hard-coded HTML, can be seen as little more than window dressing.

Built-in Templates

So, how are the actual weblog entries formatted? As you can see when you view your pMachine site, these entries aren't just raw text out of the database—they have headlines, body text, More links, and information about the author. Each of these entries is represented in your HTML templates as a pMachine tag. You can think of each tag as a placeholder that fits into the HTML documents index.php, comments.php, and so on. When pMachine displays that HTML template, it looks into the database for corresponding data and it checks the tag's own template for markup and style cues. For total control, you need to be able to access and alter each tag's own "mini" or internal templates, which you can do by clicking the Edit Templates command in the pMachine control panel. From there you'll be able to change the templates used to format the dynamic content that pMachine "pours" into your HTML document templates when it creates a page.

When you click Edit Templates, you're shown the Current Templates screen. Here you can choose to edit various groups of internal templates that are used for formatting the data that pMachine extracts from your database and adds to the HTML documents "on the fly" to replace the PHP tags you've placed in the HTML document templates. These categories include the weblog category (for templates that affect weblog entries and listings), the membership templates, e-mail templates, search-related templates, and calendar-related templates (see Figure 7-11). We can't get to all these items in this chapter, so let's focus on the weblog-related templates.

To edit the weblog templates, click the Edit link in the Weblog Templates row. You'll see a new Weblog Templates screen that displays links to all the different templates that are used to format template-related content. It may look like an intimidating list, but it's not as bad as it seems. Here's a quick roundup of the links

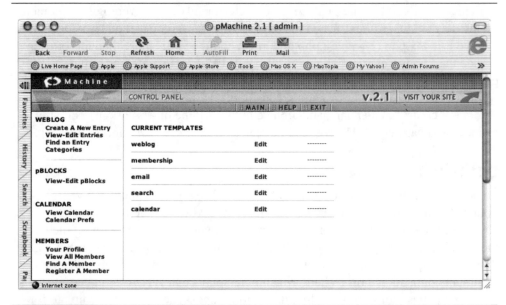

FIGURE 7-11   Here's the list that appears when you click the Edit Templates command.

to each set of internal templates as well as the associated pMachine tags that are used to add these blocks to one of your HTML document templates:

- **Weblog Multi-Entry Templates**   These are used to format the appearance of multiple weblog entries that will then be placed on your pages using the following tag:

```php
<?php weblog_entries($id, "weblog"); ?>
```

  For instance, the index page of your blog uses this tag to show multiple entries, so those entries are formatted using these templates.

- **Weblog Single-Entry Templates**   These templates are used to format weblog entries that appear on a page by themselves when added to a document template using the following tag:

```php
<?php weblog_entry_ind($id); ?>
```

  You can also format some alternative single-page entry templates that can be used for "printable version" pages and so forth. For instance, these module templates govern the look of entries that appear on More (more.php) and Comments (comments.php) pages.

- **Weblog Headlines Template**   Used to format the appearance of the headlines of multiple entries that can be added to your template pages using the following tag:

```php
<?php weblog_headlines("all","3"); ?>
```

Here, "all" is for determining the specific weblog from which to take the headlines, and "3" is a number you can set to determine how many headlines appear. (More on this in the section "Extras: Static Pages, Blurbs, and Headlines.")

- **Comment Display Templates**   These templates are used to format the display of comments added by your readers. Comments are displayed whenever you add the following PHP tag to a single-entry page:

```php
<?php weblog_comments($id); ?>
```

For instance, this tag is in the comments.php HTML template by default, which is the template used when a reader clicks the Comments link for an entry from the main index page of your site. If the reader clicks a More link for an entry, the more.php template is used, which doesn't include the comment display tag, so the comments aren't displayed.

- **Comment Form Templates**   These templates are used to change the appearance of the form(s) used to accept user comments.

- **Archive Multi-Entry Templates**   These are the templates, such as the default template archives.php, used to display multiple-entry listings on archive pages using the following tag:

```php
<?php archive_entries($id,"weblog"); ?>
```

- **Archive Misc. Templates**   These templates let you format various PHP tags that relate to archives, such as the links that appear in monthly archive pages and the page headings for archive pages.

- **Archive Summary Templates**   These templates let you format the special archives summary output that appears, by default, in the template document archive_summary.php. By default, this is a simple listing of entry titles organized by month.

■ **Nav Link Templates**   Here you can change the look of the links that are inserted into several of the HTML templates so that users can return to the weblog's main index page or main archives page.

■ **Collective Entry Form Templates**   In this area, you can format the form that appears if you opt to allow non-administrative users to submit their own entries to your blog. If you do so, you have to create a special entry page for the users to access, using the following tag:

```
<?php collective_entry_form($id,"weblog"); ?>
```

This tag causes the form that's formatted here to appear on the page. (More on this in the section "Create a Collective Weblog.")

That's the list of the different templates you can alter—and that's just the Weblog section! So, is this complicated? It may seem that way at first, but you'll soon find that these templates are here as a convenience, to make it possible to quickly alter the look of your site in many different ways. Over time, you'll get used to how they work and get a better sense of how to alter them in order to customize your site. (Eventually, you may actually dig into all the templates—including those that govern the member pages, search pages, and more!)

Let's check out one quick example. Click the Weblog Multi-Entry templates link. In the first entry box, you can edit the way that each individual weblog entry will look when it's displayed in a multi-entry scenario—such as on the index page of your site.

NOTE   *In pMachine 2.2 and higher, what I'm talking about here is the second entry box, because the first one is now the Master Date Heading field, which is used to display a date heading over individual entries that occur on the same date—it's a little "bloggier" that way. You can delete the markup in that field if you don't want to use the master date approach.*

In the Entries field, you can change things slightly if you'd like to use different formatting. For instance, here's the default template:

```
<div class="weblog">
<h3>%%title%%</h3>
```

```
<p>
%%body%%

%%more_link%%
</p>

<div class="author">Posted by: %%if_email_or_url_as_name%% on
%%date%% | <a href="%%profile_link%%">Profile</a></div>

<br />

%%comments_link%%   |  <a
href="%%comment_permalink%%">link</a>
</div>
```

Now, consider a simple possibility—you want to make the headline of your entries clickable; when the headline is clicked, the user can access the permalinked page (a link to the permanent location of the entry) and view the entire story on its own page. To do that, let's remove the permalink entry at the bottom of the entry and instead surround the headline with the permalink. We'll also move the comment portion up to the author line and remove the link to the author's profile.

NOTE   *The <div> elements are used for applying predefined style sheet classes to the markup inside them. See Chapter 8 for more on the <div> element and style sheets.*

Here's what the new code would look like:

```
<div class="weblog">
<h3><a href="%%comment_permalink%%">%%title%%</a></h3>

<p>
%%body%%

%%more_link%%
</p>

<div class="author">Posted by: %%if_email_or_url_as_name%% on
%%date%% | %%comments_link%%</div>

</div>
```

With the changes made, scroll to the bottom of the page and click the Update button. Now, load your weblog's index page to see what the changes look like. Figure 7-12 shows how the page should look in a web browser.

> **TIP** *While you're editing these templates, if you ever decide that you've made a mistake and you'd like to return to the original template, all you have to do is click the Original link at the top of every Template entry box. A window will pop up to show you the original code, which you can copy and paste into the entry box. Likewise, you can click the Variables link to see a pop-up window that shows the relevant variables you can use in this entry.*

Each entry looks pretty good, but I don't like the comments link doubling over onto the second line. This is probably something that could be handled by changing the template for %%comments_link%%, which you can also do on the

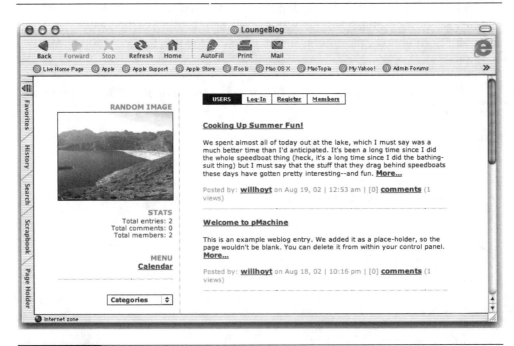

FIGURE 7-12   Here's how the altered entry looks on a multi-entry page (the index page). Headlines are now hyperlinks.

Multi-Entry Templates screen (in fact, it's the Comments Link field right below the Entries field we just edited.) Therefore, change

```
[%%comments_total%%] <a href="%%comments_url%%">comments</a>
 (%%comment_hits%% views)
```

to something simpler, like this:

```
[%%comments_total%%] <a href="%%comments_url%%">comments</a>
```

Now, without the (x views) section, it should fit on the line a little better, as shown here:

Edit the HTML Templates

Although we won't go too deep into this topic, I think you already have a good idea that you can dig into the HTML template files—index.php or weblog.php, along with comments.php, more.php, and so on—to change the look of your site and personalize it. If you want to add a banner image, for instance, you can go into your index template (index.php or weblog.php) via the File Browser and add the image. It would probably make sense right near the top but before the <div> tag that identifies the "menu" portion of the page, as in this example:

```
<body>
<img src="http://www.ourgreatsite.com/images/banner1.gif"
alt="OurSite Banner Image" />
<div id="menu">

<div class="menuitems">
```

You might also want to add your own links. You can do that in one of two ways: You could dig into the HTML code that defines the "menu" portion of the page and add a section that would display links to other blogs. For instance, right after the Mailing List section

```
<div class="menuitems">
<h4>MAILING LIST</h4>
<!-- Mailing list submission form -->
<?php mailinglist_form(); ?>
</div>
```

you could add a section that shows your favorite links:

```
<div class="menuitems">
<h4>MY LINKS</h4>
<!-- Links to my favorite sites -->
<a href="http://www.macblog.com">MacBlog</a><br />
<a href="http://www.metafilter.com">MetaFilter</a><br />
<a href="http://www.salon.com">Salon.com</a><br />
<a href="http://www.wilwheaton.net">WilWheaton.net</a><br />
<a href="http://www.metafilter.com">MetaFilter</a><br />
</div>
```

With that added, you can save the page by clicking the Save File command. The next time you view your index page, you'll see the links appear in the menu bar on the site.

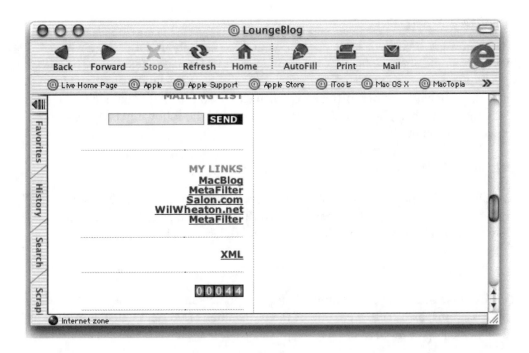

What's the other way? Create a pBlock that displays your links. Then you can even post them on multiple pages (with a pBlock tag). If you change the links by editing the pBlock, all instances of that pBlock will appear updated on the site.

NOTE   *The File Browser feature in pMachine doesn't work well with all server platforms. If you have trouble with yours, you'll probably need to edit the HTML in your template documents locally on your computer and then upload them to your server using FTP. Replace the existing templates with your edited versions using the exact same filenames (index.php, comments.php, more.php, and so on) so that the server can properly use them as templates when building your blog's pages.*

Extras: Static Pages, Blurbs, and Headlines

While you're editing, you'll likely consult the pMachine manual (which you can access by clicking Help in the control panel) on a regular basis. Still, there's a special tip or two worth looking at quickly before we finish this section.

Create a Static Page

Say you want to create a static page on your site—an "about.html" page where you tell people about yourself, or a resume or portfolio page. Yet, you'd still like to include some pMachine tags on your page—perhaps to show recently added stories or to make use of a pBlock. You can easily do this. All you need to do is save the file with a .php filename extension and add the following as the *first* line in your document:

```
<?php include("pm_inc.php"); ?>
```

Now, add the rest of your HTML markup, and feel free to include any of pMachine's tags that might be relevant. You'll link to the page like you would any normal HTML document, using the anchor element. Here's an example:

```
<a href="resume.php">See my resume</a>
```

Because of the include command and the .php extension, the file will be processed just as if there were one of the pMachine HTML template pages such as comments.php or more.php.

Use Blurbs

Whenever you create or edit a page, you're given the option of entering text in the Blurb entry box, but this box doesn't get used by default. A blurb is most useful on a secondary page, such as a static page that serves as a jumping-off point for your blog, rather than on your index page. For instance, say you have a more traditional home page at http://www.yourowndomain.com/index.php and a blog at http://www.yourowndomain.com/weblog.php. On the index page, you'd like to show the headlines and blurbs from your stories, as opposed to the headlines and the first 30 (or so) words from your stories. To do that, you'd edit the Headlines template. Here's how:

1. In the control panel, click Edit Templates.

2. Click the Edit link in the Weblog row.

3. Click the Weblog Headlines template.

4. In the template entry box, change

```
%% body%%
```

to

```
%%blurb%%
```

5. Click the Update button.

With that done, move on to the headline discussion in the next section.

Use Headlines

Regardless of whether you've elected to use blurbs with your headlines, you can add those headlines to your pages—either in the existing pMachine templates (if you feel the need) or to other pages in your site. For instance, in the example where your main index page is index.php (but your weblog's index is weblog.php), you could add headlines from your weblog in the following way. First, make sure the line

```
<?php include("pm_inc.php"); ?>
```

appears at the top of the page. Then, wherever you'd like the headlines to appear, add the following tag:

```
<?php weblog_headlines("all","5"); ?>
```

The word "all" means that headlines from all your weblogs will be included. If you want only headlines from a specific weblog, enter its name between the quotation marks. (If you don't have more than one weblog, there's no need to worry about this entry. The ability to work with multiple weblogs requires pMachine Pro.) The number "5" represents the number of headline entries you want to have displayed.

If you happen not to have changed the Headline template (and the headlines are still set to show the body of each entry, not the Blurb field text), then you can change the headline tag so that only the first x number of words will be displayed. You do that simply by adding an additional number to the tag:

```
<?php weblog_headlines("all","5","30"); ?>
```

Finally, you can choose to have only the headlines from a certain category appear, using yet another attribute in the tag:

```
<?php weblog_headlines("all","5","30","news"); ?>
```

Just add the name of the category, and only the headlines associated with that category will appear. This is a great way to make your site seem styled a little more like a magazine, without being forced to manage your articles in multiple weblogs.

Create a Collective Weblog

Want to let others add full blog entries to your site? If you simply want to add a few different authors, you can do that by changing their status, as discussed in the section "User Registration." But, if you'd like *all* your readers to be able to submit weblog entries, you can do that, too. It just takes a few steps.

The first step is to access the General Preferences screen and, in the Member Preferences section, make your choices about whether member registration will be required for adding to weblogs. Click Yes in the Member Registration: Weblogs preference if you'd like to require that users register on the site before they're able to post an entry. If you don't require that they be registered, you can require that they include an e-mail address when posting (choose Yes for the option Require Email for Non-Registered Posting). Scroll to the bottom of the General Preferences screen and click Update Preferences.

Next, you'll need to choose Weblog Management and open the preferences for the weblog to which you'd like to add the collective weblog capabilities. (If you only have one weblog, click the Preferences link for that weblog.) On the Preferences page, choose the Yes entry in the Is This a Collective Weblog menu. Then you must decide, in the next preference item, whether the collective entries should be closed by default. (That means they'll require your approval before they appear on the site, because you'll have to specifically edit and mark them as open.) Scroll to the bottom of the page and click Update Preferences.

Now you're set up for a collective weblog, but you're not quite home yet. First, you need to create the entry page that will be used to enable your users to send you an entry. You'll need to do this in a text editor and then, ideally, upload it to the same directory where your index.php and other HTML template files are stored.

At the very least, it should include the following elements:

```
<?php include("pm_inc.php"); ?>
<head>
<title>Send Us an Entry</title>
</head>
<body>
<?php collective_entry_form($id,"weblog"); ?>

</body>
</html>
```

Save that file as a plain text file called entry.php and use your FTP program to upload it to your site. (Eventually you might want to add a little more HTML and text to make the page look a bit prettier and, perhaps, to explain the rules and terms of submitting a story to your site. For now, though, this barebones page will work.)

Finally, you'll create a link—probably somewhere on your blog's index page—to that entry form page. Somewhere, perhaps in the menu area of the index.php or weblog.php page, add something like this:

```
<a href="entry.php">Add an Entry</a>
```

Save that template, upload it to your site (if necessary), and you're done. When the users visit your index page (or wherever you added the link) and click the Add an Entry link, they'll see an entry page like the one shown in Figure 7-13. This page will allow them to send an entry to your blog. (I've added some formatting and linked to the main pMachine style sheet using the <link /> element, which is discussed in Chapter 8.) If you've chosen to make entries closed by default, you'll be able to access the new entry by choosing View-Edit Entries in the control panel. You'll then be able to decide whether the entry is good enough, edit it if necessary, and then choose to make it open and, thus, publish it on your site.

More...

In this chapter you learned quite a bit about pMachine, a wonderful blogging solution aimed at the weblog author who wants to create an online community. pMachine offers some fairly unique tools, including support for collective weblogs, mailing list management, and site-wide user memberships, all in a package that's pretty easy to install and set up. This was a long chapter because there's a lot you can do with pMachine, such as add entries, manage users, edit templates, and create a collective weblog.

FIGURE 7-13   Here's the collective entry page.

pMachine is also a little different from the other tools discussed in this book because it's written in PHP and works with a MySQL database back end. This makes it a little faster, particularly as your site grows to many entries. This may also make it a little more flexible than Perl-based solutions, which must be specifically republished after changes and offer a little less dynamic flexibility. pMachine offers a ton of tags—which can take some getting used to—but they end up making pMachine very flexible in its presentation, if a bit complex. In this chapter, you saw how the internal templates work together with the pMachine tags and the external HTML template documents to build dynamic sites.

In the next section of the book we'll move on from the individual tools and focus instead on building and extending your blog. In Chapter 8, you'll get tips on writing, focusing, and designing your blog. In Chapter 9, you'll see some add-on solutions that can make your blog an even more interesting, hands-on community for your visitors.

	T	W	T	F	S		S	M	T	W	T	F	S		S	M	T	W	T	F	S		S	M	T	W	T	F	S
		1	2	3	4				1	2	3	4					1	2	3	4					1	2	3	4
	7	8	9	10	11		5	6	7	8	9	10	11		5	6	7	8	9	10	11		5	6	7	8	9	10	11
3	14	15	16	17	18		12	13	14	15	16	17	18		12	13	14	15	16	17	18		12	13	14	15	16	17	18
0	21	22	23	24	25		19	20	21	22	23	24	25		19	20	21	22	23	24	25		19	20	21	22	23	24	25
7	28	29	30	31			26	27	28	29	30	31			26	27	28	29	30	31			26	27	28	29	30	31

Part III

Extending Your Weblog

Chapter 8 Writing, Designing, and Tweaking Your Blog

Chapter 9 Add-Ons for Your Weblog

M	T	W	T	F	S		S	M	T	W	T	F	S		S	M	T	W	T	F	S		S	M	T	W	T	F	S
		1	2	3	4				1	2	3	4					1	2	3	4					1	2	3	4	
6	7	8	9	10	11		5	6	7	8	9	10	11		5	6	7	8	9	10	11		5	6	7	8	9	10	11
3	14	15	16	17	18		12	13	14	15	16	17	18		12	13	14	15	16	17	18		12	13	14	15	16	17	18
0	21	22	23	24	25		19	20	21	22	23	24	25		19	20	21	22	23	24	25		19	20	21	22	23	24	25
7	28	29	30	31			26	27	28	29	30	31			26	27	28	29	30	31			26	27	28	29	30	31	

Chapter 8

Writing, Designing, and Tweaking Your Blog

In this chapter:

- ■ What are you gonna say?
- ■ Grammar and writing tips
- ■ Weblog netiquette and ethics
- ■ CSS, HTML, and changing the look of your site
- ■ Tips for designing a blog that works

So you've settled on a blogging approach—you've chosen a host, a service, and/or a server-side blogging solution. Perhaps you've added a few entries, experimented with adding images (if your software enables you to), and, hopefully, you've even had a reader or two. In this chapter, let's move from the nitty-gritty of choosing and installing your software and focus on what you're going to say, how you're going to say it, and how it's going to look.

We'll start by discussing the nature of the content of blogging a little bit and discuss some issues, such as how you want to approach your blog, how to find the time and discipline to keep it up, and how to be well received by the reading public. Then, we'll move on to design issues, including a look at how you can tweak the look of your site, including some tips on keeping a clean and accessible design.

What Are You Gonna Say?

In most cases, you need to write some fairly interesting stuff if you're going to have an audience for your blog. I say "in most cases" because people who aren't interesting in their blogs sometimes get readers, particularly if they (1) are famous, (2) post inflammatory opinions, or (3) link to silly things and make juvenile comments about them. Even then, only one in a thousand of that sort of blogger is really getting much attention. (And as your mother probably scolded you, that's *negative* attention.)

For the rest of the blogging world, it helps to keep a number of tricks in mind for structuring the content of your blog. No, it's not a term paper or a novel, but there are a few things to focus on if you're going to keep people reading. Here's my quick list:

- Have something to say

- Say it quickly

- Say it with reasonably accurate grammar and spelling

- Let others play

In this list, there are a few things I'm *not* saying. For instance, I'm not saying that blogs need to be nice, or inviting to all, or that they all need to feature someone's opinion. A weblog can be all about business, politics, your personal life, or some combination thereof. But the challenge—and this is what many of the really good bloggers do—is to write something that holds your reader's attention. If, at the same time, your writing conforms to a statistically significant percentage of the rules we've all pretty much agreed on to keep us communicating effectively—namely, grammar and spelling—then your message will be that much more effective. Not that you need a college degree in English (and, trust me, a degree in it doesn't always help) or whatever language you're blogging in. However, a little knowledge of grammar can go a long way.

Have Something to Say

Sometimes when I dig in and read through a lot of blogs, I come up for air after a long surfing session and wonder, *Where did the time go?* That's usually when I've been reading interesting blogs or threads of conversation—whether personal, political, or what have you. The other feeling I occasionally get is, *I've lost valuable hours from my life!* This, as you'll notice, is not quite as positive a reaction, and it usually comes after some heavy wading through boring blogs that don't have much to say or don't say it effectively.

What does it mean to "have something to say"? To my thinking, it means that you have some core element or idea or item to communicate to your readers in *each* entry that you add to your blog. That something doesn't have to be earth shattering, socially significant, newsworthy or even entertaining, although those things help. In fact, an entry doesn't even necessarily have to have a point or purpose. It simply needs to communicate *something*. And how does one communicate more effectively? Through brevity, wit, and grammar, which we'll discuss in a few paragraphs.

Before we get there, though, let's backtrack and consider the question: What is it that *you* have to say? Understand that it's perfectly reasonable to have a blog that is completely about yourself—an online diary of sorts—or a blog that's completely about something else, ranging from a professional topic to a personal one. Just pick something, even if it's a different *something* with every post.

8

NOTE   *Rick, our intrepid blog-eating technical editor, points out that it's possible to find your blogging (or writing) voice over time. The best advice to finding that voice is to challenge yourself to write often—daily or more—without exhausting yourself. Write comfortable amounts every day. At the same time, read voraciously. Turn off that last half hour of reality TV and curl up with a good book—fiction, non-fiction, classic, or contemporary—particularly one written somewhere near the style you want to emulate or grow from.*

I've got two favorite kinds of blogs. The first one is a blog that tells me something about the world as the author sees it. This isn't straight opinion ("You know what makes me mad…") but rather what journalists call *narrative non-fiction*—a true story that has a plot and a purpose. The story is told in order to make a point, even if it's a small one. I've read some very interesting blog entries about motherhood, racism, politics, skateboarding, computing, and locales I've never visited. These entries have all lead to an interesting idea or an "a-ha!" that made reading the blog worthwhile. (And I've read them all in the past week.) The fact that we *can* publish stories in this way is some of the power of blogging—real people telling actual stories, not just network television or national newspapers telling stories that their producers or editors have somehow managed to hear about.

The second kind of post I enjoy reading is what I'll call a *geek-out* post, where someone really shows some lucid, poignant excitement for a particular topic. Of course, it helps if I'm interested in the topic, too, but sometimes you can read a geek-out post and appreciate it on a level that isn't just your personal interest in the topic. It's an opportunity to learn more about somebody else's interest, calling, hobby, or obsession. Even if your blog is primarily a diary, the occasional geek-out topical post ("I try not to talk too much about my obsession with choosing the right motor oil…") can be a real classic, particularly if you're able to toss in some interesting information or advice or trivia that's part of the mix of knowledge that makes you a unique person.

Beyond these types of posts, I've identified a few others for your consideration in the following list. Use this list to think more about the types of entries you might consider for your blog or even to brainstorm when you can't come up with something to say:

- **IMHO.**   Of course, opinion entries can range in their sophistication of presentation—that is to say that even writing "I'm anti-anti-establishment!" is registering some kind of opinion, even if that's as far as you go. When done well, an opinion entry can provoke thought and may prove worthy of comment and lengthy discussion by your readers.

NOTE   *IMHO stands for In My Humble Opinion, a common abbreviation in Web- and Internet-based discussion shorthand.*

- **Hey, check this out!**   This is a broad category—everything from "weird news," to serious news and opinion, to new products. Of course, what's being described here is an entire school of weblogging—acting as a content editor for the Web by linking to another story and, perhaps, offering an opinion on it. Regardless of what you write, you're saying to the reader, "I've looked at or read this and thought it was interesting. You might, too."

■ **Whatcha think?**   These entries are usually designed to bring something to your readers' attention for the express purpose of getting them to comment on it. If your blog supports reader comments, you'll probably find yourself offering up a "whatcha think" post every few days or weeks just to get the ball rolling. The topic can be anything—a pop culture happening, a new advertising campaign, a politician's latest speech, a world event, a sports match, or similar. In some ways, all "whatcha think" posts boil down to something like a poll entry or a question designed to "light up the phones" on a radio talk show. As with real-life conversation, asking people about themselves is a great way to get people to talk and, more to the point, to think you're a very interesting person.

■ **Here's a tip.**   I'm also a sucker for these entries—I like to learn things, and I love to learn things quickly. A lot of tips in regular blogs are about blogs, the Internet, or software, but they can be about anything. This is particularly handy for hobbyist blogs, but it's a great thing to insert into a blog entry *whenever* you learn something new. Also, don't forget the old standby—the review. Review movies, books, CDs, TV shows—anything you've experienced that you feel is worthy of an opinion that can help your readers determine whether they should see it, read it, listen to it, buy it, or whatever.

NOTE   *"Here's a tip" entries are a great excuse to geek out. If you have a hobby or pastime or obsession, let people know about it in your blog. Eventually, if they read you regularly, your readers will remember your tips and come back to your site to learn more about a particular topic (or write about it). It's a lot like finding out that someone in your office is a gourmet cook, former Olympian, wine connoisseur, or amateur mechanic. You know where to go to get advice.*

■ **What I did last night (or yesterday).**   Some people make decent money writing "nightlife" columns for newspapers and magazines; others make money by writing columns about their day, their life, their kids, their dreams, or their problems. There's no reason you can't do that, too (although I certainly won't promise you anything on the money front), particularly if you can write entries about your life that others can relate to and find amusing or poignant. If only your close friends read your blog, you don't need to worry about broader appeal. If you're going for a wider audience, though, you'll need to tie up the loose ends and make sure it's entertaining and, if possible, informative. ("Hey, I was reading about this great restaurant in Chicago on this guy's blog and decided to go, and you won't believe who I ran into....")

- ■ **Work (life, dating, nightlife, food) sucks (or rocks!).** These are common posts in diary-style blogs, and they certainly have their appeal to some readers—particularly if (1) you have a new twist on why whatever you're doing is either great or lousy, (2) your entry is funny, (3) it offers an interesting insight that others can relate to, or (4) only your friends read your blog anyway. If I don't know you, I'll feel this sort of entry is less interesting, unless you somehow add some universal appeal, or offer a comment on the human condition at the same time. (After all, people watch movies, read books, sit through TV shows, and giggle over comic strips about bad jobs and bad relationships, so it certainly has potential appeal in a blog.)

- ■ **Just blogging.** These entries—where someone posts to let you know that they haven't posted for a while and feel guilty about it—are at the bottom of the "have something to say" food chain. However, they can still serve a very minor purpose—trying to keep in touch with your readers and letting them know that you are still aware you have a blog. Beyond that, they're not much to look at or read.

No, that's not every type of entry, but hopefully these give you some ideas if you get stuck for something to blog about. Of course, the most important thing to do with your blog is to let your personality shine through, unless your personality really sucks. And, even then, I think it's better to be natural than to try to fake being interesting. Being interesting is a little like being tall—it takes publicists, producers, camera angles, and special effects to really fake it convincingly. So be yourself and you'll get your readers.

Say It Well

One way to keep from harpooning your chances of getting and retaining readers is to do your best to make it possible for them to read your entries without going cross-eyed. That's why we have grammar and spelling. Although it's certainly true that people are very forgiving of grammatical mistakes on the Internet, following some of the basic rules can help you stay out of your readers' way, making it easy for them to read without forcing them to block out mistakes or try to reason out what you're attempting to say.

Here, then, are a few ideas and tips (OK, they're mostly just my pet peeves) to help you improve your online writing:

- **Use a spell-checker.**   If you don't have a spell-checking blogging tool (remember, many blogging solutions let you use a Blogger-compatible editor to post your entries), you might consider writing your entries in a word processor that has spell-check capabilities and then copying and pasting the entry into your web browser (or other tool) for posting. Remember, though, that you'll want to post only a plain-text file. Therefore, make sure your word processor isn't set to create "curly" quotes, em dashes, and other special characters. They'll look wrong in your blog.

- **Consider your capitalization.**   In any situation on the Internet, using all capital letters looks like SHOUTING so it's best to avoid it. While most of your readers don't care if you follow strict rules on capitalization, you should at least strive to be consistent. The easy capitals to remember are those that start a sentence, a proper name, a day of the week, a month's name, and titles that precede a person's name ("Governor Rich Guy" vs. "Rich Guy, our state's governor").

- **Read back through your text.**   When you're done with your post, read back through it for any mistakes or typos. Many professional writers I know read their work out loud, believing that it helps them find errors that their eyes skips over—and it does.

TIP *Got some time? It's always best to let your entry sit for a while before posting it, if you feel you have the time. Get away from it for a while and do something else. Then return to it with "fresh eyes." It'll be easier to see mistakes or problems. It can also help to print an entry to read for errors, as it's sometimes easier to see problems on the printed page than it is on the screen.)*

- **Write in active voice.**   A lot of blogging is personal, so active voice is easier to write in. But as you're writing, check your voice. Are things *doing* things, or are things *being done to* things? Here's an example of active voice:

  Bob and I really hated the movie last night.

And here's an example of passive voice:

The movie last night seemed pretty boring to Bob and me.

■ **Know *which* and *that*.**   These two words are often confused, but they're easy to use correctly. *Which* introduces independent clauses; *that* introduces dependent clauses. In other words, you use a comma and the word *which* if the information isn't mandatory to make the meaning of the sentence clear. For instance, saying "Give me the pencil that has a red eraser" means a particular pencil, and the information is used to differentiate it from others. By contrast, "Give me the pencil, which has a red eraser," suggests that the identity of the pencil is not in question— the red eraser is simply additional information.

■ **Know the difference between *they're, there,* and *their*.**   These are often typos, not really grammatical mistakes, but it's good to recall what they mean when you're writing. *They're* is a contraction for "they are," as in "*They're* coming home soon." *There* is a location, as in "They've been over *there* in Mexico for a long time." *Their* is a possessive pronoun, indicating that something belongs to "them," as in "Don't forget the Bothwells are coming back from Mexico and they'll need *their* car back soon."

■ **Know when to use *it's* and *its*.**   This rule is simple, although it might seem backward: *Its* is the possessive form, indicating something belongs to "it," whereas *it's* is a contraction of "it is."

■ **Know where to place quotes and commas.**   In almost all cases, punctuation goes inside quotation marks, even if you're just putting quotes around "special words." Only use single quotes in headlines (Steinbrenner to NY: 'Drop Dead!') and inside other quotation marks, as in "Joe told me 'No way!' and I said 'Way!'," Judy said, laughing.

■ **Strive for subject/verb agreement.**   This one is easy, in theory. The idea is simply to decide if your subject is singular or plural and then make sure the verb you chose agrees with it. People usually get this right, but it sometimes gets twisted down the windy road of a long sentence, as in "The vice president, along with all his sales people, is doing a spectacular job." (Ignore *sales people* because it's part of a clause; it's the vice president we're talking about.)

8

> **TIP**   *When you've got an "or" in the sentence, the verb should agree with the subject closest to it, as in "Either mousetraps or a cat is a good solution to our mouse problem." If you use "and," then the subject is always plural, as in "A mousetrap and a cat are good solutions to our mouse problem."*

Many other rules of grammar abound, which is why they offer entire classes—even college degrees—on the subject. You'll find that using a spell-checker and reading entries aloud, which helps you determine whether they "sound" good, will result in grammatically superior writing that will be a joy to read.

Brevity Is Your Friend

I'll keep this short. (Bu-da-bum. Thanks very much. I'll be here all night. Don't forget to tip your server.) Perhaps the single coolest thing about blogs, from my point of view, is that they encourage short, pithy entries.

In fact, I've started a blog for that purpose alone. I've run a magazine-style site for years about upgrading Macintosh computers, covering the Mac news world, new products, and so forth. I've also had opinion pieces and reviews on that site for years, and I've always felt compelled to make those pieces longer (see Figure 8-1), perhaps because of the format, the expectation that the reader needs to get "value" out of the piece, and some of those little nagging fears ("I'm not good enough. People won't think I'm smart.") that keep professional writers up at night.

I've noticed on that site, however, that I wasn't as comfortable with quick, personal entries about my experience with Macs, a new technique, or my opinion on a simple topic or news item—so, I started MacBlog.com (see Figure 8-2). There, the software and the overall "feel" of the site encourages shorter articles, quick observations, and the occasional discussion piece—all the things we've been talking about throughout this text.

Maybe this is all just me, but the format and software do encourage these shorter pieces—and I'll encourage them, too. A short piece is easier to read online—you're not likely to shift in your chair four times before you finally opt to read it. Longer pieces—especially those cut into four or five pages—are how the big commercial sites sell ads for their websites. On blogs, shorter is usually better.

That's not to say a longer piece can't sneak in occasionally, although you might opt, in that case, to either use the More feature in your blogging software to "jump" to a full-page entry or create a static article and link to it via the blog entry. (This is the built-in approach when using Radio Userland, for instance, and it's

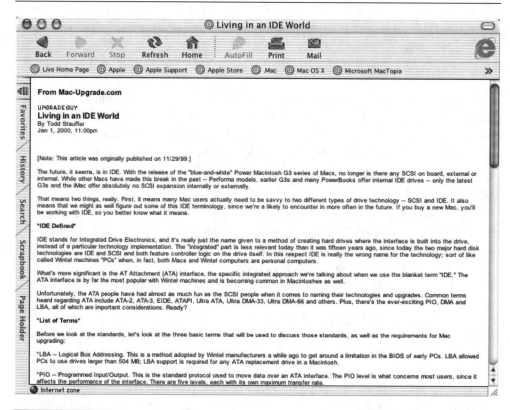

FIGURE 8-1   Sometimes the format of the website encourages longer articles.

possible with most any blog in which you can ftp to the host server.) This gives users the opportunity to determine whether they want to see the entry. It also gives you an opportunity to see how popular the entry is and how many people are clicking through to view the whole thing.

Now, some bloggers like long entries, and some like them all to appear on the index page. It's your blog. But as a reader, I appreciate short entries and the ability to scan the last 10 or 15 posts quickly without scrolling through multiparagraph entry after multiparagraph entry. If you're that prolific, at least consider looking into that More feature.

FIGURE 8-2 MacBlog.com is where I can write quicker tidbits and shorter articles.

Let Others Play

Finally, a happy blog is an active blog. If your blogging software offers the ability for users to comment on stories, then try to drum up those comments, whether it's by adding "Please comment" at the end of your entry (or some slightly more clever request) or by posting "Whatcha think?" entries every so often. Also, as host or hostess, remember not to berate your commenting public if they say something that you don't agree with, unless that's the true tenor of the blog. (For instance, I would expect Howard Stern's blog to be something like that, but yours might take a more tempered approach.)

Another human nature recommendation: Let your readers come up with answers, and then let them be right. Ironically, I've seen some very popular "community" blogs that don't offer a comment feature (both www.andrewsullivan.com and www.thismodernworld.com come to mind, which clearly means I'm using both sides of my brain to conjure them). Instead, these blogs quote a reader's e-mail in a message and then respond to it, often calling attention to and praising the individual by lavishing him or her with feedback. But sometimes they're not so nice. Whatever the case, it's surprising how community-focused these sites *feel*. Take a tip and call out your readers, quote their responses, and agree or disagree within actual blog entries, not just via the comment feature, when you feel the topic warrants it. I think you'll find that people appreciate the community feel and might just comment, e-mail, and visit more often to see if their name lights up an entry or two.

Weblog Netiquette

Before we get out of this section on content, I want to focus in on two related issues—*netiquette* (which simply means *net etiquette* or online "manners") and ethics. If you're familiar with the idea of e-mail netiquette, you're already aware of some of the basics that spill over into web-based communications. Others, particularly those that fall into the realm of "ethics" are items that have begun to emerge as weblogs have become more popular.

As the host of a weblog, your responsibilities are slightly different than as a guest on someone else's weblog. When you're a reader, most netiquette guides recommend that you *lurk*—that is, read the site without posting—for at least a little while, until you get a sense of the dynamics of the community. After a time spent just reading, you'll probably get a sense of how things work and can probably jump in quickly, if you remember some basics:

- Don't type in all caps.

- Always add to the conversation (and add something beyond "Me, too!").

- Stay on topic.

A related admonition is to read the FAQ (Frequently Asked Questions) that some discussion-focused blogs post. For a personal weblog, the FAQ may be a less formal "About this site" link or a help link of some sort. If you still have questions, it's probably best to address them directly to the site's author in e-mail, not in a public comment thread that is about another topic.

When you comment on another author's entries or add to the discussion in a discussion forum, you should keep in mind the need to be considerate and to argue your points (if you're arguing) on their merits, and not personally. If you get into an exchange of insults and epithets with another person online, you're engaging in what's called a *flame war*, where each participant is "flaming" the other with *ad hominem* attacks and uncalled-for name-calling.

You should strive to use your real name and e-mail address—or at least a link to your weblog—when commenting on other people's sites. Although it might not be true in every circumstance, at least consider this possible mantra: "If you need to say it anonymously, maybe it isn't worth saying."

As a weblog *author*, you have different responsibilities. Perhaps the most important one is to maintain the privacy of your participants' information. Blogging software will sometimes reveal to you personal information about a user. For example, users may be asked to register or to log in with a username and password, or their IP addresses may be logged. This information should be considered private. Even if you take the bare minimum of information (such as name and e-mail address), you should post a privacy statement of some kind that tells your users whether you will be selling their information or redistributing it in some way. (If you ask readers to subscribe, you should also tell them what to expect in terms of e-mail from you and how they can stop that e-mail from coming.) Note that laws govern privacy and personal information online, so you should do what you can to be aware of them and follow them.

Blogging Ethics

Ethically, your first responsibility as a blog publisher is to follow the preceding netiquette outline, particularly in regard to privacy. Also, you should consider the ethics of the way you post and edit comments. Blogging software often allows you to dig into an entry that you've posted and change it. Likewise, you can often delete comments by others and, in some cases, edit those comments so that they say something different.

Bloggers tend to agree that any changes beyond fixing the grammar and spelling of published posts (that is, any change that alters the meaning of your posts) should be marked as such in the post. (Add a line at the bottom of the entry that reads "5/6/03, 3:05 pm: I corrected a mistake in this entry where I'd inadvertently said that Dr. Rouve was dead.") You can also correct yourself in a comment added to your own story, which can be handy because it will automatically show the date and time of the correction. Likewise, if you edit a reader's comment, you should add a note to that comment saying what you edited and why.

Why is this? Because people may see your story at different times during the day, and it isn't fair to them to "change the record," particularly because they may be blogging on the same topic, refuting your argument in a comment, and so on. For you to change the entry without making note of it might simply make the other person look bad or waste their time.

As the blog author or publisher, you have plenty of power over the people who participate in your community. Because of that, you should use your power wisely and fairly—that's what being ethical is all about.

Change the Look of Your Site

As you've already seen in the chapters that specifically covered the blogging tools, all blogging solutions store the actual text of entries in databases, and HTML templates are used for the design of sites. In order for a visitor to see a particular page in your blog, it must be "published." In some cases all pages are published ahead of time; in other cases, they're published "on the fly" as they're requested. The fact that all the blogging tools use HTML templates means that pretty much any weblog site can be altered by changing those templates. In most of the previous tool-specific chapters, you saw how to change small things, such as the links that appear on the pages. In this section, we'll talk about some broader changes.

To govern appearance, most blogging software programs use CSS-based *style sheets*, which are special files used in addition to the HTML templates to determine how the blog will look. In particular, style sheet definitions are used to set the fonts, sizes, colors, backgrounds, and shadings of the various parts of the page. What's cool about using a style sheet is that you can make all these design choices in a centralized file. That means the definitions are easy to change, as you'll see in this section.

Use a Third-Party Template

Let's start the discussion with a look at the HTML templates. If you would like your weblog to look significantly different, the way to do that is to change the HTML in the underlying templates that dictate your site's design. In particular, you'll have at least one index template (for the main page of your site and perhaps for your archive index pages) and one template that governs the look of a full-page entry. If you know a little something about HTML, you can dig into those template pages—along with any others you're interested in—and go to work making changes.

As you're editing, use the blogging software's manual to make sure you're using the correct tags so that your site will still display the blog's index listing (the multiple-entries listing) as well as the full-page entry page. On a full-page entry, for instance, you'll have variables or tags that cover whether the page is properly displaying the headline, the body, and the "More" text of the entry, as well as any comments and, perhaps, even the form elements that appear on the page so that readers can enter a name, e-mail address, URL, and their own comment to add to the discussion (see Figure 8-3).

So what do you do if you don't know HTML terribly well? Your best bet might be to download a template and alter it to make it work for your blogging software. One place to start is BlogPlates.net, the home page for the BlogPlates *webring*,

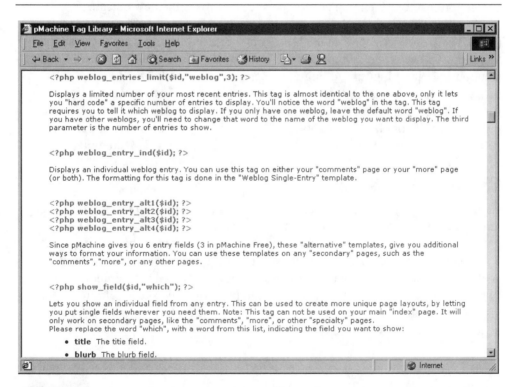

FIGURE 8-3   Here's a look at some of pMachine's tags that can be used when editing the HTML templates that create the underlying design of your site.

which is a collection of sites that offer templates for blogging. On the BlogPlates site you'll find tutorials that provide in-depth explanations of installing and using the templates for different tools (http://blogplates.net/tutorials.html).

The easiest templates to use are those designed for your blogging solution—at the time of this writing, it's common to find templates for Greymatter, Movable Type, and Blogger. pMachine is still relatively new, although a few compatible templates (or at least instructions for using templates originally designed for Movable Type or Greymatter) have popped up. In most cases, you'll need to copy images and a style sheet file (with a .css extension) to your main blog folder. Then you'll alter the main HTML templates with any changes you've made to your existing blog's templates. (Follow any instructions included with the templates carefully.) Once that changeover is made, you should be able to republish your site, if applicable. When you access the site, you'll see the new design.

Another place to get advice for changing up your blog is ScriptyGoddess (http://scriptygoddess.com/), which is simply a great place to learn more about blogging and scripting, including tips for digging into the actual code of blogging solutions, adding plug-ins, adding third-party utilities, and changing the look and behavior of your blogging software. (For instance, you'll see some solutions that use JavaScript, a scripting language recognized by many web browsers.) It's a very interesting and popular site. Although it's skewed toward Movable Type, you'll still find discussions of nearly all blogging tools based on HTML templates.

CSS and Style Sheets

If you're not the type to go in for an all-out change of your blog's HTML templates, maybe you'd like to do something that offers a bit more immediate gratification. This can be done by digging into the style sheet that accompanies a site built using blogging tools such as Movable Type, pMachine, or Blogger. A style sheet is a text file, written to the Cascading Style Sheet standard. The file (which is technically an *external* style sheet, because style sheet definitions can also be embedded in HTML documents) serves as a central repository for all the style definitions for your site.

NOTE *Style sheets have only been fully supported in web browsers in the 5.0 level (Internet Explorer 4 and Netscape 4 had only limited support for style sheets). What this means is that users of older browsers won't see your style decisions—they'll still see your text and formatting (italics, headings, and hyperlinks) but without the fonts, text sizes, and so on.*

If you've worked with Microsoft Word's styles (Normal, Heading 1, Heading 2, and so on), you're familiar with the idea—a style sheet definition is simply a preset, named set of characteristics. For instance, using a style sheet, you could define the <h3> element so that it appears in a particular font, at a particular size, and with a particular font weight, as shown here:

```
H3 {
    font-family: verdana,trebuchet,sans-serif;
    font-size:   14px;
    color:       #333333;
    font-weight: bold;
}
```

What happens is simple: When a reader's web browser downloads an HTML document, it will notice that the document includes a style definition and a link to the style sheet. Therefore, the browser will request and download the style sheet. It will then use the definitions in that style sheet to determine how the individual elements will look—if the <h1> element is defined in the style sheet, it will be rendered according to that definition.

If an element isn't in the style sheet, it will be rendered according to the browser's default settings or any preferences that the reader has set in the browser for that element. In fact, some browsers will allow you, as a user, to add your own style sheet to use as the default, thus specially formatting any page that doesn't have it's own style sheet. For instance, Internet Explorer enables you to create a default style sheet and assign it via IE's preferences settings. So, if you're viewing a page that doesn't have a style sheet, it will use your appearance preferences—fonts, font sizes, and so on.

The Why of Style Sheets

Up until recently, style sheets were considered optional and were ignored by many designers who preferred to use elements that directly marked up the text with visual commands—for instance, both Internet Explorer and Netscape (along with others) support a <font> element that can be used to change font faces, sizes, and so forth.

But the move in HTML (and XHTML) has been away from elements that directly affect the appearance of the text and toward technologies that allow you to separate the appearance and content of a website—a common refrain in web design today. When you do that, you make it possible for the content to appear on devices or in situations that you may not have even anticipated—small screens, phones, PDAs, and assistive browsers—because the content doesn't have visual instructions *embedded* in it.

For instance, the <font> element makes for a fairly typical scenario—instead of using heading elements such as <h1>, many web authors simply surround regular text with a <font> element that makes the text bigger and bold, like a heading. The problem is, if the browser doesn't recognize the <font> element (or isn't able to render it as specified), the text appears as just regular text—the browser doesn't know that the author wanted it to be a heading, because the author didn't use the <h1> (or other heading) element. With style sheets, you can define the <h1> element (in more than one way) to appear with a certain font face, size, weight, and so on. That makes for a flexible page that looks exactly the way you want it in a typical web browser, but the page can still be displayed in an appropriate way in any browser you didn't anticipate and for which you didn't explicitly design the page.

The Style Sheets

You have two ways to add style definitions to a page. The first way involves typing them directly into the HTML document, using the <style> container. (Most of the time, this is done in the <head> section of the document.) For instance, that's how Blogger's pages work—click the Template link in Blogger and you'll see the style sheet definitions at the top of the template's HTML. Here's an example:

```
<head>
<title><$BlogTitle$></title>
<!--Set the following content-values to the description and
```

```
keywords you would like search engines to associate with your blog.
-->
<meta name="description" content="">
<meta name="keywords" content="">

<style>
body   {background:white;margin: 0px;font-family: Verdana, Arial,
sans-serif;color: black;}
.blogtitle    {font-family: Lucida Console, Verdana, Arial, sans-serif;
color: white;font-size:36px;margin:2px;}
.links     {font-family: Verdana, Arial, sans-serif;color: black;
font-size:11px;}
A      {color:#0069c3;}
A:hover     {color:red;}
A.byline {color:black;text-decoration:none}
.date {font-family: Verdana, Arial, sans-serif;color: black;
font-size:14px;font-weight:bold;}
.posts     {font-family: Verdana, Arial, sans-serif;color: black;
font-size:12px;}
.byline     {font-family: Verdana, Arial, sans-serif;color: #000000;
font-size:11px;}
</style>
</head>
```

In this example, a number of different styles and style *classes* have been defined specifically for the web page this document will create. (Don't worry about how the styles actually work; we'll get to that in a moment.) The other way to add style elements—and the way that's encouraged by the XHTML standard— is to link to an external style sheet document. This has the advantage of enabling you to use the same style definitions with different HTML documents without retyping or copying and pasting the style definitions into each page. It also means that a single change to the style sheet can be seen on multiple pages all over your website. This linking method is the approach used by some of the major blogging tools—particularly Movable Type (styles-site.css) and pMachine (pm_style.css). It's done using a special link in *each* HTML document that is to be associated with that style, as in this example:

```
<link rel="stylesheet"
href="http://www.mybigsite.com/blog/styles-site.css"
type="text/css" />
```

This link element appears in the <head> container of the document (usually just after the <title> element) and generally points directly to the style sheet document using an absolute URL. So, if you opt to change to a different style sheet for a particular HTML document, you can do so by altering this link on that HTML document's page. (Similarly, you can add this element to a static page you're adding to your blog's website if you'd like that page to use the same style sheet.)

> **TIP** *Want to use a style sheet in Greymatter? Add one! Create a style sheet (it's just a plain ASCII text document—no special codes or headers required—with the filename extension .css) and add style definitions to it, as described in the next sections. Next, link to the style sheet from your Greymatter template pages using the <link /> element, as shown previously. You may also want to use third-party templates (http://foshdawg.net/gm/templates/gfx01.php) or rewrite them yourself, because the defaults are showing their age and don't conform to the latest standards.*

Style Sheet Definitions

You've seen how style sheets are embedded or linked, but what you need to know is how the actual style definitions work. You'll work with two basic types of style definitions—an actual element and a *class*. When you define an element's style, you're making choices for how that element will look every time you use it. If you create a class definition, you can assign that class to the elements you want to style in that way (for instance, <h1 class="timestamp">), whereas other instances of that element can be assigned a different class (for instance, <h1 class="title">) or no class at all.

In the case of creating a style definition for an element, you simply dig into the style sheet and add the element's name, followed by an opening bracket and then a series of style definitions, separated by semicolons. Here's an example:

```
H1 {font-family: verdana, sans-serif; font-size: 20px;
color: #33333; font-weight: bold;}
```

You can also, for the sake of readability, stack each of the attributes you're changing. The web browser doesn't care because it doesn't interpret the new lines (when you press RETURN or ENTER):

```
H1 {
 font-family: verdana, sans-serif;
 font-size:    14px;
 color:        #333333;
 font-weight: bold;
}
```

To define a class, all you need is a well-placed period. You can define classes for a particular element, as shown here:

```
H1.red {
 font-family: verdana, sans-serif;
 font-size:    14px;
 color:        #ff0000;
 font-weight: bold;
}
```

Now, in your HTML templates you can change the way some of your headings look by using something like this:

```
<h1 class="red">%%title%%</h1>
```

In a pMachine template, this change will cause the title of the entry (or multiple titles on the page, in the case of a template designed for multiple-entry pages, such as a blog's index page) to appear in red when viewed in a web browser. You could later use just a plain <h1> element, and it would be styled according to whatever is defined for <h1>, such as the gray text shown in previous examples. If no style is defined for <h1>, the browser will display it according to the browser's user preferences or the default for <h1>.

Note that you can also create a class that isn't associated with a particular element—that way, you can use this class with any element you desire. All you have to do is omit the element from the definition and simply define a class by starting it with a period, as shown here:

```
.red {
 font-family: verdana, sans-serif;

 color:        #ff0000;
 font-weight: bold;
}
```

8

Now, this class can be used with any element that makes sense, such as the paragraph element (<p class="red">) or a heading element (<h2 class="red">). It could even work for a list item (<li class="red">Item One</li>).

Change Styles

For starters, you probably won't actually add many entries to your style sheet, because most of the elements that are in your templates, by default, are defined in the style sheet. So, you'll likely start tweaking your website's appearance by changing things that already exist in your weblog's style sheet. Before you can do that, though, you'll need to know a little about how the CSS standard works, because that's what defines the actual attributes and values you'll use within a style sheet.

The CSS standard focuses on the visual portions of the web pages you create, with three major types of properties that are relevant to what we're discussing here—font, text, and block-level attributes. Let's take a look at some examples of each.

> **NOTE** *The home of CSS online is http://www.w3.org/TR/REC-CSS2/ at the W3C's website. This particular document is pretty formal and convoluted, so you might want to look for a better CSS reference, such as the Guide to Cascading Style Sheets (http://www.htmlhelp.com/reference/css/).*

Font-level attributes include the font-family, font-style, font-weight, font-size, font-variant, and color properties. Using them, you can determine a fairly exact look for the fonts used in your document. You can also experiment with the look of the elements that are already in your blog's style sheet. For instance, here's a snippet from the standard Movable Type style sheet (Figure 8-4 shows an example of this style):

```
blogbody {
    font-family:georgia, verdana, arial, sans-serif;
    color:#666;
    font-size:11px;
    font-weight:normal;
      background:#FFF;
      line-height:16px;
    }
```

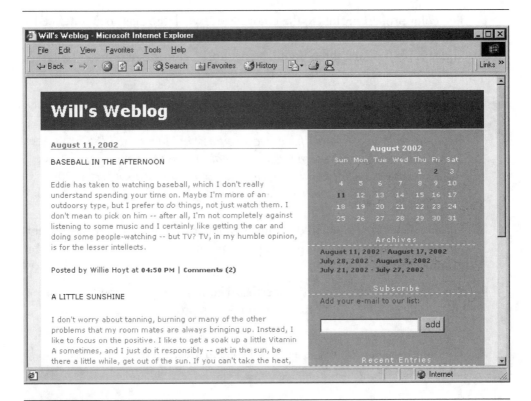

FIGURE 8-4   Here's the default look of this Movable Type style.

This class definition, as you can see, has entries for a number of the font-related properties. If you'd like to tweak them, you're free to do so—just jump in and start making changes—but with a few caveats:

- The font-family property can accept a single font name, but it's usually a good idea to include a series of font names, separated by commas, so that a browser can choose a secondary font if the first one listed isn't available on that computer. (For instance, some computers don't have the fonts Verdana and Helvetica installed, but might have Arial installed.) You should also include serif, san-serif, or monospace as the last entry so that the browser has a choice just in case none of your listed fonts is available.

■ The color property refers to the color of text when the class being defined is applied to a text container element. It's technically the foreground color. You specify it with a three-digit hexadecimal number that represents the Red, Green, and Blue values for the color.

NOTE *Hexadecimal (which means base 16, so letters are used to represent numerals over 9) color values are either three-digit hex numbers (for example, 878 or FFF) or three two-digit hex numbers (887788 or FFDDFF). HTMLHelp.com has a very handy color chart you can use to determine what colors are right for a particular property setting (http://www.htmlhelp.com/icon/hexchart.gif).*

■ The font-size property should include a number and the unit of measurement for that size, such as px for pixels, pt for point size, in for inches, or cm for centimeters.

■ Bold and italic use different properties. The font-weight property can be bold, bolder, lighter, or normal; the font-style property can be normal or italic.

■ The font-variant property is a special case that can be used to make a small-caps font.

So, knowing all this, you can change the Movable Type style sheet entry shown earlier rather dramatically, perhaps to something like the following (Figure 8-5 shows the changes):

```
blogbody {
    font-family:times, times new roman, serif;
    color:#090;
    font-size:18px;
    font-weight:lighter;
      background:#FFF;
      line-height:16px;
    }
```

TIP *If you're viewing your style sheet changes in Internet Explorer for Macintosh, note that it will sometimes fail to reload the style sheet, even if you've changed it. If you don't seem to be seeing different styles, you should jump into the IE Preferences, delete the cache, and then reload the page in question.*

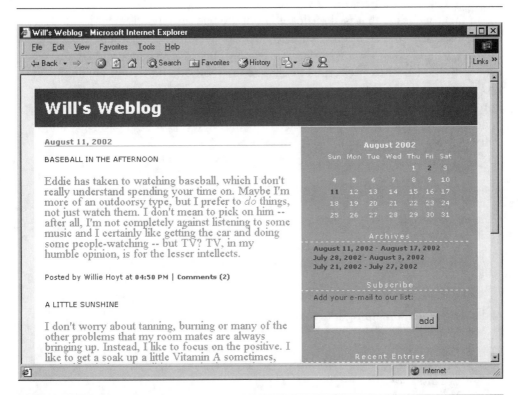

FIGURE 8-5   Here's the looks after the changes—the blog text is big, light, and green (you have to take my word on it).

Along with all these individual properties, you can also use a single font property, which can accept all the preceding values in a row (separated by spaces, if desired). Here's an example:

```
.lightext {font: arial, Helvetica, sans-serif 12px lighter}
```

This is convenient, but some browsers seem to mix elements when you add them this way, particularly browsers with earlier implementations of CSS. Another element that can be used this way (and is used this way very frequently) is the background property. Although specific background properties are available for use (such as background-image and background-position), a lot of designers seem to stick with the background property and often for a simple color choice, as in

```
{background: #00FF00}
```

In fact, one issue that is significant about the background element is that it can be used with different types of elements, such as the <p> element, to change the background color for a specific paragraph of text, for instance. It can also be used with the CSS box properties to change the look of a particular element. The box properties include top-margin, right-margin, left-padding, bottom-padding, border-style, border-width, and so on. You can use the more general margin, padding, and border properties, too. All this makes it possible to take our sample entry (shown earlier in Figure 8-5)

```
.blogbody {
font-family:times, times new roman, serif;
color:#090;
font-size:18px;
font-weight:lighter;
background:#FFF;
line-height:16px;
}
```

and change it to something like this:

```
.blogbody {
      font-family:times, times new roman, serif;
      color:#444;
      font-size:18px;
      font-weight:lighter;
      background:#CCC;
      line-height:16px;
      padding: 10px;
      margin: 10px;
      border: 1px dotted;
          }
```

The result is that each day's entries have a background color (light gray, in this case) and some padding around the text so that there's a border of color between the text, the dotted-line border, and the white of the page's background (see Figure 8-6). Without the padding, the text would appear right up against the edge of the border, which probably wouldn't look as good.

NOTE *Notice that padding adds space between the border and the text; the margin adds space between the border and the next entry (that's why the entries appear to be in separate boxes in Figure 8-6).*

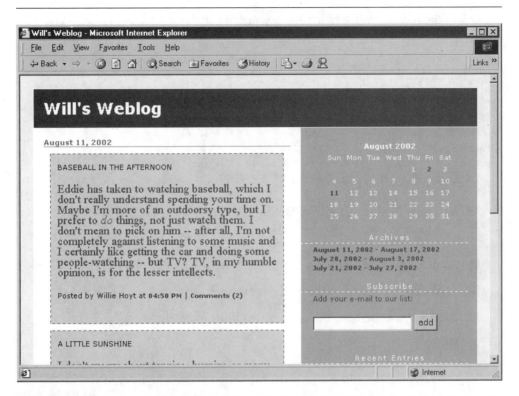

FIGURE 8-6   Here's the site now with a background color for each entry, as well as a padding, margin, and border specified.

You might also wish to play with the text properties, which include word-spacing, letter-spacing, text-decoration, vertical-alignment, text-alignment, and line-height, among others. (See http://www.w3.org/TR/REC-CSS2/text.html or http://www.htmlhelp.com/reference/css/text/ for a good explanation of each text property.) These properties enable you to alter the way text appears and behaves on the page, right down to characteristics such as spacing between letters and words. The text-decoration property is of interest, as well, because it enables you to add underlined text (text-decoration: underline), strikethrough-style text (text-decoration: line), or even blinking text (text-decoration: blink).

The last type of style sheet property I want to discuss is called a *pseudo-class*—a special series of properties that are used with the anchor (<a>) element. If you'd like your blog's pages to react to mouse movements, such as "mouseovers" (hovering the mouse over a hyperlink), you can use these special classes. Here's an example from pMachine's main style sheet:

```
a:link    { color: #000033; font-size: 11px;
font-weight: bold; text-decoration: underline; }
a:visited { color: #000033; font-size: 11px;
font-weight: bold; text-decoration: underline; }
a:active  { color: #333333; font-size: 11px;
font-weight: bold; text-decoration: underline; }
a:hover   { color: #999999; font-size: 11px;
font-weight: bold; text-decoration: none; }
```

These define the look of all the anchor elements on the page in their various states:

- **:link**   The state of the anchor text before the hyperlink has been clicked

- **:visited**   The state of the anchor text after the click

- **:active**   The state of the anchor text during the click

- **:hover**   The state when the mouse is over the link

You can change the colors and sizes (although size changes aren't recommended because it can mess up the design of a page) and even add a background property:

```
a:hover         { color: #FFCC66; background: #660066 }
```

This can make for a neat little visual effect when the user points to a link with the mouse, as shown here:

Mark Up with Styles

There's a lot more to the CSS standard, and I suggest you head out on the Web to the sites mentioned previously and in Appendix A to get a sense of the breadth of options. (They include some pretty interesting properties, including properties that can govern how text-to-speech browsers for the visually impaired should *speak* the text contained in certain elements.)

Before we move on from this section, however, it's worth discussing two important elements that are particularly useful in XHTML for designing and altering your pages to work with style sheets: the <div> (division) element and the <span> element.

It's easiest to think of the <div> element as sort of a super paragraph element that you can use to define sections of your document. In fact, entire pages can be parceled up and designed using the <div> element and some clever style sheet markup.

> **NOTE** *It's a little outside the scope of this book, but the <div> element can be used with a special style sheet specification called CSS Positioning for some very advanced web page layout tasks. See http://www.w3.org/TR/WD-positioning for the specification or http://www.brainjar.com/css/positioning/ for a tutorial.*

At the most basic level, the <div> element can simply be used to create and format large chunks of your page at one time:

```
<div align="center">
...a bunch of elements and text
</div>
```

The <div> element is also used heavily to apply certain style classes to groups of elements, as in this example from pMachine's template code for displaying multiple entries on an index page:

```
<div class="weblog">
<h3>%%title%%</h3>
<p>
%%body%%
%%more_link%%
</p>

<div class="author">
Posted by: %%if_email_or_url_as_name%% on %%date%% |
<a href="%%profile_link%%">Profile</a>
</div>
```

```
<br />
%%comments_link%%  |  <a
href="%%comment_permalink%%">link</a>
</div>
```

Note how the entire entry is enclosed in a <div> element that is used to assign the style class "weblog" to the entire entry—all the text that appears in the section that isn't overridden by another style definition will appear according to the weblog class:

```
.weblog {
  padding-bottom: 12px;
  border-bottom:1px dotted #999999;
}
```

Of course, a lot of those elements *do* have overriding style definitions—the <h3> element used for the headline has a special style sheet entry, for instance, and the variables that represent information about the entry (the author, date, and so forth) are surrounded by another <div> element that assigns the class "author" to the enclosed markup. That's the *cascading* part of Cascading Style Sheets— an overall style is in force until another one overrides it. In this example, any elements that don't specifically have a style defined will use the weblog style, but individual elements, such as the <h3> will still use their style sheet definitions.

> **NOTE**   *Note that the special align attribute can be used with the <div> opening tag if you want to align the markup that appears inside the <div> element, as in <div align="right">. Also, you can use the special style attribute to add style that isn't defined in the style sheet—for example, <div style="font-size: 16pt"> could be used to assign all fonts inside the <div> element to 16 points (unless overridden by another style definition).*

The other style element, <span>, is used when you don't want to create a block-level element using the <div> container (<div>, after all, creates white space— a line break—on either side of it, just as <p> does). You can use <span> the same way you might use the <em> or <strong> emphasis element, as shown here:

```
Posted by: <span class="red">%%name%%</span> on %%date%%
```

Of course, you can use the <span> element in regular markup (for instance, on static pages or in the static content on your template pages) as well as in conjunction with template variables, as shown earlier. After all, the template variables will simply be substituted with the actual entry's text once the page is published—that's the whole point of separating your content from your template design.

Tips for a Blog *That Works*

Although many of us will stick close to the original templates provided by our blogging tools, you may opt to head a little further out on the limb. There's nothing wrong with that—it's good to see cleverly designed sites that push the limits of both HTML and the blogging tools. I've seen some very impressive sites, and I've seen some that do less than impress.

However, if you're going to break out and start designing your own blog on any level, I can offer a few design hints within my limited repertoire:

- **Keep it simple.** Rules are made to be broken, but in general the simpler a website's design is, the easier it is to read. Present you entries, links, and static elements as simply and logically as possible to make for a well-read blog. Use as few images as you can get away with, if only to keep the site from taking a long time to download and appear in the user's browser. If you make your visitors wait for the page to download, they may just leave before reading and participating.

- **Think content first.** The nice thing about a weblog is that you can always change the design—in fact, it will likely grow and change over time as you get more ideas and the time to implement them. In the meantime, remember the real purpose of the blog—people will only want to look at its design for so long if the content isn't any good. Focus on the writing first and the design second (if you have time).

TIP

Most browsers have a View Source command. Use it when you're surfing and you see a site you like. Don't steal the design (tsk, tsk) but rather see how the designer did things and try to learn from it for your own site.

- **Use headings, paragraphs, and style sheets.** If you know something about the "dark days" of web design, you might be familiar with the <font> element, the <pre> element, the <center> element, and the <blockquote> element. These were used to manually format paragraphs. Avoid using such elements in place of the <h1> and <p> elements. If you'd like them styled differently, use style sheets to create different looks and/or different classes of each element.

- **Make your site as accessible as possible.**   Accessibility can be achieved by simply following the preceding rules as well as by being careful to use the additional descriptive attributes that some elements offer. For instance, when adding an image, use the alt attribute to describe the image for those browsers that can't display it. (Likewise, you should never have image-only links but rather duplicate them with text-based hyperlinks.) XHTML also enables you to label form elements, add summaries to tables, and provide some other special extras to help special-needs browsers.

> **NOTE**   *A good look at creating an accessible site is available online at http://diveintomark.org/archives/rooms/30_days_to_a_more_accessible_ weblog/index.html. Divided into 30 entries, this article does a great job of laying out accessibility issues as well as making them relevant to blogging.*

- **Test your site.**   The first time you view your site in a different browser, at a different screen resolution, or on a different platform (Mac vs. PC vs. Unix), you may be shocked by the differences. Various browsers and platforms render pages differently. Therefore, it's always good to test— even with older browsers—so that you have a sense of what many of your visitors are seeing.

More...

In this chapter we discussed some *post-installation* topics regarding your blog— content and design. The chapter began with a discussion of the different elements and blog entry types that you can use to keep dynamic and interesting content flowing on your blog. I also offered some advice on interesting writing, quick rules of grammar, and a consideration of etiquette and ethics in blogging.

The second part of the chapter focused on using the Cascading Style Sheet standard to change the look of your blog, particularly if it was designed using a popular tool such as Movable Type, pMachine, or even Blogger. You learned how to alter style sheet definitions, add and use style sheet classes, and dig into HTML documents to alter or add to the markup using the <div> and <span> elements.

Finally, the chapter took a quick look at some recommendations for making your site look good, just in case you decide to go well beyond the built-in templates and really change the way your site looks and feels.

In the next chapter, we'll cover some add-ons for your site—beyond just the design, you can add special programs and scripts to do all sorts of things, from managing mailing lists and discussion groups, to holding opinion polls and posting online photo galleries.

M	T	W	T	F	S		S	M	T	W	T	F	S		S	M	T	W	T	F	S		S	M	T	W	T	F	S
		1	2	3	4					1	2	3	4					1	2	3	4					1	2	3	4
6	7	8	9	10	11		5	6	7	8	9	10	11		5	6	7	8	9	10	11		5	6	7	8	9	10	11
13	14	15	16	17	18		12	13	14	15	16	17	18		12	13	14	15	16	17	18		12	13	14	15	16	17	18
20	21	22	23	24	25		19	20	21	22	23	24	25		19	20	21	22	23	24	25		19	20	21	22	23	24	25
27	28	29	30	31			26	27	28	29	30	31			26	27	28	29	30	31			26	27	28	29	30	31	

Chapter 9

Add-Ons for Your Weblog

In this chapter:

- Setting up a reply e-mail account
- Do you need a forum?
- Adding and managing a mailing list
- Adding a poll
- Adding a photoblog
- Using Blogger-compatible editing tools

If there's anything that might be even more fun than getting your own blog up and running, it's the chance—once the dust has settled—to start accessorizing it. You'll find tons of options on the Web you can add to your blog—often for free—to help make it more personal, more interesting, and more community oriented. You'll also find some tools that can make using and updating the blog a little easier, too, as you'll see in this chapter. Most of the stuff we'll talk about in this chapter is as easy to implement as the blogging software you've seen so far in this book. Although some installation and configuration may be necessary, I doubt you'll break a sweat.

Set Up a Reply E-mail Account

It might go without saying, but I'll say it anyway: you should have an e-mail account that your readers can use to get a hold of you, whether for administrative issues, to send a "letter to the editor" to respond to your posts, or both. I'd recommend separating your blog-oriented e-mail account from your other e-mail, just because e-mail accounts tend to be cheap or free, and it's nice to have the separation between your blogging life and your real life. (If you get famous or popular enough as a blogger, you might start to get a clogged e-mail account, and you'll miss messages from your real-life loved ones or colleagues.)

If you've set up one of the more sophisticated blogging tools, chances are you've already entered an e-mail address in the appropriate configuration entry box. If not, or if you're using a general e-mail account (such as your own personal, standard-issue account), then you might want to set up an e-mail account that's specifically for your blog. If you're paying for a hosting service for your blogging server software, there's a good chance your hosting company has made available a certain number of e-mail accounts and/or addresses. Set one up, if you can (see Figure 9-1). If not, you might consider a Hotmail or Yahoo! e-mail account.

Once you have the account, you'll want to add it to your blog in some way. The easiest way is to add it is as a link—you can open up the HTML template for your blog or for the blog's index page (depending on how it's organized) and add a mailto: link for the e-mail address, as in this example:

```
<a href="mailto:admin@mycoolblog.com">Contact Me</a>
```

The mailto: URL causes the e-mail address to be launched in the reader's default e-mail editor so that the reader can send you a message.

It can be useful to change the address in your e-mail links a little bit so that web "robots" can't harvest the address and add it to a "spam" (junk mail) list.

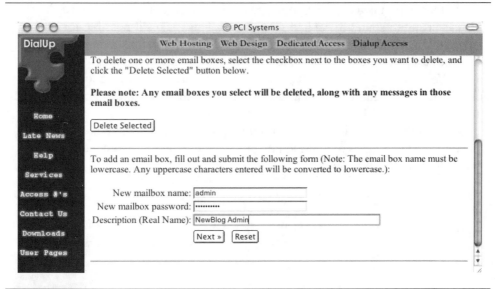

FIGURE 9-1   With many web hosts, setting up another account is easy.

9

Posting your e-mail address on a public website is a fast way to increase the number of junk mail posts that appear in your e-mail box. You can solve that problem by altering your e-mail address some, as shown here:

```
<a href="mailto:adminNO@SPAMmycoolblog.com">Contact Me (remove NO
SPAM)</a>
```

This makes it obvious, to a human, that the words *NO SPAM* need to be deleted before the message will be sent successfully. Another way to deal with this is to simply leave the domain extension off of the e-mail address, as in this example:

```
<a href="mailto:admin@mycoolblog">Contact Me</a>
```

To an automated e-mail harvester, this address won't work. For humans, it's reasonably easy to figure out that they need to add the .com (assuming it's the same as your site URL) if they're going to send a message to you successfully. If you want to be more explicit, try:

```
<a href="mailto:admin@mycoolblog">Contact Me (add .com)</a>
```

Another option is to encode your e-mail address so that a harvester can't get it (this is starting to sound like a bad sci-fi flick). This makes it possible for your e-mail address to work perfectly when clicked by a user but be meaningless (at least, for now) to the e-mail bots. Head to http://www.hivelogic.com/safeaddress/ on the Web and plug in your e-mail address. You'll get back a JavaScript that builds your e-mail address from a series of HTML special character codes for each letter (such as &#97 for *a* and &#122 for *z*).

Want another solution? If you're running pMachine, you can add a special Contact Us page, thanks to a pMachine tag. Create a page called contact.php (or something similar) that looks like this:

```
<?php include("pm_inc.php"); ?>
<head>
<title>Send Us an Email</title>
<link rel="stylesheet" type="text/css" href="pm_style.css" />
</head>
<body>
<h2>Send Us a Message</h2>
<?php contact_form("subject line","email@address.com"); ?>

</body>
</html>
```

When you create this page, substitute an actual subject line for the message in the first set of quotation marks, and substitute your e-mail address for *email@address.com*. (You can actually leave this second attribute out if you want the message sent to the default e-mail account specified in the Admin E-mail entry inside General Preferences.) Now, from your index page and wherever else, create a hyperlink to the contact.php page you just created. When readers click that link, they'll see the page that appears in Figure 9-2.

> **NOTE** *Rick Ellis (creator of pMachine and tech editor of this book) is a busy man. He has developed a special tag in pMachine 2.2 and higher that can encode an e-mail address that you add to your page: <?php encoded_ email("you@yoursite.com", "click here to email me!"); ?>. Using this tag instead of a mailto: anchor element causes the address to be encoded, and bots shouldn't be able to grab it.*

Even if you don't have pMachine, you can still add a contact page with Perl, although it would be a little more complicated. You'll need to create an HTML file that includes the requisite HTML form elements and then link it to a form-to-mail

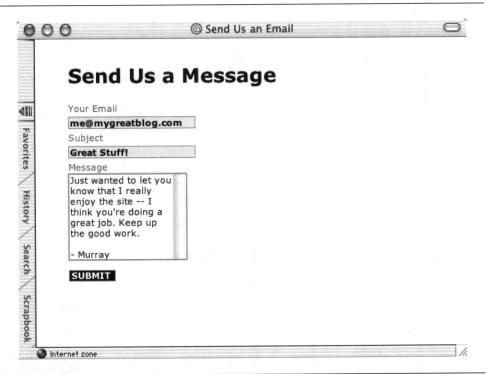

FIGURE 9-2   Here's the simple contact form that pMachine enables you to generate.

CGI script. Try http://www.ftls.org/en/examples/cgi/Form2Mail.shtml for a self-installed script or look into a service such as HostedScripts.com (http://www.hostedscripts.com/formmailer.html), which allows you to create your form and link it directly to their form-to-e-mail solution.

Do You Need a Forum?

A discussion forum makes for an interesting addition to a weblog, particularly if you're working to create a large, active community. A forum gives your readers the opportunity to choose the topics of discussion and participate on an even footing with you on your site. Not that users can't participate with a regular blog, because most blogging software enables you to sign up more official authors, if desired. (Plus, with pMachine, you can create a collective weblog in which anyone can send an item.) But a forum tends to be even more democratic than that, with users able to sign in and post more freely and more quickly.

Deciding whether a forum is good for your site can be something of a balancing act. If you don't get a lot of visitors per day—in the hundreds or thousands—then a forum may not be as important as focusing on good content in your blog. After all, with most blogs you can solicit comments from your readers, and those comment discussions can be just as dynamic as any discussions in special forum software. For smaller sites, sticking to comments is the way to go.

However, if your blog grows to where you have a devoted and outspoken following of readers, you might consider adding discussion forums. In these forums you can register your users, create an abundance of topic areas, and allow for all sorts of questions, discussions, and observations (see Figure 9-3). In fact, the forum software gives you an outlet for some of the "off topic" discussions that

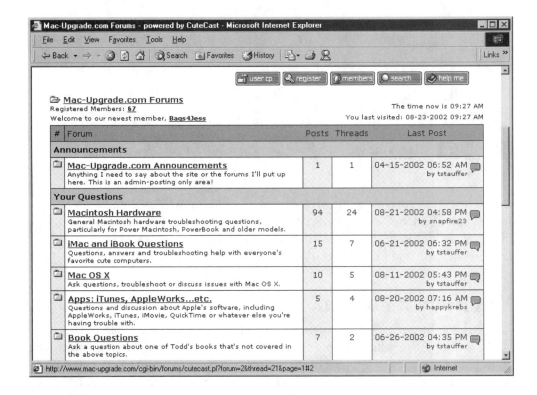

FIGURE 9-3   Here is a discussion forum I've set up on one of my sites.

are bound to pop up on a popular blog. For example, if you'd prefer that all the "shout outs" between your readers happen somewhere other than in the comments to your blog entries, a forum is a good idea.

> **TIP** *Speaking of shout outs, another common weblog add-on is the "shout box," in which people enter just a line or two of text in a small window. Check out http://www.tag-board.com/ for a free, hosted solution.*

Adding discussion forum software to your blog site is, in some ways, like getting and configuring an entirely new blog. From the point of view of a user, the two are reasonably similar—you have entries, replies, index pages, and archives. On a technical level, there are also similarities—you can get Perl-based software, PHP-based software, hosted solutions, server-side solutions, and so on. You can also get totally free options, nearly free options, and some rather costly options. I'll work from the assumption that you want to keep it cheap.

> **NOTE** *I've discussed this PHP and MySQL business earlier, but let me reiterate it here because I know it can be confusing. PHP is an embedded scripting language that allows you to add dynamic content to web pages. PHP requires a server that supports it and documents saved with ".php" extensions instead of ".html" extensions. Many PHP tools such as discussion forums (and pMachine blogging software, for instance) also require MySQL, which is a web-based database server. If you decide to use a PHP/MySQL-based web application, you'll simply need a web hosting account that supports those technologies; they're readily available from most any IPP.*

The easiest way to add a forum to your blog is to use a hosted service and link to it. When your users click the link to your discussion forum, they actually leave your site and go to the forum host's special board that has been set up for you.

A number of hosted forum services abound, including quite a few that offer their services for free because they run advertisements on the board pages. That's a tradeoff you'll have to consider—especially if you don't run ads on your blog's pages. (Some of the services will let you pay a nominal fee to do away with their ads.) In choosing a service, you'll also want to consider how much control you need over the design of the hosted message board pages. Do you need them to look like you chose the colors? Should they look similar to your own site?

NOTE *Because a hosted forum is on someone else's site, you'll need to conform to their terms of service. Read these carefully before signing up and make sure there's nothing in their agreement that you can't live with. (You might also check to make sure they run backups to restore your entries in case of a server problem and that you can export past entries for use in another message board at a later date, if those are considerations.)*

For a very basic forum you can use the message board from HostedScripts.com (http://www.hostedscripts.com/). It comes with all the other scripts they offer for free. The forum created is very plain and has pop-up ads that greet your readers, but you can change the color scheme and it's a fairly easy type of board for people to grow accustomed to (see Figure 9-4). It has the advantage of looking pretty active, even if you have relatively few posts and responses, because the screen fills up quickly. However, it has the disadvantage of getting cluttered. What's more, if you do get a lot of messages, earlier topics will soon be gone from sight.

ProBoards (http://www.proboards.com/) offers free, hosted message boards that are cast in the very popular Ultimate Bulletin Board (UBB) vein. UBB was once a free bulletin board application that's now much pricier. It pioneered a certain look and feel that the vast majority of forums—either hosted or server based—have based

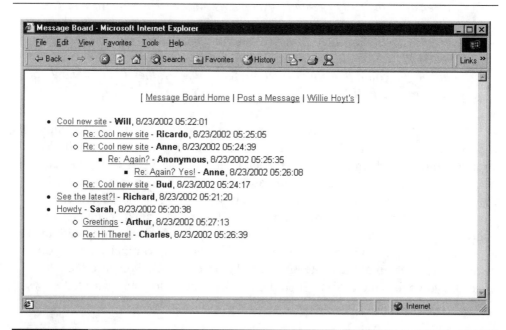

FIGURE 9-4   HostedScript.com's basic message board is, well, basic.

themselves on. ProBoards, shown in Figure 9-5, is ad driven, although you can pay a fee in order to remove the ads from your pages. The feature set is pretty good: readers will be able to format their postings, add small images (called *avatars*) to personalize their posts, get a notification when a post of theirs is responded to, and so on. The look of the default site is dark, but you can dig into the colors and change that, too.

NOTE

One of the upshots of UBB's popularity is the fact that a great deal of forum software offers compatibility with UBB codes, *which are special codes that format text much like HTML, without actually allowing HTML in your users' posts. (For instance, you can use [b] and [/b] for underlining and [url=http://www.mycoollink.com]click here[/url] to add a link.) The UBB codes offer fewer and less-sophisticated markup, meaning there's less chance of a user doing harm with their HTML skills (or lack thereof). See http://www.iuma.com/bb/ubbcode.html for a list of codes commonly used.*

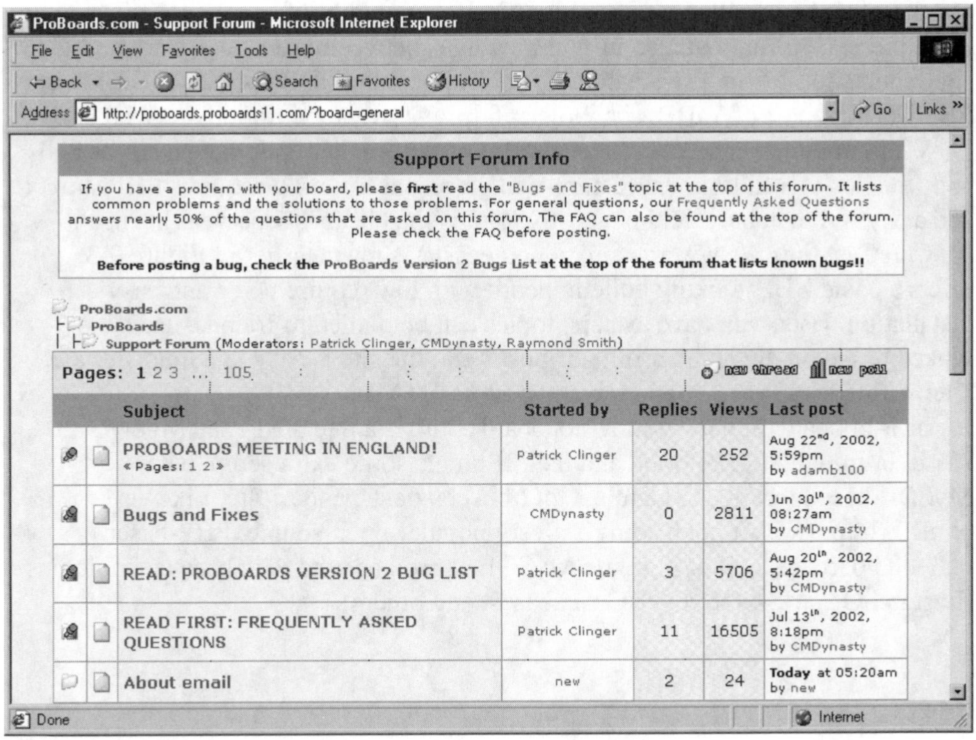

FIGURE 9-5   ProBoards is a more sophisticated, graphical solution for a hosted forum.

ezBoard (http://www.ezboard.com/) is another very popular offering that allows for many of the same features as ProBoards—users register with the site, they can check out the different topics you've created, and they can add their own posts or reply to others. ezBoard doesn't offer quite as much customization for the user (no avatars are apparent, at least not in the current release), but the boards themselves are easy to customize, with prebuilt themes available to board managers. Another feature is the ability to e-mail all members. You'll see a lot of ads and up-sell, but the ad-free option is offered at a reasonable price.

> NOTE   *Other hosted options include the very simple www.instantmessageboards.com and the UBB-like www.forumco.com, both ad supported but very different in implementation.*

As for server-based forum software, you have plenty of options, most of them based loosely on UBB. YaBB (Yet Another Bulletin Board), which can be found at http://www.yabbforum.com/, is a popular, free forum system that runs in Perl and can therefore be installed on basic servers. It is incredibly feature rich, offering not just a message forum but also instant messages between users, templates and CSS style sheets for layout, private boards, and support for UBB codes. (YaBB SE is a PHP/MySQL port of YaBB, available at http://www.yabb.info/ on the Web.)

VBulletin (http://www.vbulletin.com) is also a popular option, with all the bells and whistles of a full-blown, feature-rich graphical forum. It requires PHP support and a MySQL database, and it's costly ($85 is the cheapest one-year license).

CuteCast (http://www.artscore.net/cutecast/), shown earlier in Figure 9-3, offers a basic UBB-looking bulletin board with low requirements and easy installation. Users can have avatars, topics can be mailed to friends, users are ranked based on the number of their posts, and the site is easy to administer and alter with colors, images, and top and bottom HTML.

Invisionboard (http://www.invisionboard.com/) is a free, PHP- and MySQL-based forum with a UBB look and feel. It'll take some extra setup, but a MySQL-based forum can handle a lot of users, posts, and traffic. Likewise, phpBB (http://www.phpbb.com) is a very popular open-source, PHP-based bulletin board system that can use MySQL as well as other database technologies (PostgreSQL, MS-SQL, ODBC databases, and others).

TIP *If your server or web hosting account will support a MySQL/PHP discussion forum, this might be the right way to go. These forums tend to be much faster and more capable than Perl-based boards, particularly once you have hundred or thousands of users and thousands or hundreds of thousands of posts.*

Phorum (http://www.phorum.org/) offers a plain but very clean-looking open-source PHP/MySQL bulletin board solution. The software doesn't provide a lot of graphics, avatars, or burning folder icons (which are common on other sites) but rather much simpler text-and-link entries. It's a good choice for a more business-like approach to your forum.

If those don't satisfy you, know that tons of other options are available in all shapes, sizes, and prices. Start at http://directory.google.com/Top /Computers/ Software/Internet/Servers/Discussion/ and click around to see whether any of the software suits your fancy.

NOTE *Wondering about the actual, original Ultimate Bulletin Board? It's still there—it has just gone corporate. You can get it for a price (currently $199 for a single license) at Infopop.com, which also offers UBB.x (hosted forums), UBB.threads (a MySQL implementation of UBB), and OpenTopic (enterprise-level hosted boards).*

9

Finally, if you're working with pMachine for your blog, you may want to consider using its built-in forum templates to create a forum. (The templates actually build upon the collective weblog concept, enabling users to post their own "entries," which then get comments—it's the same thing, just a different format with some tweaks to the information presented.) In order to get the pMachine forum templates you have to upgrade to pMachine Pro ($45 for noncommercial use), but that does give you one significant advantage over other forum options: your users can have one login for both the blog's community features and the forum software. (If you add any of the forum software mentioned earlier to an existing blog, your users have to register and sign in to the forum separate from the blog.) The downside is that the pMachine forum isn't as graphical or flexible as many of the UBB-style forums, but it has a good, clean look and gives you basic functionality (see Figure 9-6).

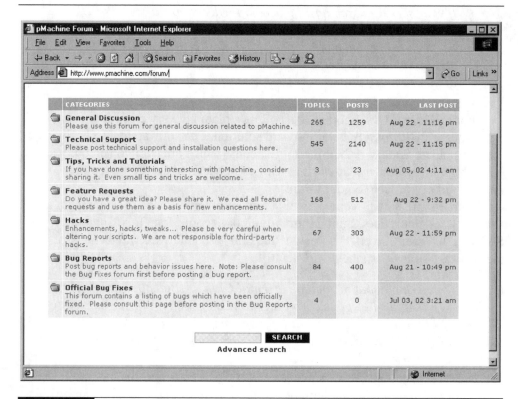

FIGURE 9-6   Here's an example of the pMachine forum template—none other than the discussion forum at pMachine.com.

Add and Manage a Mailing List

Another tool for building community is the mailing list. Lists that are managed using sophisticated software can be a pleasure to work with—all of the headaches of actually managing the people who subscribe or unsubscribe to your list can be taken over by the software so that you can concentrate on the content of the e-mail messages you want to send. And despite the universal abhorrence that people have for junk e-mail, the truth is that opt-in e-mail newsletters are one of the segments of the Internet that have seen the most growth recently in terms of actual paid subscribers or advertising revenue. That suggests, at least, that people appreciate receiving e-mail newsletters if they have decent content and if their readers have the opportunity to opt in and out easily.

For your community, the advertising revenue may not be the most important thing, in which case a mailing list offers two other opportunities: it can be used to drive traffic to your weblog, and it can be used to foster conversation among the recipients of your list. Which of these it does basically depends on how you set up your mailing list. Most mailing list software gives you the option of creating either an *announce-only* list, where messages go out only from you to the readers, or a *discussion* list, where readers can also post their own messages.

The magic of a mailing list is that users can manage their own relationships to it. With a basic mailing list (for instance, the mailing list capability built in to pMachine), the user can opt in and opt out of the list fairly easily. In pMachine's case, the reader can change his status by altering his personal profile page or by clicking the link that appears at the bottom of each mailing list message. Integration between its mailing list and its site-wide user registration feature is one of the major community advantages of pMachine. It's nice not to make users register twice for something, although pMachine's mailing list doesn't offer the features of a full-blown mailing list server, such as the ability to subscribe to digests of messages (daily or weekly collections instead of individual messages) and the ability to stop a message list from showing up for short vacation periods.

With the more sophisticated mailing list managers, the reader will generally have the option of sending commands to a particular e-mail address (listserver@ *yoursite*.com, for instance). In some cases, you can even write to the list for help, getting back an explanation of the features (see Figure 9-7).

So where do you get a mailing list? First, check with the IPP that supplies your blog's hosting service—many of the competitive IPPs, including the cheaper ones, offer some sort of mailing list–management feature, and it's often something that you can set up from whatever control panel interface you use to make other choices about your hosting account. Clearly, the quality of service offered can range considerably—some mailing list server software will only accept commands via e-mail messages; others will provide a web-based interface for your reader to subscribe, unsubscribe, and make other choices.

If your IPP doesn't offer a mailing list or you don't like the way it looks or functions, you can consider installing your own mailing list software on your server or you can look to a hosted solution. Hosted solutions range from for-pay models to ad-driven options.

Topica (http://www.topica.com) offers both ad-driven, free mailing lists and subscription-based, ad-free lists. The mailing lists offer sophisticated features, such as messages addressed directly to readers, support for HTML, AOL and plain-text messages, and a web-based interface for the reader to change list options. In fact, an archive of the list is kept online and can be quickly accessed for reading previous messages. If there are any disadvantages, it's that the site is a little e-commerce focused (not *too* annoying, at least at the time of writing), and your

9

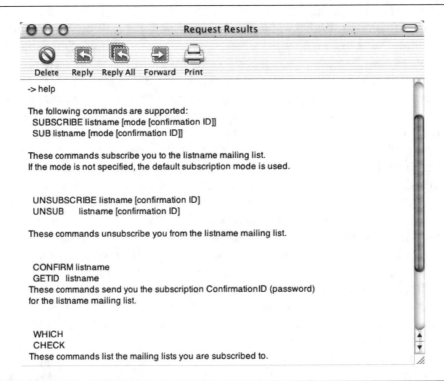

FIGURE 9-7 The mailing list feature offered by this IPP can automatically respond to a request for help sent to the main listserver address.

users will have to become Topica members in order to receive the list, which is a greater commitment than simply adding an e-mail address.

Yahoo! Groups (http://groups.yahoo.com) has bought and rolled a few well-known list-hosting services into its Groups service. The Groups service goes beyond simple mailing lists by providing a forum, photos area, calendar, and more. In fact, the only real problem with using Yahoo! Groups for your mailing list is that it's very full featured and could serve as a community destination in its own right—potentially making your blog superfluous. Groups isn't exactly a blog; it's really a hosted, ad-driven mailing-list server with polls, chatting, and other features. However, it does post the latest mailing list messages on the home page and serves as an archive for an active mailing list—particularly a discussion list where readers of the list respond and interact via the list. Figure 9-8 shows a Yahoo! Group in action.

Going back to the well again, HostedScripts.com (http://www.hostedscripts.com/) also offers a basic announce-only mailing list that you can use for your site. (Yes,

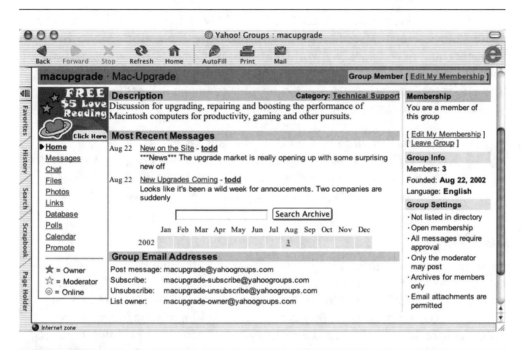

FIGURE 9-8   Here's the main page of a Yahoo! Group.

they also have a poll, so brace yourself—I'll talk about polls in the next section!) The HostedScripts.com mailing list is ad supported, but, fortunately, the ads in an e-mail message aren't quite as intrusive as the pop-up ads on their forum software. (Users will still see the pop-ups when subscribing or unsubscribing.) It's very basic, but it works for site announcements.

Your other option is to download and install mailing list–management software via your server. Again, if you've managed to install a server-based blog, then adding the e-mail server shouldn't be too difficult. In most cases, you'll need to know if and how Sendmail is configured on the server computer. If you don't know this, you may need to consult your IPP or systems administrator.

The granddaddy of mailing list managers is the still-free Majordomo (http://www.greatcircle.com/majordomo/), which is written in Perl and can be installed on a server relatively easily. If there's one problem with this mailing list manager, it's that Majordomo is distributed as source code, meaning you'll need to compile it a bit and have some admin access to your server. If you don't have that level of access (or interest), try MojoMail (http://mojo.skazat.com/), a free Perl-based script for managing a mailing list. Also, Mail List V (http://www.cgi-factory.com/ maillist/index.shtml) is free for users with Unix-based servers, and MultiList Manager (http://www.webscriptworld.com/scripts/mlm.phtml) is a free PHP-based solution. Besides those, there are literally hundreds of free and commercial mailing list options that you can install and run on your computer, depending on the scripting languages and permissions you have to install files on your server.

> **TIP** *HotScripts.com (http://www.hotscripts.com/) is one of the best places to find Perl, PHP, and many other types of scripts that are good for websites and other tasks. At the time of this writing, it lists over 100 Perl-based scripts just for managing a mailing list!*

Add a Poll

Another popular way to encourage repeat visitors and a little sense of community is to offer a clever or interesting poll or survey on your site. Although the results will never be scientific (after all, this is a cross-section of people who are self-selecting readers of *your* site), they can be an interesting insight into how the group feels on various topics. Such a survey or poll can also be helpful to you if you can manage to get people to respond about issues such as the design of your site and new features they may or may not want you to add.

> **TIP** *Don't want to add a poll? You might still have fun completing a poll, survey, or personality test and then posting it to your blog—this is a popular pastime for bloggers. Start with the Friday Five (http://www.fridayfive.org/), which many people like to answer in their own weblogs. Then, move on to the Geek Quiz (http://www.thudfactor.com/geekquiz.php), The Life Expectancy Test (http://www.longtolive.com/), or try the Fun Test and Quizzes Page (http://www.wizardrealm.com/tests/fun.html) or the QueenDom.com tests (http://www.queendom.com/tests/ minitests/index.html). As you surf other people's blogs, you'll find links to many more tests and games, many of which give you the HTML to post the result on your own blog.*

Implementing a survey or poll script is generally as simple as downloading a Perl or PHP-based script and installing it. The complexity is in the archiving, the way the script reports results, and the intricacy and flexibility of the layout. Some scripts will simply accept values from HTML forms that you create, whereas others will manage the look and feel of your poll. Hundreds of downloadable polls

abound—see PlayVote (http://www.playhouse.com/Software/PlayVote.shtml), CGI
Factory's Survey (http://www.cgi-factory.com/software/packages/), and EZPOLMKR
(http://mannyjuan.com/ezpolmkr.htm), shown in Figure 9-9. Note that some
"survey" scripts will enable you to ask more than one question, whereas many
"polls" are aimed at a single issue. (Of course, that's only a guideline.)

A number of sites offer hosted polls that you can link to or, in some
cases, embed in your pages. (Generally, when users click to the results page,
that's when they'll visit the poll hosting company and that's when they'll see
the advertisement offered by same.) Using a hosted solution is a quick way to
get your poll online, although you'll have much less control over it. Try
WebEnalysis (http://www.webenalysis.com/onlinepolls.asp), HostedScripts.com
(http://www.hostedscripts .com), WebPollCentrl (http://www.webpollcentral.com),
or SiteGadgets (http:// www.sitegadgets.com).

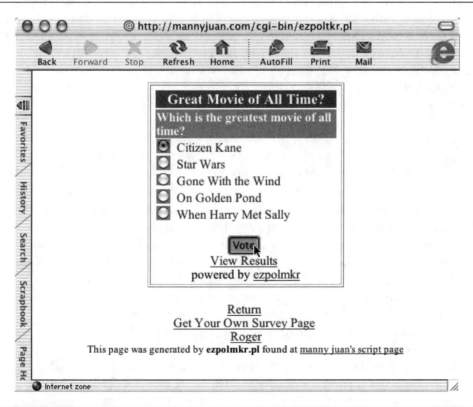

9

FIGURE 9-9 Here's a poll created using EXPOLMKR.

 *If you'll allow for the fact that the entire genre of free, hosted Web add-ons tends to be a little heavy on annoying pop-up ads, then FreeCenter (http:// www.freecenter.com/hostcgi.html) isn't a bad place to start if you're looking for hosted scripts and solutions.*

Add an Image Gallery

Got photos to share? How about adding a virtual photo album or image gallery to your site? You can get software that offers an automated presentation of those images, usually by displaying thumbnails first and then displaying larger images when a thumbnail is clicked.

One way to add your photos is to create what some call a *photoblog*—a second weblog (if your software supports it) where you post images and descriptions instead of standard blog entries. Each entry can begin with a description of the images. When readers click the More link, they're taken to the More section of the article where you've put a series of thumbnails of those images, perhaps arranged in an HTML table. This is particularly easy to do in Movable Type, which happens to be able to create thumbnails from your images. It's also not that difficult to do in other blogging software like Greymatter or pMachine, although it may eventually get tedious if you're trying to add more than five to ten images per blog entry or if you have literally hundreds of photos to share.

NOTE   *Want to create a special MT template for your photoblog? Try http:// blogstyles.com/photo/photoview.html for a good look at how it can be done. (Also, check the links on this page to other photoblogs.)*

The ideal image gallery will simply allow you to place your images in a directory on the web server, where they will then be automatically placed on gallery pages (per your specifications) and thumbnails will be created. When a thumbnail is clicked, the full-size image is revealed. Image galleries are also easier to deal with as server-side scripts—and much easier to *find* that way, because not too many hosting services will offer you cheap access to the bandwidth it takes to host images. (One that I'm aware of is the .Mac subscription-based tool from Apple, which offers the HomePage tool that you can use to turn images into thumbnails rather easily.)

The Image Display System (IDS; http://ids.sourceforge.net) is a free Perl-based solution that offers support for exactly what we're talking about here—it takes images that you place in directories on your web server and creates thumbnails from them, enabling you to post them in a gallery format. It's a bit tough to install (it requires command-line access to your server), but if your host enables you access at the command line, it's a good option for an image gallery.

Need Blogging Cash? Solicit Donations

A fair number of hosted CGI sites offer to do away with the advertising if you'll subscribe to the service for a certain number of dollars per month, quarter, or year. In some cases, it can be a good idea to pay up—it may be cheaper than buying and installing the software outright, and it might be nice to rely on their servers for some of the bandwidth. But where do you get the money?

It's becoming more common to beg for it—although that's not what it's called. A number of Web-based services will enable you to solicit donations from your site visitors—PayPal and Amazon are two respected names that offer such a service. With PayPal, you'll first need to set up an account—it's free. Next, log in and click the Donations link. (It's currently found under the Sell tab, in the Sell on a Website area.) You can then create a button to place on your website that enables visitors to donate to your site.

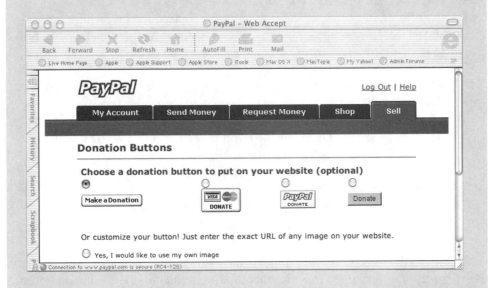

Amazon's service is similar. It's called the Amazon Honor System, and it allows you to make a pitch to readers asking them to pay for the great content they're getting. (Head to Amazon.com and look for the Honors System link; the URL is a little too amorphous to print here.) Readers can donate as little as $1 in appreciation of your content. And, believe it or not, some bloggers are finding that they make some money with these donations, particularly if the site is popular and/or offers a unique service or value. Likewise, the blogging software folks themselves—Greymatter, Blogger, and Movable Type—all solicit donations.

Amazon also offers the Wish List feature, another popular link on blogs. On the Wish List, you enter the items from Amazon that you'd most like to have—sort of a wedding registry for bloggers. Then, you can link from your site to your Amazon Wish List, letting people know what books, music, electronics, and so forth you're interested in getting as a present. If people really like your blog, maybe they'll buy you a gift. (And, if they happen to be friends and you publicize your birthday on your site....)

If your server supports PHP, Gallery (http://gallery.sourceforge.net) is an impressive application for setting up and managing web-based image galleries. The software creates thumbnails, allows for easy captioning, and has a login feature that gives visitors more control over what they see. PhotoFrame (http://photoframe.sourceforge.net) is another PHP-based freebie, with a frames-focused interface. Images appear on one side of the page as thumbnails, with full-size images, captions, and visitor comments showing up in the "viewer" window.

NOTE *With photo album software, you'll need to check the requirements carefully and make sure you can use the software with your web host. Some IPPs don't compile the GD library (an image manipulation package) into their PHP installation, which may be required by the software. (It's something you could do relatively easily if you have full access to the server, but you'll have to ask your IPP about it if you have a shared hosting account.) Check with your IPP to find out what they have available, or choose software (such as Gallery, discussed earlier) that uses an image manipulation library (such as NetPBM or ImageMagick) that can be installed easily.*

In fact, PHP seems to be very popular for writing photo galleries. Based on my experience, some very good tools for that task are written in PHP. For many more options, see http://www.hotscripts.com/PHP/Scripts_and_Programs/Image_Galleries/ on the Web.

If you're interest is in using images to keep people coming back to your site (or to build a gallery of images over time), you might try the free, Perl-based Schlabo's Scripts (http://www.schlabo.com/) for the Picture of the Day script, which offers a gallery, slide show–like presentation and, of course, the "picture of the day," which enables you to put a picture from your gallery on a different page—perhaps the index page of your blog. It's not exactly an automatically generated thumbnail gallery, but it's a great script if you want to add photos to your blog daily to keep everyone's interest up.

Add Comments

If you're working with blogging software that doesn't have a comment feature (notably Blogger, but others as well), you still have an option—hosted comments. A number of hosted services allow you to link from your blog entries to the host, making it appear that your entries seamlessly support comments. Among the options is NetComments (http://netcomments.co.uk/). An easy-to-use service, NetComments requires a minimum of setup, is free, has no advertising, and allows you to choose from a number of different comment templates. It generates the correct code for a number of different tools and even enables you to add comments to static pages. Others that work in a similar way include BlogOut (http://www.klinkfamily.com/BlogOut/blogout.html) and Enetation (http://enetation.co.uk/). Perhaps the most popular, particularly among Blogger aficionados, is YACCS (http://rateyourmusic.com/yaccs/), which offers integration with Blogger, support for 15 different languages, and the ability to dig into the design and make your comment page look exactly the way you'd like it to.

In all these cases, you add the comments to your blog's templates by adding special JavaScript code in the head of the document. Then you add a call to that script function from the body, where you'd like the comments link to appear. (YACCS does offer support for non-JavaScript browsers, but the default is JavaScript.) When the comments link is clicked, either a new page is loaded or a new window appears with the comments ready to be read and added to.

Blogger Editing Tools

As mentioned in Chapter 4, support for the Blogger API is something that programmers can add to their own blogging applications, and some of them have. In particular, both Movable Type and pMachine allow you to use one of these third-party blog-editing applications to update your blog. If you're familiar with the bookmarklet concept, then using a third-party application won't seem so strange—even if you're not using Blogger. (Because they're actual standalone applications, each is generally compiled for a specific operating system, so you'll need to get one that matches your computer's OS.) Some of these third-party applications include the following:

- **BlogBuddy (http://blogbuddy.sourceforge.net) for Windows**   Basic, but handy.

- **w.bloggar (http://wbloggar.com)**   Offers a great feature set, including extra support for HTML tags, the ability to preview posts, a find-and-replace feature, and direct support for editing the Blogger templates. It's also well-tested with other servers.

- **iBlog (http://iblog.soapdog.org) for Mac OS X**   Still a preview beta at the time of this writing, iBlog offers support for AppleScript, drag-and-drop text, a search-and-replace feature, and a history feature that makes it possible for you to repost items you've posted in the past. (Currently, iBlog is hard-coded to work with Blogger and doesn't support other Blogger-compatible weblog servers.)

- **BlogApp (http://www.webentourage.com/blogapp.php) for Mac OS X**   Offers basic Blogger-compatible functionality as well as a spell checker and quick access to basic HTML commands.

- **Blognix (http://blognix.sourceforge.net/)**   Offers many of the same Blogger-like features in a graphical client for Linux.

- **Jericho (http://jericho.sourceforge.net/)**   A Java-based offering that can be used in nearly any Java-compatible operating system.

When used with Blogger, most of these tools are very straightforward. But Blogger offers a special application programming interface (the "Blogger API") that the programmers of other blogging applications can take advantage of, too. Some, such as Movable Type, do take advantage of this API, making it possible for you to edit your blog using a Blogger tool. All you need to know is the proper way to access the API—you'll need to look for XML-RPC support in the blogging application. For instance, Movable Type makes this interface available via the script mt-xmlrpc.cgi. So, if you're using Movable Type and you have a Blogger-compatible editing application that enables you to choose a new location for your XML-RPC support, you can enter the URL to that mt-xmlrpc.cgi (for example: http://www.*yoursite*.com/cgi-bin/mt-xmlrpc.cgi) and then your editing software can log in to the MT blog as if it were Blogger. In pMachine, simply point to the file at http://www.*yoursite*.com/*pm*/xmlrpc/pmserver.php (where *pm* is the name of the directory you created and configured for your pMachine scripts).

NOTE *The Blogger API, because it was written for Blogger, is actually a touch limited. Although most blog software allows you to have titles and blurbs and so on, Blogger entries are usually just text and markup. So, if you're using a Blogger application with other software, you'll generally add these special fields using special HTML-like tags, such as <title>More News From Abroad</title>, and so on. See your blog software's documentation for details.*

More...

As if sparkling content and amazing personality weren't enough, this chapter introduced you to a number of different ways to improve your blog by adding community features. You learned how to add a contact e-mail address, a discussion forum, a mailing list, a poll or survey, and a photoblog. Also discussed were some of the third-party Blogger-compatible applications that can be used to update any weblog that supports the XML-RPC interface.

In the last section of the book, we'll take a look at two important topics. Chapter 10 covers publicizing your weblog (in a uniquely "bloggish" way), and Chapter 11 offers ideas for using your blog in an organizational or business setting.

9

M	T	W	T	F	S		S	M	T	W	T	F	S		S	M	T	W	T	F	S		S	M	T	W	T	F	S
		1	2	3	4					1	2	3	4					1	2	3	4					1	2	3	4
6	7	8	9	10	11		5	6	7	8	9	10	11		5	6	7	8	9	10	11		5	6	7	8	9	10	11
13	14	15	16	17	18		12	13	14	15	16	17	18		12	13	14	15	16	17	18		12	13	14	15	16	17	18
20	21	22	23	24	25		19	20	21	22	23	24	25		19	20	21	22	23	24	25		19	20	21	22	23	24	25
27	28	29	30	31			26	27	28	29	30	31			26	27	28	29	30	31			26	27	28	29	30	31	

Part IV

Publicity and Possibilities

Chapter 10   Publicizing Your Weblog Site
Chapter 11   Using Weblogs in Organizations

	T	W	T	F	S		S	M	T	W	T	F	S		S	M	T	W	T	F	S		S	M	T	W	T	F	S
		1	2	3	4				1	2	3	4					1	2	3	4					1	2	3	4
	7	8	9	10	11		5	6	7	8	9	10	11		5	6	7	8	9	10	11		5	6	7	8	9	10	11
	14	15	16	17	18		12	13	14	15	16	17	18		12	13	14	15	16	17	18		12	13	14	15	16	17	18
	21	22	23	24	25		19	20	21	22	23	24	25		19	20	21	22	23	24	25		19	20	21	22	23	24	25
	28	29	30	31			26	27	28	29	30	31			26	27	28	29	30	31			26	27	28	29	30	31	

Chapter 10

Publicizing Your Weblog Site

In this chapter:

- Win readers and influence people
- Join weblog directories
- Join webrings and banner swaps
- Submit to search engines
- Syndicate and be syndicated
- Build a mailing list
- Sidebar: Get the Media Interested

You've got your site up and you're posting like a mad dog (were a mad dog something or someone who felt inclined to post to a weblog a lot). I mean tons. You've got stuff to say, you're saying it, you're linking to it…and nobody seems to care. You're not getting comments or e-mail messages, and you're not seeing the page counter tick over the way it should. What can you do?

Publicize. You need to get out there and let people know that your site exists, let them know that you're kicking and screaming, and that you've got things to say. I'm not telling you to get in people's faces about it or to "go Hollywood" all of the sudden and start calling the press. And I'm not going to sell you a $59 series of e-books outlining winning strategies for driving more traffic to your blog. (Although, come to think of it, that's not a bad idea.) It so happens there are some perfectly reasonable, blog-savvy ways to start generating traffic and getting loyal readers. That's what I'll cover in this chapter—ways to get noticed, get involved, and, eventually, get some folks visiting your site (hopefully on a regular basis).

How to Be Seen

The key to getting people to your site is to let them know about it. There are millions and millions of websites out there. Millions. Maybe even *gagillions*.

Let's say for the sake of argument that you're an interesting person. (Not your blog—I mean the actual *you*.) How do *I* know that you're interesting? I don't know you. You live in a different place. We've probably never met. It's highly unlikely that we'll have a phone conversation soon.

It's the same thing on the Web. It's excruciatingly unlikely that thousands or millions of people will stumble upon your blog by accident—unless your site happens to have an address that is an easy typo away from an extremely popular site (such as microsift.com or something. Of course, somebody already has that one). Put your blog there and then see if anyone reads it.

NOTE   *That's not to say you can't make it more likely that people will happen upon your site by accident. We'll discuss that later in the section "Get Listed and Searched."*

If having a knockoff domain name doesn't work, the solution is going to have to go beyond "If you build it, they will come." You'll need to get out there and let people know you've built a site. Fortunately, you can do that in a number of ways without being cheesy, irritating, or making up annoying sales copy. You'll publicize your site in three ways:

- By participating in the weblogging community and in other web-based communities

- By getting listed in various places

- By sharing headlines with others

We'll cover these three different approaches to publicizing your site, plus I'll toss in some ideas along the way, including a look at how to try to get the media interested in your blog, if that's appropriate.

> TIP
>
> *Here's a neat trick suggested by Rick Ellis, our technical reviewer: Once you get involved in the blogging community, you can become famous by doing something in the interest of the blogging community. Like what? Create quizzes (http://www.wannabegirl.org/quiz/), give awards (http://www.fairvue.com/?feature=awards2002), or develop a blog-related expertise and post about it (http://diveintoaccessibility.org/). If you can render bloggers a service, it's probably a good way to get on their link lists.*

10

The Art of Conversation

As has been mentioned previously, there's a spectrum of types of weblogs, with the link-heavy "editorial" weblog on one end of the spectrum and the personal, diary-like weblog on the other end. Most blogs end up somewhere in the middle, cheating their way toward one side or the other. A news junkie may focus entirely on linking to stories, or she may comment on them or start to offer personal anecdotes that relate to the headlines, thus sliding along the spectrum. A diarist might write in his blog as if speaking to his psychiatrist, but eventually a link or two to daily events might creep in. A particular news story will catch his eye and he'll talk about it, perhaps in a very personal way.

Knowing this about the spectrum, you can decide where your blog falls and then try to consider how, exactly, to "promote" the site by letting others know about it. By promotion, I don't mean a throaty PR dame calling "all the right people" at the New York tabloids, and I don't mean sending out thousands of spam e-mail messages or posting "Come See My Blog" messages on other sites' discussion forums. I mean looking at the idea from a community point of view. Identify the blogging community (or any topic-focused web community) you want to participate in and then go about making yourself known in that community. You'll do that by participating.

Want bulleted points? Here are some tips to consider when you're ready to get busy and get people to gravitate to your blog:

- **Learn your audience.**   Find yourself on the spectrum described previously and then look for similar sites. Note the sites that bloggers put in their "favorite links" sections, and notice the other blogs and sites they link to in their entries. Visit all those sites and try to get a sense of whether you fit in. If your site is about the inner turmoil you feel over losing a job or moving to a different city, it's unlikely that a fast-blogging "weird news" site is the right place to find appreciative readers. When you find some sites that do offer some synergy, look to see what *webrings* (discussed in the next section) these bloggers belong to or what services or tools they use for their sites. You'll eventually find sites that strike a chord of common interests or goals with your blog.

- **Lurk.**   The term *lurk* is used throughout the online world to suggest "reading without chiming in"—if it were a conversation, you'd be listening. When you find a site that resonates with you—it seems to offer similar content, a similar voice, or a shared message—then the first thing to do is *read*. The idea is to simply page through the bulk of a site that interests you—read the comments, read the archives, read the About page, read the Frequently Asked Questions document, if there is one. This is how you'll get to know the people who participate, the people who run the blog, and so on. You'll also get a sense of the norms of this particular little community. Are they open to new people? What's the best way to approach them? Who are the leaders?

- **Surf.**   One of the benefits of lurking is that you'll tend to spend more time reading other people's comments. Therefore, you'll encounter more comments than you might if you were more focused on writing your own. Don't just read what people are talking about but click the links to their sites as well. (Most blogging software will make the name of the author of a post or comment into either an e-mail address or a hyperlink to their home page or site. Click the link to see what sort of site that person has put together.) Doing so will help you learn more about the dynamics of the communities that you find interesting and the people in them.

Once you've found some blogs that interest you and you've gotten a sense of the people who participate in them as well as the words being said, you'll naturally be led to participate in the conversation. I say *naturally* because if your first inclination is to rush to a site that seems a lot like your site and your first post is something along the line of "Yup! That's exactly what I said here at my blog," then you may not get the results you were hoping for. You might jostle the regulars.

Instead, lurk, read and, when you're comfortable, comment on posts and diligently fill in your URL when the blogging software requests it. Your comment will be linked to your name, and your name will be linked to your blog. Slowly, people will find you interesting and be ready to learn more about you. As you participate in the community, more people will visit and read your site— eventually, some may even start to refer to your entries, linking back to your blog. Some may put you on their "hot links" list. Just remember that at the same time you're doing all this participating, you also need to be keeping up your blog with constant and interesting content, too.

On Being a Joiner

Once you've done some lurking and have begun to stake out a set of favorite sites to call your personal "community," you should look around for resources that help others find that same community. After all, it may have been easy for you to find all these great sites, because they were linking to one another—maybe there's one "central" site where everyone seems to congregate, or perhaps there's a site that's actually devoted to linking to entries and sites on particular topics. (In one of the online communities I participate in, the Macintosh computing community, the site http://www.macsurfer.com/ serves as an important jumping-off point for news stories, opinion, and all sorts of daily links to Mac-related content.) That site may be a registry, a webring, or something less formal—just the main site people tend to gravitate toward.

10

NOTE   *I don't mean to suggest, by using words like "community" that these things are always easy to pin down. For instance, there isn't one single "Macintosh computing community" that all such sites participate in. I only mean that, after surfing for a while, you'll start to get a sense of what blogs seem linked to other blogs and so on, forming a community or clique of some sort.*

Get Thee to a Registry

One place to start is listing yourself in directory sites that cater to blogging. For instance, the Globe of Blogs (http://www.globeofblogs.com/) is a site where thousands of blogs are organized by author, title, topic, birthday, gender, and location. Registration is a little involved (after all, they need to know your name, blog's name, topics, birthday, and so on), but it's definitely an opportunity to experience the occasional synergy when a reader is clipping through the Globe of Blogs for something interesting and comes across your site.

BlogTree (http://www.blogtree.com) is a fun take on the registry concept—it's a genealogy of blog relationships. It works like this: You sign up on the site and tell the site who your blog's "parents" are, meaning the blogs that inspired you to create your blog. As more and more people register, you can start to see the relationships between the blogs, which can also help you to find blogs that might interest you. It also gives you a sense of the popularity and "pedigree" of certain blogs, as the site puts it—some of the most popular sites have many siblings and children, suggesting they've influenced many others. It's a cool concept.

The Truth Laid Bear (http://www.truthlaidbear.com/ecosystem.shtml) includes the Ecosphere page, which compares its member sites against one another to see who has the most links, the fewest links, and what sites are doing the most linking to other sites. It isn't updated as automatically as Blogging Ecosystem (http://www.myelin.co.nz/ecosystem/), which does the same thing but (apparently) in real time. If you're a prolific linker (or link*ee*), you should add your sites to these directories and see whether you can move up in the list.

Other blog-focused registries include the following:

- The Portal at Uncorked.org (http://uncorked.org/portal.html)

- The Blog Portal (http://www.eatonweb.com/portal)

- BlogDex (http://blogdex.media.mit.edu)

- Boing-Boing (http://www.boingboing.net)

For more, check out http://www.lights.com/weblogs/directories.html for a list of blogging directories and registries.

Ring-a-Ding-Ding

One way to make random visits to your blog a bit more likely is to join a *webring* or two. Webrings are groupings of websites, generally using a common URL to list themselves, as well as special code that appears on each participating page to help a web visitor move from one site in the ring to the next, or perhaps to a random site that is part of the ring. Look around on the pages of blogs you like to see whether they belong to any webrings.

EVERYTHING ELSE

RINGS
« × Blog×Philes × »
« ? greyLOGS # »

In the blogging world, being part of a ring usually doesn't cost anything, although it may require approval. When you identify a webring that makes sense for your site and appears to be active and interesting, go ahead and apply for membership. If you get in, make sure you implement the code for the webring and do what you can to encourage your visitors to check out the other members of the webring. (If you feel you don't like or appreciate the other members' sites, that's an indication you're in the wrong ring.)

Although a number of rings are specifically for blogging sites (see http://www.xanga.com/blogrings/default.asp and http://www.blogphiles.com/webring.shtml) and blogging tools—the GreyLOGS (http://grey.glory-box.com/), MT Ring (http://www.brookelyn.org/mtring/), MT Blog Ring (http://www.kiwinessie.net/rings/mtblog/), and the pMachine ring (http://pmachine.phpdiva.com/ring.php)—you can also look for webrings (using http://www.ringsurf.com/, for example) that cover topic areas and interests related to your blog so as to get some traffic from non-blog sites as well as blog sites.

Wander-Lust (http://www.wander-lust.com/) sort of fits the webring category, but this interesting site is really quite a bit more than that, because it serves as both a content-aggregating site and a random webring. When you join and add the Wander-Lust button to your site, you allow visitors to click that button and be taken to other blogs at random. Wander-Lust also posts links to member sites and culls content from them, posting blurbs on the front page.

Get Listed and Searched

Early in your site's life you might want to head to the major search engines and get yourself signed up. Doing so lets those engines know that you're out here. Eventually, they'll send a *bot* (a robot script) your way to check out your site and attempt to catalog it. This can actually be a slight advantage for sites that offer published pages (those, such as Blogger and Movable Type, that don't build pages dynamically), although some of the more advanced search engines, such as Google and Alltheweb.com, handle both kinds of blogs pretty well.

To sign up, head to the site of the search engine in question and look for a link for the submission. Google, for instance, actually uses the Open Directory Project for its listings, and you can add your site directly (http://dmoz.org/add.html). To add a site to Alltheweb.com, visit http://www.alltheweb.com/add_url.php. Use http://www.altavista.com/addurl to submit to AltaVista. For MSN, head to http://search.msn.com/ and click the Submit a Web Site link.

For Yahoo! (http://docs.yahoo.com/info/suggest/) the process is fairly simple: Find the area of the Yahoo! directory where you'd like your site to appear; then find and click the Suggest a Site link, which generally appears at the bottom of these pages. If you want to be added to Yahoo!'s Weblog listing page, it's at the unwieldy URL of http://dir.yahoo.com/Social_Science/Communications/ Writing/Journals_and_Diaries/Online_Journals_and_Diaries/Web_Logs/. You should also consider heading to topic areas relevant to your blog and attempting to get listed there, if it makes sense (particularly for hobbyist and professional-oriented blogs).

Another interesting option is DayPop, which is something like a weblog registry, but it also serves as a weblog and general news search engine. It's popular among many bloggers, partly because it's fairly easy to add to your site—if you'd like a DayPop search box on your index page, for instance. In any case, it's a good idea to add your site (http://www.daypop.com/submit.htm), especially if you cover any news or current events in your blog.

Once you've submitted your site to a directory or two, you've got another priority. You need to dig into your HTML templates and add some code—called *metadata*—that the search engine's bots will find useful. Metadata means "data about data." In this particular instance, it means using a special HTML element so that you can suggest important items to the search engines, such as keywords for your site and a description.

Inside the head section of your document, add the following <meta> elements:

```
<head>
<title>your site's title</title>
<meta name="keywords" content="blog, news, libertarian, democrat,
green party, republican, movies, books, Star Wars" />
<meta name="description" content="A weblog that covers news,
politics, current events and, of course, science fiction." />
</head>
```

The name attributes and values should be formatted exactly as shown, but the content attributes are yours for the changing. With these elements added, you should republish your website (or at least your index page) if your blogging software requires it. Now, you'll find that many search engines will pick these items up (over time) and use them to help categorize and describe your site.

Want to learn more than you ever need to know about search engines? Head to http://www.searchenginewatch.com/, where you can read articles on how to get into search engines, how they work, and more. Wondering what the most popular search engines are? See http://www.searchenginewatch.com/ reports/netratings.html, where they regularly track the leaders.

Link and Ping

You can begin to see from this discussion why tools such as Movable Type's TrackBack feature, discussed in Chapter 6, are a good idea. In the case of TrackBack, it only works for Movable Type blogs, but it works in a very *bloggish* way—by linking between blogs to show threads of discussion or argument. Consider how this could be helpful for your new blog: not only are you able to comment on other sites' entries and link to them, but you can have them automatically link *back* to your blog ("track back" to it). Therefore, you're likely to generate a few visitors from that link. In a way, it's an approved method of piggybacking off of popular blogs, and one that isn't terribly intrusive. (After all, even if I have a hugely popular site I'm not going to be terribly upset to see that my TrackBack feature is being used a lot.)

Aside from the TrackBack approach, you have two similar methods to consider for generating traffic and creating relationships between blogs. The first is linking to other sites. You've seen in each of the chapters how to accomplish this for the particular blogging software, but you might be interested in a more automated solution. Blogrolling.com (www.blogrolling.com) is that solution, and it's incredibly popular.

Blogrolling gives you a central location for managing your links and some interesting tools to do it with. You register, log in, and create your *blogroll*, where links to other blogs or sites will be stored. Now, you can add links in one of two ways. The first way is to simply type the links into your blogroll's entry page, giving a title, description, and the URL. Blogroll will put the links together for you automatically and help you manage them. I can tell you're underwhelmed.

The other way is the cool one. With your blogroll created, you can add a bookmarklet by dragging the link up to your Favorites toolbar in your browser. Now, as you're surfing and reading blogs, if you find one that interests you, click the bookmarklet. A window appears in which you can quickly edit the essentials

10

of this link. Edit to taste and then click the Add Link button. The link is added to your blogroll, with no hand-coding on your part. Now that's cool.

Back on the Blogrolling site, you can click the Get Code link to access the code for your blogroll, which you then paste into your blog's template. (You can paste it in pretty much the same place where you would manually type in links for display on your index or other pages.) When the code has been pasted, republish your site (if appropriate). The Blogroll list of links should appear.

When it's this easy to add them, you'll start to recognize that the links on your blog's index not only benefit your readers, but you, too. (When I have to physically edit the template to add the links, it feels more like I'm doing it for presentation, not for my own convenience.) Once you've got the code published as part of your site, you don't have to edit HTML or republish in order to show new links. Just keep surfing and adding to your blogroll. You can return to the site to delete links, if necessary, as well as to set preferences for your blogroll. Also, when you're logged into the Blogrolling site, look for a link that allows you to back up the list, which is a good idea to do periodically. Just copy the links to a text file and store them somewhere so you can get at them when necessary.

TIP   *The author of Blogrolling, Jason DeFillippo, accepts donations on his site, in exchange for which you can get even better service. It's definitely worth considering a donation if you use the service, if only to help keep it around.*

The other trick to getting more hits to your site is to *ping* websites (send a quick message) to let them know when you've updated your site. The granddaddy of ping sites is Weblogs.com. Using Radio Userland, Movable Type, pMachine, and others, you can set your software to send a message to Weblogs.com whenever you change your site. That ping is noted, and the URL to your index is linked on Weblogs.com (see Figure 10-1). Of course, the site gets a lot of pings, so your link will scroll down and off the page relatively quickly, but it's still a way to get a few hits and some publicity, especially if you update often and want *someone* to know about it.

10

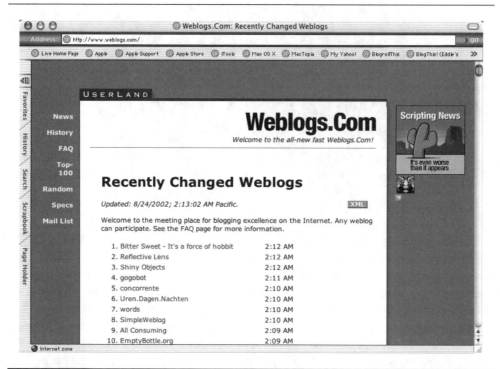

FIGURE 10-1   Weblogs.com accepts pings from weblogs around the world and posts their URLs when they are updated.

So how do you ping Weblogs.com? It may be built in to your software. Radio Userland does it by default, unless you turn the option off in the preferences. Movable Type offers the option on Blog Config's Preferences screen. Note that you can also ping the Recently Updated list that appears on Movable Type's homepage, but only if you have contributed a donation for the software and received a Recently Updated key, which you also input on the Preferences screen.

pMachine lets you turn on pinging in each weblog's preferences. You also have the option of specifying the name of your blog as you want it to appear at Weblogs.com. (If you have pMachine Pro and multiple weblogs, you can set up Weblogs.com pinging individually for each.)

Blogger doesn't ping Weblogs.com, but it does offer you the option of making your blog public or private in its settings. A public blog shows up in Blogger.com's own Fresh Blogs listing and in the Blogger directory; a private blog does not. You will find, also, that many third-party Blogger API tools (such as w.Bloggar and others mentioned in Chapter 8) will enable you to ping Weblogs.com. The fact that these tools can update any weblog that implements the Blogger API means you can use them to write blog entries and ping Weblogs.com under a variety of circumstances.

> **NOTE** *If you want to update Weblogs.com manually (for instance, your site doesn't have a Weblogs.com feature), then use the form at http://newhome.weblogs.com/pingSiteForm on the Web.*

Weblogs.com is useful in other ways, aside from simply listing your site's changes for a few minutes. For instance, Blogrolling, discussed earlier, can check submissions to Weblog.com and note which of the blogs you link to have been updated recently. Also, Weblogs.com is posted as XML, which can be used to display the links as headlines on your own blog—if your software supports XML syndication, discussed next.

Headline Syndication

One of the most universal methods that blogging software uses to publicize sites is to offer RSS (*Rich Site Summary* or *Really Simple Syndication*, depending on who you ask) headline feeds that others can "syndicate" (place on their own site), thus linking back to the originating site.

Many of the blogging software solutions automatically offer this XML page to anyone who wants it. As you're surfing (or even as you're looking at your own site) note the link or image that users can click to see the syndicated page. Figure 10-2 shows an RSS page as viewed by a web browser (which, of course, isn't something you'd typically find useful).

> **NOTE** *These pages are good for more than putting someone else's headlines on your site. The standard format (usually RSS 0.91, but more recent versions of RSS are becoming popular) makes it possible for other devices, sites, and web applications to read the headlines and offer links to the stories. RSS feeds provide one way to get headlines for Palm OS handhelds and cell phones, as well as for personal-portal desktop applications that aggregate interesting content in the way that Yahoo! and Netscape.com do.*

XML is the Extensible Markup Language—a language in which other markup languages can be created. (One such creation is XHTML, which is HTML *recast* to conform to XML syntax and rules.) In this case, XML is the basis of RSS, which is simply a standard way to display summaries of websites. Once the specification is created and agreed upon, developers are free to use the new "language" in whatever way seems to fit their needs. That's what's going on with RSS—blogging software programmers have noted its usefulness and are rolling it into the software.

NOTE   *As you can see in Figure 10-2, the typical RSS page is actually pretty simple. RSS is just a basic specification that includes XML tags for the title (<title>), link (<link>), body (<description>), and a few other elements that make up the basics of each of your weblog's entries. XML tags are similar to HTML tags, so it's actually pretty easy to hand-code an RSS page if you'd like.*

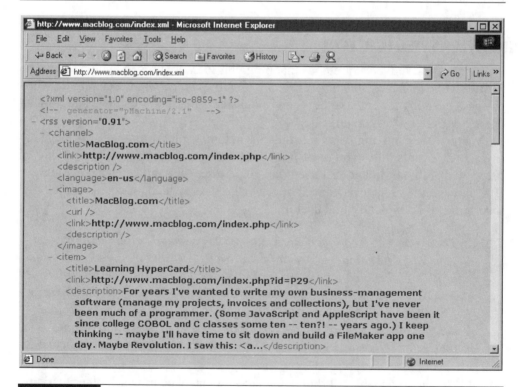

FIGURE 10-2   Here's what an RSS page looks like if you view it in a web browser.

Publish Your Feed

Publishing your RSS feed is usually easy and automatic—by default, Blogger, Movable Type, pMachine, and Radio Userland all have an RSS feed link that appears on the page automatically. Someone who wants to syndicate your headlines can do so simply by clicking the XML or RSS link on your index page to figure out the correct URL. And within your blogging software, you can generally dig into the template area and change the RSS template, if desired. (For instance, you might want it to show a shorter "description" after the headline than is typical.)

Where "automatic" breaks down a little bit is in the version that your software uses—RSS 1.0 is the latest standard, but it differs considerably from 0.91, which is often used as the de facto standard because it has been around longer and is implemented widely. Movable Type, for instance, offers two different RSS templates: a 1.0 and a 0.91 option. By default, the 1.0 feed is posted, but you can manually change that by editing your blog index's template.

Read Feeds

So what does one do with these feeds once they're created? Well, you can sit back and hope others will syndicate your headlines, which they may in fact do. As mentioned, a number of applications exist to read syndicated headlines, such as Radio Userland (see Chapter 4), News is Free (http://www.newsisfree.com/), FeedReader for Windows (http://www.feedreader.com/), AmphetaDesk for Windows (http://www.disobey.com/amphetadesk/), Slashdock for Mac OS X (http://homepage.mac.com/stas/slashdock.html), and many others.

Using these applications, you can subscribe to your favorite blogs and news sites, view them all in one interface, and then quickly see their headlines and blurbs. Then you can make the decision to click a story that interests you.

If you'd like an online way to view and manage your favorite blog headlines, try BlogHog (http://www.bloghog.com/). BlogHog follows the most popular blogs that it has registered, making it easy to quickly check their headlines. You can also personalize the service so that headlines show up for your personal favorite blogs (see Figure 10-3).

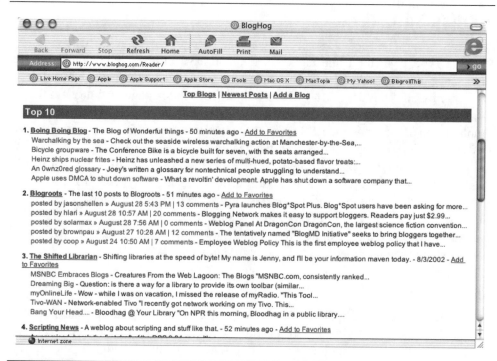

FIGURE 10-3   BlogHog can track headlines on multiple blogs at once, giving you the opportunity to scan stories to decide what to read.

> **TIP**
>
> *According to a tip on BlogHog, you can make your site friendlier to these headline readers by adding the following to the head of your index template: <link rel="alternate" type="application/rss+xml" title="RSS" href="url_to_your_RSS_file" />. In the href attribute, enter the URL to your RSS feed's file (for example, http://www.yourblogsite.com/index.xml) so that headline software can automatically launch that file instead of asking the user to locate the proper RSS page.*

Publish Others' Feeds

So you've seen how to read the headlines of other people's sites. But what about adding those headlines to your own page? At the time of this writing, only pMachine Pro offers the built-in ability to place other people's feeds on your website. (Radio Userland offers very sophisticated RSS tools, including the News Aggregator, which enables you to subscribe to other sites' headline feeds, read them from within the Radio tool, and post individual stories to your site for comments. It doesn't, however, help you post the actual headlines from other sites on your own blog—for instance, in a "headlines" column on your index page—in the same way that pMachine does.)

With pMachine Pro, you begin by creating and editing an RSS template by clicking the RSS Parser Template link in the Admin section. Enter a name for the template and click Create New. The new template is added to the template list; click the Edit button in that template's row in order to edit it. As you'll see, the template and available template variables are pretty basic.

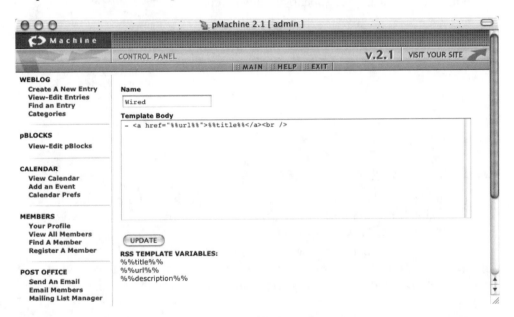

You might consider deleting the description variable, for instance, if you only want to show headlines. In any case, make your changes and click Update.

Now, armed with the name of this template and the URL to the RSS feed you want to add, you'll need to edit an HTML template page (or create a new HTML template page) for the feed to appear. (If you add the RSS headlines tag to your pMachine index page, it will conform to the division or table elements it's placed in—for instance, if you place the feed in the "menu" area, it will conform to that size.) Here's the tag to add:

```php
<?php show_rss_page("template","RSS_url","n");?>
```

In this case, "template" is the name of the template you just created, "RSS_url" is the URL to the RSS feed page that you want to include, and "n" is the number of headlines you want to show. Here's an example:

```
<?php
show_rss_page("Wired","http://www.wired.com/news_drop/netcenter/net
center.rdf","5");?>
```

With that added, the next time you view your page, you should see the headlines appear, as shown here:

WIRED NEWS

- **Telescope Big as the Eye Can See**
- **Sky's Limit for Telescope Tech**
- Is This One Nation, Under Blog?
- **For Simone, 'Fake' Is Flattery**
- **Palm Handed Suit Over Colors**

Get the Media Interested

All this talk of headlines and news feeds makes one think of the traditional press. Wouldn't it be cool to get your blog written up in the newspaper, weekly alternative, or perhaps even talked about on television? Right now, while blogging is hot and relatively new, probably isn't a bad time to try and make that happen, if you're interested. Here are some suggestions for how to get the traditional press to notice you and your blog and to put both of your names in lights:

- ■ **Talk about blogging.** The best way to get a reporter to write about you is to know a colleague of that reporter. (Knowing the reporter too well might make her *not* write about you because of a potential conflict of interest.) Talk to a reporter or a reporter's colleague about blogging and the future it presents and mention you have an interesting example that you're running. (Try to be more charming than earnest.) She might file it away and bring it up as a story idea in the future or in response to a query from an editor or fellow reporter.

- ■ **Write a press release.** Reporters and magazine writers really do read press releases (or at least glance at them) and will sometimes write about the pitched topic if the story is good enough. The press release should be professional, addressed directly to the editor or writer in question (don't use a generic opener), and should be on topic for that publication. Provide full contact info, including, of course, the blog's URL. Don't e-mail the release if the editor doesn't want you to (call and ask how they like their press releases but *don't* pitch the story on the phone unless asked to), but be sure to follow their instructions on e-mailing attachments if e-mail is okay with them.

- **Pitch a good story.**   The real trick with a press release is to successfully pitch a *story* and not just write up your bio or resume or a bulleted list of your achievements and merits. (Your mom *might* want to read that, but no one else does.) If you can, instead, pitch a good story idea that includes your site (such as "More and more of the DJs in Memphis clubs have their own blogs" and "Investment websites—and particularly investor 'blogs'—are focusing more on ROI in the companies they track"). This way, you're more likely to be read by the reporter. A great release makes the reporter's job easier, even if she ultimately writes about you in a different context.

- **Think small.**   I mean two things by this. First, be willing to focus on smaller, more local publications and media outlets—the smaller they are, the more likely they are to be interested in taking a chance on your story. Second, think small in terms of your expectations—even if the resulting story only has a mention of you and your blog, not a two-page spread exclusively about you, count it a success. It's publicity, and it can be used in the future to show another reporter that you have an interesting and important story.

10

More...

In this chapter we focused on getting your blog a little publicity and, hopefully, getting some readers to visit it. In particular, you read about the different tools and tactics you can take to make your weblog a popular one with thousands of adoring fans clamoring constantly for more. (That's the downside about the Internet—you can rarely hear your fans screaming.) You also read about webrings and blog directories, TalkBack, linking, pinging, and headline syndication.

In the next, and final, chapter, we'll explore some of the more professional and organizational possibilities that blogging presents. If you've got something that needs to be organized, recorded, remembered, or talked through—particularly if the participants are remote and self-directed—then using a blog might be an interesting approach.

M	T	W	T	F	S		S	M	T	W	T	F	S		S	M	T	W	T	F	S		S	M	T	W	T	F	S
		1	2	3	4					1	2	3	4					1	2	3	4					1	2	3	4
6	7	8	9	10	11		5	6	7	8	9	10	11		5	6	7	8	9	10	11		5	6	7	8	9	10	11
13	14	15	16	17	18		12	13	14	15	16	17	18		12	13	14	15	16	17	18		12	13	14	15	16	17	18
20	21	22	23	24	25		19	20	21	22	23	24	25		19	20	21	22	23	24	25		19	20	21	22	23	24	25
27	28	29	30	31			26	27	28	29	30	31			26	27	28	29	30	31			26	27	28	29	30	31	

Chapter 11

Using Weblogs in Organizations

In this chapter:

- ■ Can weblogs be serious?
- ■ Collaborate online
- ■ Blog your customers
- ■ Blogs and nonprofit organizations
- ■ Weblogs for education

Can a weblog be serious business? I think so, at least in many organizations and companies. Although a weblog can't substitute for certain types of interaction—face-to-face conversations, telephone calls, and e-mail messages all have their place—today's weblog software does offer you an opportunity to build and maintain an online, collaborative community website that can be useful in a variety of settings. Blogs can help project team members collaborate, share information, and track their progress, even if team members are all over the country or the world. Blogs can also be quite useful in organizing, both at the grassroots level as well as in more traditional corporate and institutional settings. Also, blogs can be very effective for education, not just for electronic and distance education, but for supporting regular grade school and college classes, as well, not to mention for teacher team-building, college department management, and professional development.

Can Weblogs Be Serious?

Throughout this book, at least in the sections that weren't taken up with procedural stuff, I've pounded home the notion that blogs are an extension of a traditional journaling concept now taken to the Web, thus making for an interesting opportunity to build interactive communities online. A blog presents time-based, searchable nuggets of information and discussion topics, while enabling others to respond to it using reasonably sophisticated tools for communication. Although many use their blogging software to offer personal, emotional, spiritual, or humorous insight (or, sometimes, drivel), it isn't the medium that dictates the type of topics but rather the author.

This means weblogs can be great for organizations—businesses, charitable organizations, political campaigns, and schools. They can be project-specific or ongoing. They can be focused and diligent organizing tools or organic and less-structured discussion tools for brainstorming ideas. They can foster communication in some situations, and they can draw teams of people together—particularly those working from a distance—in ways that might not be as easy with traditional websites, e-mail, phones, and teleconferences. What's more, under different circumstances, blogs can be useful for communicating with your customers as well as with colleagues and employees. If your goals for a business website are similar to those for a personal weblog—you want to create community, promote repeat visitors, and build "stickiness"—a well-executed blog may be the way to do it.

However, having said all that, a weblog can also be the wrong choice for your organization or undertaking, depending on the circumstances. Let's look at the advantages, the drawbacks, and how to decide whether a blog makes sense.

Blog Advantages for Organizations

The weblog is different enough from many of the communication tools used in business and organizations today—such as e-mail, the phone, and static websites—that we should look at its advantages and disadvantages for the organization a bit more closely. Let's consider a few characteristics that weblogs have that can make them useful in an organizational setting:

- **Asynchronous**   Nicholas Negroponte (http://web.media.mit.edu/ ~nicholas/) in the book *Being Digital* defined and discussed the merits of asynchronous communication, meaning simply communication that doesn't require both parties to participate at the same time. It's e-mail versus the telephone; if you write, I can get back to you when I pull my head out of my work and take a break; if you call, I've got to stop at that moment and talk to you (or let your call go to voicemail). Weblogs offer basically the same asynchronous opportunity that e-mail does—you can read the messages posted to it and respond when you get a free moment. Plus, for groups, this is more efficient and less intrusive than something such as a mailing list or an ongoing message with many CC recipients, where messages are broadcast to each user, perhaps many times in a day. With a weblog, you can stop and take in the group's discussion whenever it makes sense for your schedule.

- **Structured**   Another advantage—or, at least, difference—that weblogs have over e-mail is that weblogs offer more hierarchy and structure. A weblog can have an editor (or editors). This person can be a team leader or manager or someone else designated to moderate or facilitate the discussion. The entries themselves give structure to the conversation—an entry starts a topic (or a branch of a topic) and conversation ensues. For instance, a teacher can post lessons or examples on a blog, and a conversation can result from each entry. Unlike e-mail, the entry that started a discussion is easy to reference (it's right there at the top of the page, in most cases), and the structure of the blog messages can help keep conversations on topic. Plus, the time-based nature of the blog can be helpful both in setting

11

priorities and in encouraging the group to let a topic or thread end as others appear and take priority.

■ **Archived**   An immediate advantage over e-mail is that blogging software, by default, effortlessly archives conversations so that they can be accessed at a later date. With the right software, you can also perform keyword searches, thus answering questions such as "What was that idea we had in June about shipping containers?" The archive can also serve as meeting "minutes" or a virtual transcript of the ideas and discussions that the group has had, making it easier to refer back to all the points of an earlier discussion. A blog can serve as a collective memory and may, in some cases, be a big list of things to remember for your group—posts that aren't conversations or brainstorming might instead be sort of "virtual sticky notes" aimed at adding to a body of knowledge with links and ideas that are stored for the group.

> **TIP**   *One day, perhaps soon, a killer app could come along that encourages us to use graphic tablets and pens for computing input. One reason could be to add images and drawings to a collaborative environment such as a blog, particularly if your group deals with visual ideas that need to be knocked around and discussed. You could create the images, optimize them for the Web (if necessary), and link to them or embed them directly in entries and/or replies. Of course, that works for any sort of image, as well as links to other files such as PDFs or Microsoft Office documents.*

■ **Conversational**   Weblogs happen in a more public "space" than e-mail, which can help build toward a conclusion a little more fluidly than an e-mail conversation does. With a blog, you can see what everyone else has said on a given topic, and you can a see a "conversation" unfold where ideas are shared and built upon. For instance, a project leader asks for ideas for a new marketing campaign. The first responses are brainstorming; then later responses take ideas from the first and build on them. ("I like Carol's idea about the billboard, but what if….") The popularity of "quoting" e-mail messages—sometimes to absurd lengths—can suggest the usefulness of being able to remind ourselves of the thread of a conversation as we try to make decisions or reach consensus. The format of a blog is conducive to seeing those threads.

■ **Communal**   The social component is just a guess, but I think the structured, archived nature of a blog creates a sense of community that e-mail doesn't, by being more public and less isolating. In other words, in a blog you may get slightly more polite, thoughtful, and carefully worded responses (particularly in an organizational setting) that can be, nonetheless, off the cuff and informal. I'm not saying that blogs will improve an individual's particularly bad "e-mail" voice, but the public presentation of a blog (again, in an organizational environment) may make the e-mail firebrand think twice about breaking the norms of the community.

These bulleted points show that, as a business tool, the weblog is an evolutionary idea, not a revolutionary one. (Actually, that's true regardless of where the blog is implemented, and regardless of whether it's a personal blog or professional one.) A weblog is a website, so it's similar to any other website, either on the Internet or on organizational intranets. It offers some of the same tools as e-mail, mailing lists, discussion groups, and groupware software.

If there's a particular advantage over those other discussion tools, it's the format and presentation. A weblog makes it a little easier to see the big picture, using a tool—the web browser—that most of the people in your organization have likely conquered and with which they have grown comfortable. People who use weblogs in organizational situations sometimes report that it's easier to get a handle on what everyone else is doing and saying via a blog, particularly compared to e-mail. Many people also report that it's easier to scan a blog with 40 posts, for instance, than it is to read 40 e-mail messages or access 40 posts in an online discussion forum.

Make the Choice

All these issues and advantages don't necessarily make a weblog ideal under all circumstances. For instance, e-mail is better for one-to-one conversations that would clutter a weblog. E-mail or instant messaging is better for scheduling appointments or requesting information from a single person. A regular website (or intranet site) is better for the presentation of static documents—files that can be downloaded, policies, maps, white papers, assignments, syllabi, sales literature, and so on. And the similarities between a weblog and a web-based discussion group can't be denied—if you find a particular piece of discussion software better suited to your organization's goals, then by all means use it. The difference between weblogs and discussion forums is mostly the presentation and the features of the software.

11

That said, the major advantage that weblogs have over discussion forums in organizational settings is the structure—each entry, in effect, has an author who "owns" that entry. The way a blog works, the initial entry appears higher in the hierarchy than the follow-ups, because you read the originating entry on the index page of the blog. For whatever it's worth, that makes the initial post appear to drive the topic of the comments that follow. In a discussion group, the first poster chooses the topic and starts the thread, but it's a slightly more democratic presentation, where follow-up posts basically have equal footing. Aside from that difference, the decision between a blog or a forum becomes a question of the tools available and the preferences your team expresses. Some blogging software offers better tools for aggregating news, linking to other sites, or dealing with multimedia. In other cases, the look and feel of a blog may just sit better with your group.

NOTE   *You may find that you get less resistance from colleagues when implementing a weblog versus a discussion forum, if only because some people are less familiar with online discussion areas than they would be with a weblog, which is just a slight twist on a typical website.*

And then there's the final caveat: meeting in person is still the easiest way to share an idea by drawing it on a paper napkin. Metaphorically, I mean it's important not to try to make the tool fit the communication, particularly if it ends up longer and less efficient to use a weblog (or any other technology) when a meeting, coffee break, or transatlantic flight is the most efficient solution. And, yes, you can still scan the napkin into a computer file and post it on the blog, if necessary.

None of this is to say that implementing a weblog will be easy. You may also find that the less technology-literate (or is it technology-*obsessed*) the colleague is, the more resistance he might have to implementing a blog to facilitate group communications. People may resist the switch from e-mail even if a blog is a better choice because they're comfortable with their e-mail program; they may also not want to have to take the time to decide when to make a blog entry versus when to send an e-mail. Some may also appreciate the sense of accomplishment that comes from sending broadcast e-mails or one-way directives. Others may just like sitting in front of their e-mail program reading replies. Fortunately, some blogging software allows for posts by e-mail (Userland-based sites in particular), which could help overcome this objection, as will the popularity of, and hence more familiarity with, weblogs.

Ideas for Organizational Blogs

Decided to try a blog for your business or organization? The next step is to think about the approach to take and to determine how to implement your blog. The decision you make will depend on the people you're trying to reach and the task you're trying to accomplish. Let's look at some of those potential areas of focus in the rest of this chapter.

Store and Share Knowledge

One reason larger organizations seem to have an interest in blogging software is the same reason many companies have been using discussion forums and collaborative software such as Lotus Notes for a quite a while—the opportunity to put the company's ideas, its nuggets of intellectual capital, into a database and archive them. Blogging software is just another option for doing that. It's appealing because the paradigm of the Web is one that a lot of people understand quickly, and blogging software is reasonably inexpensive to own and operate.

In a small group—made up of marketing creatives, product-development folks, or a sales team, for example—you might encourage blogging to *capture* ideas. If someone has a stray thought that they think might be useful to others on the team, they can post it on the blog. It might be nothing, or it might *seem* like nothing but become important quite a bit later. In many cases, the idea will start a conversation, or at least some brainstorming to see whether it's worth using or analyzing further or whether it can be used in conjunction with other ideas and synthesized into something useful.

In fact, a blog is particularly handy if the idea or knowledge being captured for your organization's use is something that's already on the Web. This isn't requisite, but if you use the blog as a repository for hyperlinks to sites that you think your team should see, you're using the tool to its fullest. Aggregating news in this way can be handy because it gives you a central place for it; you can make sure the members of your team are aware of it and you have a forum for discussing it.

In additional, there's the advantage that you can archive that knowledge—with most blogging tools you can access posts archived by week or month (depending on your preference settings) and search for information by keyword. It's reasonably easy to dig back into this collective memory and pull out an important nugget, which is difficult to say for e-mail, unless you diligently store and categorize it. Granted, you could do a lot of this with online discussion forums, although most discussion forums tend to be organized by topic, not by timestamp, and the learning curve that a discussion forum requires versus using a web-based interface

11

might keep some users from searching a discussion forum as readily as they might a weblog with a Search entry box on the index page.

Collaborate Online

A blog can be a strong tool for collaborating online, particularly (but not exclusively) if you work with people in different locations. Let me give a hypothetical example that's close to home—a blog to help create a computer book. As you'll see, the scenario could be applicable to many other project collaborations where a blog could shine (see Figure 11-1).

I've never used a weblog on a book project, but I may lobby for it on the next book I write. I'm beginning to see how a project-based weblog could work very

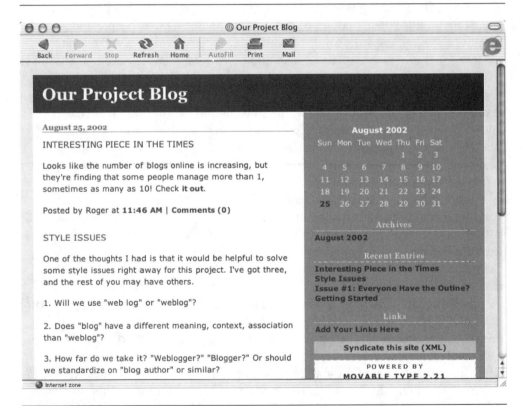

FIGURE 11-1   Here's a fictitious project blog in its earliest stages. It took about five minutes to create the new blog (on an existing site with MT installed) and add the project members as authors.

well to bring the different players in a book's production to the same place to share thoughts, ideas, and schedules. Putting together a book like this one requires the direct participation of six to ten people, usually a mix of corporate employees with onsite offices, salaried telecommuters, and freelance contractors. Often the different parties are distributed across time zones, occasionally three or four hours apart—perhaps even more, and the distribution might change if members of the team are traveling.

In my direct experience, and perhaps yours as well, this sort of distributed project is increasingly common, both in the book industry and in many other creative and professional fields. I've been writing computer books for about ten years, and over that time I've seen a marked increase in freelance and contract employees who collaborate on these projects from their home offices, from different cities, and in various time zones. Everyone has different schedules, vacations, family emergencies, and other projects to consider.

For such distributed projects (and for many projects where all the participants *do* meet, but also spend a lot of time online) a weblog can make a lot of sense. Consider the items that could be effectively communicated in the blog:

- **News and resources**   While working on a book, an editor might want to bring an article to the attention of the author and others, or a technical editor may find some important online resources for research. So, they post a blog entry and links using a bookmarklet set up for that purpose.

- **Directives**   A blog entry could include a new schedule, outline, or other missive that the corporate workers need to communicate to the contractors. Using a blog, the presentation can be brief and informal but still documented and archived. You could even implement a rule that people should comment on certain types of messages to confirm that they've seen them (each comment would automatically include the date and time, thanks to the software).

- **Questions and brainstorming**   Questions—for the author, managers, or technical consultants—can be posted to the blog if the answers will be helpful to the entire group. Individual scheduling and private communication still happen in e-mail, but questions such as "Does anyone think there's a better way to structure Chapter 19?" or "What's the appropriate style— 'web log' or 'weblog'?" would work well in this collaborative environment, because the members can self-select the information they need to know or that they care to respond to. (That means no more "Argh! I need to forward all these e-mails to Bob because I keep forgetting he should know this!" moments.)

11

- **Group scheduling and management**   Although you'll likely use more formal tools for scheduling (recognizing that some blogging tools, such as pMachine Pro, actually offer an events calendar), you can use the blog to discuss scheduling issues and conflicts and to redirect workflow on a more intimate basis. For example: "Hey, all, we need to get more chapters into production. Instead of first drafts, let's focus on finalizing the chapters that are already copyedited for the next few days." The blog can also be used to discuss holidays, vacations, trips, and conferences that might affect the project's schedule or flow.

- **Submissions**   Depending on the technology available, you may be able to use the blog (instead of e-mail attachments or FTP sites) for uploading important components of the project, particularly if more than one member of the group needs access to them. In our example, it would be book chapters and the graphics for each chapter. If they're uploaded to a central place, the various editors who need to work with the files could have access to them on their own time instead of receiving large e-mail attachments.

- **Group hugs**   The blog may be one way to build a little morale and help to get team members a little more familiar with one another. The occasional post can be congratulations for reaching a milestone, a declaration of solidarity, encouragement in the face of deadlines, or a link to a cute cartoon that hits the mark.

As you can see, these are issues that I'm close to, but you'll find that they're applicable to many different situations where group collaboration could really shine with a weblog component. If you can get all members to participate and collaborate, a weblog can significantly augment e-mail while building a small sense of community for the duration of your project.

NOTE   *Worried about having this project online? You should set up two levels of security—username and password for each author and a username and password for the blog's public directory online. If you host the blog on a corporate server, your IT department should be able to help you figure out how to assign a password to the directory where the blog resides. Even inexpensive web hosts tend to offer easy password protection for individual directory hierarchies. Sign in to your web-hosting account's control panel and look for a password-protection option or ask your IPP for help.*

Reach Customers

If you run a small business and you have the dedication and wherewithal to keep it up, a blog may be a great way to gain and retain customers. I say this with caution, however, because I think you should only take on a blog if you feel it's something that you can maintain and/or your product or service is something that will fly in a collaborative atmosphere. An empty blog or a blog filled with meaningless filler material would be more damaging to a consumer-oriented website than well-written static materials.

Therefore, when considering a blog, stop to think about what you—and your customers—have to say and whether it fits the model. If you do have enough to say and you're willing to be honest, "real," and perhaps a little personal and candid, I think a blog can help the small businessperson build a loyal customer base.

Here are some businesses and professionals who might benefit from a blog that reaches out to customers:

- **Real estate agents and property/resort managers**   If you really love your neighborhood or properties, then a blog might work for you. By keeping up with local news in a neighborly way, you might sell your regular readers on the area. You could also add new listings to the blog as you get them, although I'd also offer a database or link to your regional listing service for easy searching. If you can be honest in your blog, I'd encourage it. In other words, avoid PR drivel. For instance, don't post a blog entry with canned copy from your professional association about "how to get a mortgage" or "ten inspection tips everyone should know." Put these in your static pages and link to them. In the blog, focus on this week's current mortgage rates, special offers, open houses, and events in the neighborhood.

- **Bars, music venues, and restaurants**   Again, you need news to do this. If you own a bar or restaurant that offers live entertainment, group functions, or community activities, you may be blogger material. As the owner, chef, or manager, post about your bands, your specials, new foods you want to experiment with, or even get a little personal. If you have fun with it, you might build a following of customers who feel they know you and want to be loyal to your business.

- **Media members, musicians, and artists**   Anyone who people want to get closer to or learn more about should consider a blog, particularly

11

members of the media, who are already known for expressing opinions, and musicians and artists, who are known for their cult of personality.

- ■ **Small business e-commerce**   This one can be tough, but I've seen owners and managers of e-commerce businesses who have succeeded in creating a certain amount of personality and community for their business. (Most of the examples I can think of are computer "shops" that establish credibility with us geeks via intelligent articles and personal tips from the CEO.) If you can provide good, timely information that readers appreciate, they may send more business your way.

- ■ **Customer support**   Online discussion forums are great for technical customer service, but you may find that a blog works well for web-based customer service, too. Although you might not want your customers posting all their complaints, a weblog format can be good for fielding some of them (in e-mail, for instance) and offering honest answers and solutions. You can also blog on changes to your products, plans for new services, and so on.

In general, simply blogging about your prices and the quality of your merchandise is probably not enough to keep people engaged, unless you're selling to enthusiasts or, well, geeks. But a weblog can add a personal, dynamic, and sticky component to any website that's aimed at customers. A well-written weblog can help build loyalty in your customers and help give them a sense that there's a person behind the logo of an online business or service—particularly a small business.

Grassroots Organizing

There's no question that having a web presence is important for grassroots organizations, particularly those who are interested in garnering support for professionals and younger people. Students, academics, and young professionals (not to mention many retirees) are comfortable with the Internet and expect certain of your organization's resources—cause statements, calendars, calls to action, tax and donation information—to be available online. As was mentioned in Chapter 9, it's even relatively easy to add a donation component to your site using PayPal, Amazon, or a similar service. And there are certainly more sophisticated online giving mechanisms, as well.

As for whether a blog should be part of that presence, you'll find blogging is useful on two fronts in a charitable or political organization. First, the front page of your site is a great place to use a blog format to post news, calls to action, events,

Blogging "The Man"?

Should big business have blogs? Only if you can keep them honest. Press releases are already posted to most corporate websites in timestamp format, so there's no point in rehashing them in a more "personal" venue. Other news and product items can also benefit from the timestamp format, but big corporations have been doing that for years on their websites. As for creating community, I'd say that most, if not all, Fortune 500 CEOs, vice-presidents, and managers would probably feel too compromised in a public setting to be personal, warm, or revealing in a blog. Say the wrong thing and the stock tanks.

One place where some larger companies have had luck is in allowing their more technical staff—engineers, designers, and product managers—to let their hair down a bit and get personal with customers. This can be a great way to get candid feedback from customers, and there are plenty of social theorists around to suggest that being intimate and honest with your customers is the best way to learn and survive in business this century. (See, in particular, the Cluetrain Manifesto at http://www.cluetrain.com/.) However, one must assume that corporate paranoia—about intellectual property, employee loyalty, public image, and/or competitive advantage—will likely keep blogging and similar communication to a minimum. Were I a betting man, I'd expect more television ads repurposed for the Web and fewer personal journals of discovery and community. But I could be wrong.

11

and other important information. Although you'll likely want the blog moderated (so that an official in the organization can make the final decision as to what appears), you should consider creating a collective weblog that enables your visitors to post news and information. At the very least, any organization that casts a wide net can give posting permission to regional directors or communications officers, who can then write in with the latest news.

The front-page blog is also an opportunity to invite comment from the outside world—perhaps people who agree, disagree, or have questions. Building a sense of community is important for this sort of activity, and a front-page blog can go a long way toward making that happen.

I'd also recommend a second scenario for using a blog in organizing, because the advantages discussed earlier in the section "Collaborate Online" are equally applicable to a nonprofit or political site. Using an "internal affairs" blog in a charity or political organization is a great idea, because it presents an opportunity to keep people involved in a project even though they may have many other obligations. Consider the possibility that your key volunteers, organizers, investors, and directors can check in throughout the day or week to see what's happening within the organization, taking a moment here and there to further the dialogue, brainstorm, and help drive decision-making and problem-solving.

As I mentioned earlier, most web hosts make it reasonably simple to create a password-protected part of your public website, which enables you to give access to this internal blog to just the strategic organizers, board members, and other leaders who need it. Then, much like project management in a business, the blog can be used to schedule, manage problems, share ideas, and brainstorm solutions. (This could also be a handy way to involve community leaders or big donors without inviting them over to the office all the time—give them the password and let them participate or advise via the blog so that they can keep a foot in the daily operations from their own offices or homes.)

Again, the blog serves as a collective memory for your group. It serves as a knowledge-capturing tool and an archive of the ideas and discussions the group has been through. Depending on how much of your communication is channeled through the internal blog, it can serve as part of the historical transcript of such an organization, which can be useful for answering questions or referring to the original foundation of the organization so that future members don't repeat past mistakes. Consider some possible entries that could make their way onto the blog:

- **New ideas**   When a director or field worker comes up with a new strategy or solution, that person can post it and its supporting arguments. The group can then discuss the merits and fine-tune the solution.

- **Goals and milestones**   Post the goals you want the group to meet and let the conversation ensue as to how to go about meeting them, determining whether they're realistic, or what other goals haven't been considered. Also, post when a milestone has been reached so that all your principals can know immediately and begin passing the word around.

- **New resources**   Consider a scenario in which you come across a potential resource, an interesting person, a news story, or some new information, but you're not sure what to do with it. Post it and see what others come up with. Someone may pick up the baton and take advantage of the resource. This helps to capture useful information from volunteers or members, encouraging them to share it, even if it doesn't fit their job description or expertise.

- **Scheduling**   Start a discussion asking for recommendations for an upcoming event. People on the list may have good ideas, special contacts, or solutions to the catering, music, or meeting space that you haven't thought of.

- **Development**   Asking for help raising money might not be something you do in polite conversation with your current donors, mentors, or volunteers, but it could be nonthreatening online. The money people (or the friends of your organization who have all the contacts) can self-select and respond if they feel like it.

- **Networking and contacts**   Need to reach out to a new constituency or make contact with a new business, foundation, or organization? Put the word out to your blog and see if anyone has connections you didn't know about.

- **Share materials or expertise**   Often, organizing is about strategizing, succeeding, and then replicating that success. Using a blog, you can chronicle different experiments and find out what's working—you can also share that information with your group and, perhaps, keep others from making the same mistakes or wasting time reinventing the wheel. If your organization is distributed in different locales, a blog can be a great way to keep everyone on the cutting edge of your ideas and strategies.

These are all items that could be handled on the phone, in meetings, and via e-mail—and surely none of those tools can be completely replaced by a blog. But the timestamp nature of the blog and its approachable, familiar format may go a long way toward streamlining some of this day-to-day involvement, particularly if your group is willing to participate actively in the online community. With the blog requiring perhaps only a few minutes a day to scan and respond to, it's possible that the asynchronous advantages could kick in, enabling the group to pull additional productivity, help, and wisdom out of its members. If these people check the blog daily, they'll constantly keep the organization's goals, needs, and the shared knowledge base in mind, even while fulfilling other obligations. And, of course, the advantages are multiplied if the members of your group are in different locales or time zones. If you have a distributed organization that needs to be pulled together, a blog may be a big part of the solution.

Blogs in Education

Education is another setting in which a weblog has tools to offer. A weblog run by a teacher or professor, for instance, offers the opportunity to discuss ideas beyond the walls and timetables of the classroom. A professor's blog can offer additional information, help on assignments, links to important resources, and any special information about the class—rescheduling, room changes, and so on—in such a way that it's easy for the class's group dynamic to continue outside the regular meeting hours.

A high-school or grade-school teacher's weblog can be useful for many of the same reasons. It might also be a forum for students to help one another on assignments and problems, for the display (or posting and critique) of students' work, as well as an opportunity to boost morale, increase the team spirit of the class, and add to or highlight the web publishing, research, and other Internet-based skills of the students.

Today's weblog software is almost ideally suited to distance learning. With just a few tweaks (particularly to Movable Type and pMachine), I fully believe you could put together an online classroom and teach over the Web. Consider some possible components:

- **Lectures**   A single blog entry can serve as the week's lecture, with follow-ups posted throughout the week. Students can discuss the lecture in comments that follow it, with clarifications offered by the teacher, also via comments.

- **News, events, and related links**   The teacher can keep the blog active throughout the week by recommending other online resources, linking to relevant news stories, current events coverage, or other items found on the Web. For instance, in a writing class, a teacher could quickly blog (perhaps using a bookmarklet) about a newspaper article that offers a great example of a clever introduction or good use of quoted sources.

- **Critiques**   If the subject matter is suitable for the medium, you can allow students to post their work online for critique by the class. For instance, I have taken online writing workshops in the past where students post their work online and others criticize it, usually following the "three positive comments, three negative comments" rule, which forces students to consider the positives and point them out before launching into the negatives. The original author was then allowed to respond and provide insight into why they made the decision they made or to ask for additional feedback. A weblog entry would work very well for that, with the entry

being the submission and the comment feature used for critiques and a
discussion by the teacher and peers.

■ **Ongoing community**   You could even offer, in some situations, to leave
the blog up and running for the group of students to maintain community
after the class has ended. Even if the teacher isn't obligated to participate,
the students could continue to discuss, critique, network, or just check in
with one another every so often.

Again, you could picture such a blog being password protected so that only
your authorized (and/or paying) students can get in and see the content or participate.
You could also see that site outlasting the duration of the class, at least for as long
as the group uses it.

Another possibility, particularly suited to grade school and high school students,
is to simply use the blog concept the way it was intended—as an online journal.
Entire classes can track the progress of something—field trips, science experiments,
and group research projects—in the blog, thus "publishing" their findings very
readily. Likewise, language and composition teachers might find either individual
blogs or a collective blog useful for allowing each of their students space for
expository writing, which instantly gives the students a sense of accomplishment,
while making the class's journaling work available on the Web for presentation to
parents and peers.

Finally, the collaborative tools available to business project teams and nonprofit
participants are also available to principals, teachers, department heads, professors,
and graduate students. Start an internal blog to capture ideas, allow for brainstorming,
discuss new techniques, gather feedback on decisions, post professional development
opportunities, collaborate on grant proposals, and post new policies or directives.
(If the posts are about new policies regarding shutting down the teachers' lounge
early or adding extra class periods, you might post them as "closed" entries that
don't invite comment.)

This provides the possibility for increasing productivity, building morale among
your teachers or professors, and finding surprising opportunities for synergy—
maybe the debate students can come along on a field trip that the history teacher is
planning or maybe professors can collaborate across departments on their research.
With the blog making it easier to share ideas and to offer forums for these sorts
of discussions, you just might find it's a great idea to add one to your arsenal of
teaching and management tools.

11

More...

In this chapter, I blogged a bit—for lack of a better word—on some of the possible applications one might find for blogs in the workplace, in organizations, and in education. Although weblogging may be more evolutionary than revolutionary, I think today's weblogging software can be a valuable tool for both communication and collaboration. In all cases, the goal is to foster community—with your colleagues, your project team, your charity's donors, your students, or your customers. The use of collective weblogs, commenting tools, and even multiple weblogs and password protection can help improve the way organizations communicate internally and externally.

As for what's next—that's it! Turn to Appendix A for a convenient list of most of the websites and resources mentioned throughout this book. Feel free to visit me at http://www.blogonbook.com/ and let me know how your blog is going. You can also ask questions, express concerns, and engage in discussions regarding the book. Thanks for reading. Be well, and hopefully I'll see you online!

	T	W	T	F	S		S	M	T	W	T	F	S		S	M	T	W	T	F	S		S	M	T	W	T	F	S
		1	2	3	4				1	2	3	4					1	2	3	4					1	2	3	4
7	8	9	10	11		5	6	7	8	9	10	11		5	6	7	8	9	10	11		5	6	7	8	9	10	11
14	15	16	17	18		12	13	14	15	16	17	18		12	13	14	15	16	17	18		12	13	14	15	16	17	18
21	22	23	24	25		19	20	21	22	23	24	25		19	20	21	22	23	24	25		19	20	21	22	23	24	25
28	29	30	31			26	27	28	29	30	31			26	27	28	29	30	31			26	27	28	29	30	31

Appendix

Internet Resources

This appendix is designed as a quick reference to the sites discussed throughout the book, including links to popular blogs, software and services, add-ons, and so forth. In some cases, you might come across a link that wasn't mentioned in the book but is still worth visiting. As with any list of links, some of these will begin to rot after a while. Therefore, be sure to visit http://www.blogonbook.com/ for an updated list.

Popular Sites

In this section you'll find some popular and well-known blogs listed, including some of the stars, founders, and most-linked-to bloggers, covering all sorts of genres, design types, and blogging approaches.

Blogs

Adam Curry (live.curry.com)
Andrew Sullivan (www.andrewsullivan.com)
Camworld (www.camworld.com)
Chris Pirillo (chris.pirillo.com)
Doc Searls (doc.weblogs.com)
Gnome-Girl (www.gnome-girl.com)
Inside Gretchen's Head (gretchen.pirillo.com)
Jane Galt (www.janegalt.net)
Jason Kottke (kottke.org)
Jeffery Zeldman (www.zeldman.com)
Lawrence Lessig (cyberlaw.stanford.edu/lessig/blog)
Leoville (www.leoville.com/mt)
MightyGirl (mightygirl.net)
Rebecca Blood (www.rebeccablood.net)
Scripting News (www.scripting.com)
Shifted Librarian (www.theshiftedlibrarian.com)
This Modern World (www.thismodernworld.com)
The Truth Laid Bear (www.truthlaidbear.com)
Wil Wheaton (www.wilwheaton.net)

News and Roundup Sites

Macsurfer (www.macsurfer.com)
MetaFilter (www.metafilter.com)
Plastic.com (www.plastic.com)

Salon (www.salon.com)
The Scoop (www.thescoop.org)
SlashDot (www.Slashdot.com)
The Web Today (www.thewebtoday.com)

Weblog Philosophy

History of Weblogs (newhome.weblogs.com/historyOfWeblogs)
Rebecca Blood's Weblog History
(http://www.rebeccablood.net/essays/weblog_history.html)
Journal vs. Weblog (www.diarist.net/guide/blogjournal.shtml)

Weblog Software and Services

This section covers the tools of the trade, including hosted blogging software, server-based software, hosting companies known to focus on blogging, and inexpensive (as well as the well-known) domain name registrars.

For a roundup of many different tools and applications:
Yahoo! Directory of Weblog Tools
(directory.google.com/Top/Computers/Internet/On_the_Web/Weblogs/Tools/)

Hosted Blogging Software

Blogger (www.blogger.com)

- Blog*Spot free hosting (www.blogspot.com)
- Blogger Unofficial FAQ (archives.blogspot.com)

Radio Userland (radio.userland.com)

- Radio Docs (radiodocs.userland.com)
- Salon.com Blogs (www.salon.com/blogs)

LiveJournal (www.livejournal.com)

- Create a Journal (www.livejournal.com/create.bml)
- LiveJournal Community (www.livejournal.com/community)
- DeadJournal (www.deadjournal.com)

A

Crimsonblog (www.crimsonblog.com)
Diaryland (www.diaryland.com)
Pitas.com (www.pitas.com)

Server-Based Blogging Software

Greymatter (www.noahgrey.com/greysoft)

- Support forums (foshdawg.net/forums/index.php)

- Greymatter for Dummies (wiccked.com/gmfd)

- Greymatter templates (foshdawg.net/gm/templates)

Movable Type (www.movabletype.org)

- Default templates (www.movabletype.org/default_templates.shtml)

- Movable Type BlogStyles (blogstyles.com/mt/)

pMachine (www.pmachine.com)

- pMachine Hosting (www.pmachinehosting.com)

Others

- BigBlogTool (www.bigblogtool.com)

- Drupal (www.drupal.org)

- GeekLog (geeklog.sourceforge.net)

- Manila (manila.userland.com)

- PostNuke (www.postnuke.com)

- PHPNuke (www.phpnuke.org)

- SlashCode (www.slashcode.com)

Hosting Companies

BlogoMania (www.blogomania.com)
CornerHost (www.cornerhost.com)
LogJamming (www.logjamming.com)
WebLogger (www.weblogger.com)

Domain Name Registrars

GoDaddy (www.godaddy.com)
Domainmonger.com (www.domainmonger.com)
Namezero.com (www.namezero.com)
Register.com (www.register.com)
VeriSign (www.netsol.com)

Site Design

This section brings together links that focus on designing, augmenting, or completely changing the templates that make a blog what it is—at least on the outside. Links include replacement templates and references to CSS and HTML for editing your existing templates.

Templates and Design

BlogSkins (www.blogskins.com)
Elegant Inspirations (elegantinspirations.com/index.php)
GirlyMatters Tips (www.thegirliematters.com/tips)
Love-Productions Graphic Sets (www.love-productions.com/graphics/setlist.html)
PhotoBlog (blogstyles.com/photo/photoview.html)
ScriptyGoddess (scriptygoddess.com)
Userland Themes (themes.userland.com)

HTML and CSS References

30 Days to a More Accessible Weblog
(diveintomark.org/archives/rooms/30_days_to_a_more_accessible_weblog/index.html)
BrainJar's CSS Positioning (www.brainjar.com/css/positioning/)
The W3C's CSS Overview (www.w3.org/Style/CSS/)
The W3C's CSS 2 Standard (www.w3.org/TR/REC-CSS2)
The W3C's CSS 2 Text (www.w3.org/TR/REC-CSS2/text.html)
HTMLHelp CSS Reference (www.htmlhelp.com/reference/css/)
Web color codes (hotwired.lycos.com/webmonkey/reference/color_codes/)
Web color hex chart (www.htmlhelp.com/icon/hexchart.gif)
Webmonkey tips and tutorials (www.webmonkey.com)
World Wide Web Consortium (www.w3.org/)

A

Add-ons

Here you'll find links to all the goodies discussed in Chapter 9—virtual town halls (discussion forums), virtual voting booths (polls and surveys), and virtual art shows (graphics galleries). This section's extensive links also include mailing list managers, hosted commenting solutions (for comment-challenged weblogs), and Blogger API–compatible editing software.

Here are some general add-on sites that don't fit the more specific categories:
Download.com (www.download.com)
HotScripts (www.hotscripts.com)
PayPal Donate (www.paypal.com)
Google Discussion Topic
(directory.google.com/Top/Computers/Software/Internet/Servers/Discussion/)

E-mail

Form2Mail (www.ftls.org/en/examples/cgi/Form2Mail.shtml)
HostedScripts.com FormMailer (www.hostedscripts.com/formmailer.html)
Safe E-mail Address (www.hivelogic.com/safeaddress/)

Hosted Discussion Forum

ezBoard (www.ezboard.com)
Instant Message Boards (www.instantmessageboards.com)
The Forum Company (www.forumco.com)
HostedScripts.com forum (www.hostedscripts.com)
OpenTopic (infopop.com/products/opentopic/)
ProBoards (www.proboards.com)

Server-Side Discussion Forums

CuteCast (www.artscore.net/cutecast)
Invision Board (www.invisionboard.com)
Phorum (www.phorum.org)
vBulletin (www.vbulletin.com)
Yet Another Bulletin Board (YABB; www.yabbforum.com)
YABB SE (www.yabb.info)

Mailing List Managers

Majordomo (www.greatcircle.com/majordomo)
MailList (www.cgi-factory.com/maillist/index.shtml)
Mojo Mail (mojo.skazat.com)
MultiList Manager (www.webscriptworld.com/scripts/mlm.phtml)
Topica (www.topica.com)
Yahoo! Groups (groups.yahoo.com)

Polls and Surveys

CGI Factory (www.cgi-factory.com/software/packages)
EZPOLMKR (mannyjuan.com/ezpolmkr.htm)
PlayVote (www.playhouse.com/Software/PlayVote.shtml)
SiteGadgets (www.sitegadgets.com)
Web Poll Central (www.webpollcentral.com)
WebEnalysis Online Polls (www.webenalysis.com/onlinepolls.asp)

Photo Galleries

Gallery (gallery.sourceforge.net)
Image gallery listings
(www.hotscripts.com/PHP/Scripts_and_Programs/Image_Galleries/)
Image Display System (ids.sourceforge.net)
PhotoFrame (photoframe.sourceforge.net)

Hosted Comments

BlogOut (www.klinkfamily.com/BlogOut/blogout.html)
eNetation (enetation.co.uk/)
YACCS (rateyourmusic.com/yaccs/)

Blogger API Clients

BlogApp (www.webentourage.com/blogapp.php)
BlogBuddy (blogbuddy.sourceforge.net)
Blognix (blognix.sourceforge.net/)
iBlog (iblog.soapdog.org)
Jericho (jericho.sourceforge.net/)
w.Bloggar (www.wbloggar.com/)

A

Publicity

This final section of links focuses on places and services that help you get your blog's name in lights. Here's where you'll find directories, weblog registries, ranking services, linking services, news feeds, news feed readers, webrings, and links to search engine submission guidelines.

General Publicity Sites

BlogRolling (www.blogrolling.com)
Weblogs.com (www.weblogs.com)
Yahoo! Weblogs Directory
(dir.yahoo.com/Social_Science/Communications/Writing/Journals_and_Diaries/
Online_Journals_and_Diaries/Web_Logs/)

Registries and Directories

List of Directories (www.lights.com/weblogs/directories.html)
The Blog Portal (www.eatonweb.com/portal)
BlogComp (www.urldir.com/bt/)
BlogDex (blogdex.media.mit.edu)
Blogging Ecosystem (www.myelin.co.nz/ecosystem/)
BlogTree (www.blogtree.com)
Boing-Boing (www.boingboing.com)
Globe of Blogs (www.globeofblogs.com)
The Portal at Uncorked.org (uncorked.org/portal.html)
The Truth Laid Bear (www.truthlaidbear.com/ecosystem.shtml)

Webrings

BlogPhiles (www.blogphiles.com/webring.shtml)
BlogRings (www.xanga.com/blogrings/default.asp)
GreyLOGS (grey.glory-box.com/)
Moveable Type Blog Ring (www.kiwinessie.net/rings/mtblog/)
MT Webring (www.brookelyn.org/mtring/)
pMachine Ring (pmachine.phpdiva.com/ring.php)
RingSurf (www.ringsurf.com)
Wander-Lust (www.wander-lust.com/)

Search Engine Submissions

AllTheWeb (www.alltheweb.com/add_url.php)
AltaVista (www.altavista.com/addurl)
DayPop (www.daypop.com/submit.htm)
Open Directory Project (dmoz.org/add.html)
Yahoo! Suggest a Site (docs.yahoo.com/info/suggest)

Headline Syndication and Readers

AmphetaDesk (www.disobey.com/amphetadesk)
BlogHog (www.bloghog.com)
FeedReader (www.feedreader.com)
NewsisFree (www.newsisfree.com)
RSS News Feeds (blogspace.com/rss/writers)
SlashDock (homepage.mac.com/stas/slashdock.html)

A

Index

A

Accounts, setting up reply e-mail, 272–275
Active blog, 249
Active voice, write in, 245
Ad-driven, free mailing lists, 283
Ad-free lists, subscription-based, 283
Add a Member screen, 211
Add a New Entry page, 131
Add-ons for your weblogs, 271–293
    adding comments, 291
    adding image galleries, 288–291
    adding mailing lists, 282–286
    adding polls, 286–288
    Blogger editing tools, 291–293
    managing mailing lists, 282–286
    needing forums, 275–282
    setting up reply e-mail accounts, 272–275
Adding
    authors, 129–130
    categories, 207–209
    comments, 291
    entries, 59–60, 78–81
    entries in pMachine, 202
    hyperlinks, 62–63
    image galleries, 288–291
    images, 63–66, 99, 203–206
    mailing lists, 282–286
    new entries, 59–66
    new hyperlinks, 59–66
    new images, 59–66
    notification entries, 180–181
    pBlocks, 209–214
    polls, 286–288
    static pages, 143–145
    template variables, 144
    your first entries, 54–56
    your own links, 178–180
    to your weblog, 102–105
Addresses
    e-mail, 129
    encoding e-mail, 274
    learning user's IP, 170
    not banning your own IP, 138
Administering weblogs, 134–138, 169–176
Agents, real estate, 327
Aggregate news, 110–111
Alt text, editing, 205
Anchor elements, 62
Announce-only list, 283
API, Blogger, 293
Appearance, separating content and, 27
Applications
    client, 92–95
    Radio, 112–114
Archive miscellaneous templates, 225
Archive multi-entry templates, 225
Archive path, local, 160
Archive summary templates, 225–226
Archive URL, 160
Archives, managing, 86–87, 174–175
Archiving, 116
    past posts, 66–68
Articles
    posting exceptionally long, 21
    writing shorter, 249
Artists, 327–328
ASCII mode, 120
Attributes

alt, 66
border, 66
font-level, 260
href, 62
src, 65
Audience, learning your, 300
Authors
    adding, 129–130
    editing, 129
    multiple, 117, 149
Authors, managing, 129–130, 169–170
    adding authors, 129–130
    editing authors, 129
Automated weblog, 30–39
    preferring server-side weblogs, 36–39
    using hosted weblogs, 33–36
Automatic formatting, 205

B

Background color, 265
Badges, 6
Banning
    censoring and IP, 117
    IPs, 137–138, 170–171
Bars, 327
Berkeley DB (DB_File Perl), 150
Berkeley DB installation, steps for, 152–154
Billing, monthly, 44
Binary mode, 120
Blog
    active, 249
    are more of a slang term, 4
    in education, 331–333
    entries visible on, 207
    front-page, 329
    getting and configuring entirely new, 277
    use of word, 4
    and weblog are used interchangeably, 4
Blog advantages for organizations, 319–321
    archived, 320
    asynchronous, 319
    communal, 320–321
    conversational, 320
    structured, 319
Blog-focused registries, miscellaneous, 302

Blog, getting people to gravitate to your, 300
    learning your audience, 300
    lurk, 300
    surf, 300
Blog, ideas for extending your, 68–71
    adding static pages, 69
    consider using other scripted tools, 70
    integrating your blog into another site, 70
    learning CSS, 69
    learning to use HTML tables, 69
    play with design, 68
    using thumbnails to link to bigger images, 69
Blog, ideas for organizational, 323–333
    blogging the man, 329
    blogs in education, 331–333
    collaborating online, 324–326
    grassroots organizing, 328–331
    reaching customers, 327–328
    storing and sharing knowledge, 323–324
Blog, items effectively communicated, 325–326
    directives, 325
    group hugs, 326
    group scheduling and management, 326
    news and resources, 325
    questions and brainstorming, 325
    submissions, 326
Blog, reasons for considering using, 19–20
    you want feedback and participation, 20
    you want regular visitors, 20
    you want to inform, 19
Blog, reasons not to use, 20–21
    you don't have much to say, 20
    you want pages individually designed, 21
    you've got tons to say, 20–21
Blog, requirements for simple, 50–68
    adding new entries, 59–66
    adding new hyperlinks, 59–66
    adding new images, 59–66
    archiving past posts, 66–68
    building basic weblog page, 52–56
Blog, simple, 49–71
    ideas for extending your blogs, 68–71
    requirements for simple blog, 50–68
Blog, tips for, 269–270
    keep it simple, 269

making your site as accessible as possible, 270

testing your site, 270

think content first, 269

using headings, 269

using paragraphs, 269

using style sheets, 269

Blog, writing, designing, and tweaking your, 239–270

blogging ethics, 251–252

brevity is your friend, 247–249

changing look of your site, 252–270

have something to say, 241–244

let others play, 249–250

say it well, 244–247

weblog netiquette, 250–251

What are you gonna say?, 240–252

Blogger, 33–34, 76–89

adding entries, 78–81

API, 293

changing looks, 81–86

don't ping Weblogs.com, 308

editing tools, 291–293

sign up, 77–78

Blogging

ethics, 251–252

and fair use, 21–22

the man, 329

talking about, 314

Blogging cash, need, 289–290

Blogging community, getting involved in, 299

Blogging software

hosted, 337–338

server-based, 338

Blogging voice, finding your, 241

BlogHog, 311, 312

Blogrolling, 305

Blogs

happy, 249

multiple, 149

name, 159

Blog's core setup, editing, 159–160

archive URL, 160

blog name, 159

local archive path, 160

local site path, 159–160

site URL, 160

timezone, 160

Blog*Spot, 78

BlogTree, 302

Blurb field, 202

Blurbs, 231, 232–233

Bookmarklet link, 88

Bookmarklets, 150, 171, 209

Border attribute, 66

Borders, 265

Borders and text, 264

Bot defined, 303

Box, shout, 277

Brainstorming, questions and, 325

Brevity is your friend, 247–249

Browser feature, File, 231

Browsers

enabled, 61

have View Source command, 269

web, 64

Built-in templates, 223–229

Business e-commerce, small, 328

Business-like presence: Radio UserLand, 99–114

C

Capitalization, 245

Cascade Style Sheets (CSSs), 184

Case sensitivity, Greymatter and, 130

Cash, need blogging, 289–290

Categories, 149

adding, 207–209

creating, 162–164

editing, 162–164

and template tags, 183–184

Categories page, Edit, 164

Censoring and IP banning, 117

Cgi-bin directory, 123

CGI scripts

changing permissions on, 122

placing, 123

storing Greymatter's, 121

Changelog, dated, 28

Changing

index's name, 200–201

looks, 184–185
settings, 87–89
styles, 260–266
templates, 87
your themes, 107–108
Classes, different styles and style, 257
Client application, 92–95
Closing entries, 132–134
Codes, forum software compatibility with
    UBB, 279
Collaborating online, 324–326
Collective entry form templates, 226
Collective weblog feature, 199
Collective weblogs
    creating, 234–235
    dynamic, 17
Color, background, 265
Commands, browsers have View Source, 269
Commas, 246
Comment
    display templates, 225
    form templates, 225
Commenting features, 31
    turning off, 17
Comments, 116, 148
    adding, 291
    community, 17
    deleting, 136–137
    editing, 136–137
Commercial sites are kinda cool, 10
Community
    comments, 17
    getting involved in blogging, 299
    weblogs building, 16–17
Community living: LiveJournal, 90–99
Companies, hosting, 338
Config.php, editing, 194
Configuring
    Greymatter, 124–130
    Movable Type, 155–156
    pMachine, 196–199
    your weblog, 199–200
Contact form, 275
Container tag, 184
Containers, 52
Content

consider your, 17–18
    dynamic, 18
Content and appearance, separating, 27
Contracts, long-term, 44
Control panel, pMachine, 197
Conventions
    Unix-style, 121
    using different naming, 175
    XHTML-based, 53
Conversation, art of, 299–301
Create New Entry screen, 162
Creating
    categories, 162–164
    collective weblogs, 234–235
    LiveJournal, 90–92
    MySQL database, 193
    pages, 52–54
    special MT templates, 288
    static page, 144
    static pages, 232
    thumbnails of images, 168
Critiques, 332–333
CSS and style sheets, 254–269
CSS-based style sheets, 252
CSS online, home of, 260
CSSs (Cascade Style Sheets), 184
Customer support, 328
Customers, reaching, 327–328
    bars, music venues, and restaurants, 327
    customer support, 328
    media members, musicians, and artists,
        327–328
    property/resort managers, 327
    real estate agents, 327
    small business e-commerce, 328
Customizing text, 53
Customizing your LiveJournal, 97–99
CuteCast, 280

D

Data import, 149
Database server, MySOL is web-based, 277
Databases
    creating MySQL, 193
    Movable Type has created, 157

Date-and-time format, 18
Date Heading field, Master, 226
Date-specific variables, 142
Dated changelog, 28
Dates of entries, editing, 165
DayPop, 304
Definitions, style sheet, 179
Deleting
    comments, 136–137
    entries, 105, 166, 206–207
    prior entries, 96–97
Democratization, sense of, 9
Designing, and tweaking your blogs, writing,
    239–270
Destination menu, Upload, 204
Directives, 325
Directories, 119, 276
    setting up, 124–126
Directory, cgi-bin, 123
Discussion forum, MySQL/PHP, 281
Display templates, comment, 225
<div> elements, 227, 267
Documents, HTML, 40, 52
Domain name
    knockoff, 298
    registrars, 339
Donations
    accepting, 307
    soliciting, 289–290
Downloadable templates, 178
Downloading
    Greymatter, 119–123
    and installing mailing lists, 285
    templates, 138
Dynamic collective weblog, 17
Dynamic content, 18
Dynamic pages, published pages vs., 32–33

E

E-commerce, small business, 328
E-mail accounts, setting up reply, 272–275
E-mail addresses
    encoding, 274
    without home pages, 129
E-mail messages, 31

Edit Categories page, 164
Edit Entry screen, 165, 166
Editing
    alt text, 205
    authors, 129
    blog's core setup, 159–160
    categories, 162–164
    comments, 136–137
    config.php, 194
    dates of entries, 165
    entries, 105, 132–134, 159–168, 206
    HTML templates, 229–231
    mode, power, 166
    prior entries, 96–97
    template HTMLs, 82–86
    templates, 138–143, 176–185
    templates yourself, 138–143
    your LiveJournal, 92–98
Editing tools, Blogger, 291–293
Education, blogs in, 331–333
Elements, 52
    anchor, 62
    <div>, 227, 267
    empty, 52
    <h2>, 68
    <h3>, 268
    HTML, 61
    <img />, 65, 66, 79
    paragraph, 56
    phrase, 61
    placing images inside anchor, 66
    text markup, 61
    <title>, 53
Email Members, sending, 218–220
Email, sending, 218–220
Empty elements, 52
Empty tags, 52
Enabled browsers, 61
Encoding e-mail address, 274
Engines, search, 305
Entries
    adding, 59–60, 78–81
    adding in pMachine, 202
    adding new, 59–66
    adding notification, 180–181
    adding your first, 54–56

altering, 206–207
archiving past, 66–67
are great excuse to geek out, 243
closing, 132–134
deleting, 105, 166, 206–207
deleting prior, 96–97
editing, 105, 132–134, 159–168,
  201–209
editing dates of, 165
with hyperlinks, 63
posting, 130–132, 159–168, 201–203
posting and editing, 201–209
visible on blog, 207
Entry management, 150
Entry screens
  Create New, 162
  Edit, 165, 166
Entry Selection screen, 133
Ethics, blogging, 251–252
Etiquette, net, 250
Events, 332
Extensible Markup Language (XML), 309
External style sheets, 254
EzBoard, 280

F

Fair use and blogging, 21–22
FAQs (Frequently Asked Questions), 250
Features
  commenting, 31
  File Browser, 231
  Movable Type's, 148–150
  turning off commenting, 17
  using TrackBack, 171–174
Feeds
  publishing others', 312–314
  publishing your, 311
  reading, 311–312
Fields
  Blurb, 202
  Master Date Heading, 226
File Browser feature, 231
Files
  rebuilding, 134–135
  uploading, 135–136, 167–168

Flexibility, 30, 33
Flexible storage, 148
Folders, 119
  accessing script, 197
Font-level attributes, 260
Form, contact, 275
Form templates, collective entry, 226
Form templates, comment, 225
Formats
  date-and-time, 18
  PNG is great, 64
  weblog and its, 5
Formatting
  automatic, 205
  basic, 60–61
Forum services, hosted, 277
Forum software compatibility with UBB
  codes, 279
Forum template, pMachine, 282
Forumco.com, 280
Forums
  discussion, 276
  MySQL/PHP discussion, 281
  needing, 275–282
  ProBoards and hosted, 279
  very basic, 278
  and your sites, 276
Forums software, server-based, 280
Frequently Asked Questions (FAQs), 250
Friday Five, 286
Friendliness, user-, 39
Friends and groups, 94–95
Front-page blog, 329
FTP, 77
  servers, 78
Future logins, 130

G

Galleries, adding image, 288–291
Geek out, entries are great excuse to, 243
Geek-out post, 242
General Preferences, 198, 205
Goals, consider your, 18–22
Good stories, pitching, 315
Grassroots organizing, 328–331

Greymatter
  and case sensitivity, 130
  downloading, 119–123
  installing, 119–123
  using style sheets in, 258
  who it is for, 118
Greymatter, configuring, 124–130
  diagnostics and repair, 127–128
  miscellaneous configuration options,
    126–127
  setting up directories, 124–126
Greymatter decision: features and requirements,
  116–118
  archiving, 116
  censoring and IP banning, 117
  comments, 116
  images, 117
  multiple authors, 117
  templates and variable-based sites, 117
Greymatter, setting up and using, 115–145
  adding static pages, 143–145
  administering Weblog, 134–138
  editing templates, 138–143
  get started, 118–130
  Greymatter decision: features and
    requirements, 116–118
  post and edit entries, 130–134
  troubleshooting and backup, 145
Greymatter's CGI scripts, storing, 121
Greymatter's server requirements, 118
Group hugs, 326
Group scheduling and management, 326
Groups, friends and, 94–95
Groups service, 284

H

<h3> element, 268
Happy blog, 249
Heading field, Master Date, 226
Headline syndication, 309–315
  getting media interested, 314–315
  publishing others' feeds, 312–314
  publishing your feeds, 311
  reading feeds, 311–312
Headlines, 231, 233–234
  syndicate, 176

Headlines templates, weblog, 225
Hex number, 185
Hexadecimal defined, 262
Home pages, e-mail addresses without, 129
Hosted blogging software, 337–338
Hosted forums, ProBoards and, 279
Hosted polls, 287
Hosted services, choosing, 74–76
  Blogger, 74–75
  LiveJournal, 75
  others, 76
  Radio UserLand, 75
Hosted weblogs, 33–36
Hosted weblogs, using, 73–114
  Blogger, 76–89
  business-like presence: Radio UserLand,
    99–114
  choosing hosted services, 74–76
  community living: LiveJournal, 90–99
  popular choice: Blogger, 76–89
  Radio UserLand, 99–114
HostedScripts.com, 278
Hosting companies, 338
Hosting services, choosing good, 42–44
Hosts, web, 273
HotScripts.com, 286
HTML documents, 52
HTML templates, editing, 229–231
HTMLs
  editing template, 82–86
  familiarity with, 53
Hugs, group, 326
Hyperlinks, adding, 59–66, 62–63

I

IDS (Image Display System), 288
Image Display System (IDS), 288
Image galleries, adding, 288–291
Images, 117
  creating thumbnails of, 168
  trouble uploading, 205
  uploading, 211
Images, adding, 59–66, 63–66, 99, 203–206
<img /> element, 66
IMHO (In My Humble Opinion), 242
Import, data, 149

In My Humble Opinion (IMHO), 242
Index page, how formatted, 199
Index-Related Templates page, 142
Index's name, changing, 200–201
Installation, steps for Berkeley DB, 152–154
Installing
        Greymatter, 119–123
        mailing lists, 285
Instantmessageboards.com, 280
Interface, visual aspects of, 179
Internet protocol, 62
Internet resources, 335–343
        add-ons, 340–341
        popular sites, 336–337
        publicity, 342–343
        site design, 339
        weblog software and services, 337–339
Invisionboard, 280
IP addresses
        learning user's, 170
        not banning your own, 138
IP banning, censoring and, 117
IPPs
        choosing good, 42–44
        early stages of getting to know your, 44
        support staff of, 152
IPs, banning, 137–138, 170–171
Ipso facto ergo, 10
ISPs (Internet service providers), 40

J

Jargon, 6
Jargon, weblog server, 39–42
        CGIs (Common Gateway Interfaces),
            40–41
        HTML documents, 40
        Internet Presence Provider or hosting
            company, 40
        ISPs (Internet service providers), 40
        MySQL is web server-based database
            solution, 41
        Perl is scripting language, 41
        PHP hypertext processor, 41
        SSIs (server-side includes), 41
        web hosting account, 40

        web server computer, 39–40
Joiner, on being a, 301–303
        get thee to a registry, 301–302
        ring-a-ding-ding, 302–303
Journals
        modifying your, 97–98
        online, 6

K

Knowledge, storing and sharing, 323–324

L

Language, PHP is embedded scripting, 277
Lectures, 332
Link and ping, 305–309
Links
        adding archive, 68
        adding your own, 178–180
        aggregating to interesting sites and
            stories, 29
        Archive Settings, 86
        Archive Template, 87
        bookmarklet, 88
        Original, 228
List-hosting services, 284
Lists
        ad-driven, free mailing, 283
        adding mailing, 282–286
        announce-only, 283
        downloading and installing mailing, 285
        getting mailing, 283
        magic of mailing, 283
        mailing, 220–222
        managing mailing, 282–286
        subscription-based ad-free, 283
LiveJournal, 34, 75, 90–99
        creating, 90–92
        updating via Web, 95–96
LiveJournal, customizing your, 97–99
        adding images, 99
        modifying your journal, 97–98
LiveJournal, editing your, 92–98
        using client application, 92–95
Living, community, 90–99
Loading Movable Type, 156–158

Local archive path, 160
Local paths, 124
Local site path, 159–160
Login screen, using full username for MT, 158
Logins, future, 130
Long articles, posting exceptionally, 21
Long-term contracts, 44
Look, changing of your site, 252–270
    CSS and style sheets, 254–269
    using third-party templates, 252–254
Looks, changing, 81–86, 184–185
    changing settings, 87–89
    choosing new templates, 81–82
    editing template HTMLs, 82–86
    managing archives, 86–87
Lurk, 300

M

MacBlog.com, 249
Mailing list managers, granddaddy of, 285
Mailing lists, 220–222
    ad-driven, free, 283
    adding, 282–286
    downloading and installing, 285
    managing, 282–286
Mailings, managing users and, 214–222
    Post Office, 218–222
    user registration, 214–217
Majordomo, 285
Management
    entry, 150
    group scheduling and, 326
Management settings, Weblog, 198
Managers
    granddaddy of mailing list, 285
    property/resort, 327
Managing
    archives, 86–87
    authors, 129–130, 169–170
    mailing lists, 282–286
    users and mailings, 214–222
    your archives, 174–175
Manila, 34
Manila-based sites, 35
Manners, online, 250

Margins, 264, 265
Master Date Heading field, 226
Media members, 327–328
Menus
    Post Status, 162
    Upload Destination, 204
Messages, e-mail, 31
Metadata defined, 304
Microsoft Windows-based solution, Unix-based
    vs., 42
Miscellaneous templates, archive, 225
Modes
    ASCII, 120
    binary, 120
    power editing, 166
Monthly billing, 44
Mouseovers, 266
Movable Type, 38
    configuring, 155–156
    decision, features and requirements,
        148–151
    has created databases, 157
    loading, 156–158
    running, 156–158
    upgrading of, 151
    who is it for, 150
Movable Type (MT), 148
Movable Type, setting up and using, 147–185
    configuring Movable Type, 155–156
    download and configure, 151–154
    editing entries, 159–168
    get started, 151–158
    loading Movable Type, 156–158
    posting entries, 159–168
    running Movable Type, 156–158
    upload and set permissions, 154
Movable Type style, default look of, 261
Movable Type style sheet, 262
Movable Type's features, 148–150
    bookmarklets, 150
    categories, 149
    comments, 148
    data import, 149
    entry management, 150
    flexible storage, 148
    multiple authors, 149

multiple blogs, 149
multiple templates, 149
TrackBack, 150
Mt-check.cgi script, 155
MT login screen, using full username for, 158
MT (Movable Type), 148
MT tags, understanding, 181–183
MT templates, creating special, 288
<MTCategories> tag, 183
Multi-entry templates, archive, 225
Multiple authors, 117, 149
Multiple blogs, 149
Multiple templates, 149
Music venues, 327
Musicians, 327–328
MySOL
	is web-based database server, 277
MySQL
	values, 194
MySQL database, creating, 193
MySQL/PHP discussion forum, 281

N

Name registrars, domain, 339
Names
	blog, 159
	changing index's, 200–201
	knockoff domain, 298
Naming conventions, using different, 175
Naming pBlock, 210
Narrative non-fiction, 242
Nav link templates, 226
Netiquette, weblog, 250–251
New blogs, getting and configuring entirely, 277
New entries, adding, 59–66
New Entry screen, Create, 162
New hyperlinks, adding, 59–66
New images, adding, 59–66
New templates, choosing, 81–82
News
	aggregate, 110–111
	events, and related links, 332
News and resources, 325
Non-fiction, narrative, 242
Notification entries, adding, 180–181

Notification, Send, 165
Numbers, hex, 185

O

Online, collaborating, 324–326
Online, home of CSS, 260
Online journals, 6
	and weblogs, 6
Online manners, 250
Online writing, improving your, 245
	consider your capitalization, 245
	read back through your text, 245
	using spell-checker, 245
	write in active voice, 245
Options, server-side, 36–37
Organizational blogs, ideas for, 323–333
	blogging the man, 329
	blogs in education, 331–333
	collaborating online, 324–326
	grassroots organizing, 328–331
	reaching customers, 327–328
	storing and sharing knowledge, 323–324
Organizations
	blog advantages for, 319–321
	using weblogs in, 317–334
Organizing, grassroots, 328–331
Original link, 228
Original templates, returning to, 228

P

Padding, 264, 265
Pages
	Add a New Entry, 131
	adding static, 143–145
	e-mail addresses without home, 129
	Edit Categories, 164
	Index-Related Templates, 142
	published pages vs. dynamic, 32–33
	static, 231
	testing your, 56–59
	typical RSS, 310
	uploading your, 56–59
Pages, building basic weblog, 52–56
	adding your first entries, 54–56
	creating pages, 52–54

testing your pages, 56–59
uploading your pages, 56–59
Pages, creating, 52–54
Pages, creating static, 144, 232
Paradigm, 9
Passive voice, example of, 246
    know difference between they're, there, and their, 246
    know when to use it's and its, 246
    know where to place quotes and commas, 246
    know which and that, 246
    strive for subject/verb agreement, 246
Passwords, 326
Past posts, archiving, 66–68
Path statement defined, 153
Paths
    local, 124
    local archive, 160
    local site, 159–160
    website, 124
PBlocks
    adding, 209–214
    naming, 210
Perl, not knowing correct path to, 152
Permissions, 121, 122
Phorum, 281
Photoblog defined, 288
PHP discussion forum, MySQL/, 281
PHP is embedded scripting language, 277
Phrase elements, 61
Ping, link and, 305–309
Ping websites, 307
Pings
    TrackBack, 173, 174
    Weblogs.com accepts, 308
Play, let more users, 81
PMachine, 275
    adding entries in, 202
    configuring, 196–199
    control panel, 197
    downside of, 190
    forum template, 282
    running, 274
    template, 259
PMachine 2.2, 274

PMachine decision, features and requirements, 188–191
PMachine Pro, 313
PMachine, setting up and using, 187–236
    adding categories, 207–209
    adding images, 203–206
    adding pBlocks, 209–214
    altering entries, 206–207
    changing index's name, 200–201
    configuring pMachine, 196–199
    configuring your weblog, 199–200
    creating collective weblogs, 234–235
    deleting entries, 206–207
    digging into templates, 222–234
    download and install, 191–196
    editing entries, 206
    get started, 191–201
    managing users and mailings, 214–222
    pMachine decision, features and requirements, 188–191
    posting and editing entries, 201–209
PMachine's main style sheet, 266
PNG is great format, 64
Poll script, implementing survey or, 286
Polls
    adding, 286–288
    hosted, 287
Post Office, 218–222
Post Status menu, 162
Posting
    entries, 130–132, 159–168, 160–162, 201–203
    exceptionally long articles, 21
Posts
    archiving past, 66–68
    geek-out, 242
Power editing mode, 166
Preferences
    General, 198, 205
    setting, 108–110
Presence, business-like, 99–114
Press releases, writing, 314–315
Prior entries, editing, 96–97
ProBoards, 278, 279
Property/resort managers, 327
Protocol, Internet, 62

Providers, finding good, 43–44
    check for backup strategy, 44
    choose good customer service, 43
    consider company that focuses on
        blogging, 43–44
    don't get overcharged for extras, 43
    look for signs of life, 43
    make sure numbers are up-to-date, 43
    think local, 44
Pseudo-class, 265
Publicizing your weblog site, 297–316
Published pages vs. dynamic pages, 32–33
Publishing
    others' feeds, 312–314
    your feeds, 311

Q

Questions and brainstorming, 325
Quotes, 246

R

Radio application, 112–114
Radio, getting started with, 100–102
Radio UserLand, 34, 99–114
    adding to your weblog, 102–105
    aggregate news, 110–111
    changing your themes, 107–108
    deleting entries, 105
    editing entries, 105
    getting started with Radio, 100–102
    Radio application, 112–114
    setting preferences, 108–110
    writing stories, 106–107
Real estate agents, 327
Rebuilding files, 134–135
Registrars, domain name, 339
Registration, user, 214–217
Registries, miscellaneous blog-focused, 302
Registry, get thee to a, 301–302
Reply e-mail accounts, setting up, 272–275
Resort managers, 327
Resources
    Internet, 335–343
    news and, 325
Restaurants, 327

Ring-a-ding-ding, 302–303
RSS page, typical, 310

S

Say
    have something to, 241–244
    it well, 244–247
    what are you gonna, 240–252
Scheduling and management, group, 326
Screens
    Add a Member, 211
    Create New Entry, 162
    Edit Entry, 165, 166
    Entry Selection, 133
    using full username for MT login, 158
Script folders, accessing, 197
Scripting language, PHP is embedded, 277
Scripts
    changing permissions on CGI, 122
    implementing survey or poll, 286
    mt-check.cgi, 155
    placing CGI, 123
    storing Greymatter's CGI, 121
Search engines, 305
Security levels, usernames and passwords, 326
Seen, how to be, 298–303
    art of conversation, 299–301
    on being a joiner, 301–303
Send Notification section, 165
Sending
    Email, 218–220
    Email Members, 218–220
Server-based
    blogging software, 338
    forums software, 280
Server, choosing weblog software and, 25–45
    getting web server for your weblog,
        39–44
    types of weblog software, 26–39
Server jargon, weblog, 39–42
Server requirements, Greymatter's, 118
Server-side options, 36–37
Server-side weblogs, preferring, 36–39
Server software, using special weblog, 12
Servers

FTP, 78
getting web, 39–44
MySOL is web-based database, 277
Windows NT-based, 119
Services
choosing good hosting, 42–44
choosing hosted, 74–76
Groups, 284
hosted forum, 277
list-hosting, 284
weblog software and, 337–339
Settings
changing, 87–89
Weblog Management, 198
Sharing knowledge, storing and, 323–324
Shout box, 277
Shout outs, 277
Simple blogs, 49–71
ideas for extending your blogs, 68–71
requirements for simple blog, 50–68
Simple blogs, requirements for, 50–68
adding new entries, 59–66
adding new hyperlinks, 59–66
adding new images, 59–66
archiving past posts, 66–68
building basic weblog page, 52–56
Single-entry templates, weblog, 224
Site path, local, 159–160
Site URL, 160
Sites
changing look of your, 252–270
Manila-based, 35
publicizing your weblog, 297–316
templates and variable-based, 117
Slang term, blogs are more of, 4
Small business e-commerce, 328
Small, think, 315
Software
forum, 279
hosted blogging, 337–338
server-based blogging, 338
server-based forums, 280
using special weblog server, 12
weblog, 18
weblog-management, 30
Software and server, choosing weblog, 25–45

getting web server for your weblog,
39–44
types of weblog software, 26–39
Software and services, weblog, 337–339
domain name registrars, 339
hosted blogging software, 337–338
hosting companies, 338
server-based blogging software, 338
Software tools, sophistication and accessibility
of, 8
Software, types of weblog, 26–39
automated weblog, 30–39
basic weblogs, 26–30
Solutions
hosted weblog-management, 33–34
Unix-based vs. Microsoft
Windows-based, 42
Space-time, 9
Special MT templates, creating, 288
Special variables, 175
Spell-checker, 245
Staff, IPP's support, 152
Statement, path, 153
Static pages, 231
adding, 143–145
creating, 144, 232
Storage, flexible, 148
Stories
pitching good, 315
writing, 106–107
Storing and sharing knowledge, 323–324
Style classes, different styles and, 257
Style, default look of Movable Type, 261
Style sheet definitions, 179
Style sheets, 256–258
CSS and, 254–269
CSS-based, 252
definitions, 258–260
external, 254
Movable Type, 262
pMachine's main, 266
using in Greymatter, 258
why of, 256
Styles
changing, 260–266
marking up with, 266–269

visual, 61
Subject matter, personal nature of, 6
Subject/verb agreement, strive for, 246
Submissions, 326
Subscription-based, ad-free lists, 283
Suckiness, 10
Summary templates, archive, 225–226
Support, customer, 328
Support staff, IPP's, 152
Surf, 300
Survey or poll script, implementing, 286
Syndicate headlines and ping others, 176
Syndication, headline, 309–315

T

Tags
 categories and template, 183–184
 container, 184
 empty, 52
 <MTCategories>, 183
 understanding MT, 181–183
Teaching over Web, 332–333
 critiques, 332–333
 lectures, 332
 news, events, and related links, 332
 ongoing community, 333
Technology doesn't define weblogs, 11
Template HTMLs, editing, 82–86
Template tags, categories and, 183–184
Template variables, 142, 144
Templates
 archive miscellaneous, 225
 archive multi-entry, 225
 archive summary, 225–226
 choosing new, 81–82
 collective entry form, 226
 comment display, 225
 comment form, 225
 creating special MT, 288
 downloadable, 178
 downloading, 138
 how they work, 222–223
 multiple, 149
 nav link, 226
 pMachine, 259

pMachine forum, 282
 returning to original, 228
 third-party, 252–254
 and variable-based sites, 117
 weblog headlines, 225
 weblog multi-entry, 224
 weblog single-entry, 224
Templates, built-in, 223–229
 archive miscellaneous templates, 225
 archive multi-entry templates, 225
 archive summary templates, 225–226
 collective entry form templates, 226
 comment display templates, 225
 comment form templates, 225
 nav link templates, 226
 weblog headlines templates, 225
 weblog multi-entry templates, 224
 weblog single-entry templates, 224
Templates, digging into, 222–234
 blurbs, 231
 editing HTML templates, 229–231
 headlines, 231
 how templates work, 222–223
 static pages, 231
Templates, editing, 138–143, 176–185
 downloading templates, 138
 editing templates yourself, 138–143
Templates, editing HTML, 229–231
Templates, editing yourself, 138–143
Templates page, Index-Related, 142
Testing your pages, 56–59
Text
 customizing, 53
 editing alt, 205
 read back through your, 245
Text, borders and, 264
Themes, changing your, 107–108
Therapy, 11
Think small, 315
Third-party templates, 252–254
Tidbits, writing quicker, 249
Timezone, 160
<title> elements, 53
Tools
 Blogger editing, 291–293

sophistication and accessibility of
software, 8
Topica, 283
TrackBack, 150
features, 171–174
pings, 173, 174
Truth Laid Bear, 302

U

UBB codes, forum software compatibility with, 279
UBBs (Ultimate Bulletin Boards), 278
Ultimate Bulletin Boards (UBBs), 278
Uniform Resource Locators (URLs), 62
Unix-based vs. Microsoft Windows-based solution, 42
Unix-style convention, 121
Updating
via Web, 95–96
weblogs, 14–16
Upgrading of Movable Type, 151
Upload Destination menu, 204
Uploading
files, 135–136, 167–168
images, 211
your pages, 56–59
Uploading images, trouble, 205
URLs (Uniform Resource Locators), 62
archive, 160
site, 160
User-friendliness, 39
User registration, 214–217
UserLand, Radio, 34, 99–114
adding to your weblog, 102–105
aggregate news, 110–111
changing your themes, 107–108
deleting entries, 105
editing entries, 105
getting started with Radio, 100–102
setting preferences, 108–110
writing stories, 106–107
Usernames, 326
Users and mailings, managing, 214–222
Post Office, 218–222
user registration, 214–217

User's IP address, learning, 170
Users, let them play, 81

V

Variable-based sites, templates and, 117
Variables
adding template, 144
date-specific, 142
special, 175
template, 142
VBulletin, 280
Venues, music, 327
Verb agreement, strive for subject, 246
View Source command, browsers have, 269
Visual aspects of interface, 179
Visual style, 61
Voice
finding your blogging, 241
finding your blogging or writing, 241
writing in active, 245
Voice, example of passive, 246
know difference between they're, there, and their, 246
know when to use it's and its, 246
know where to place quotes and commas, 246
know which and that, 246
strive for subject/verb agreement, 246

W

Wander-Lust, 303
Web-based database server, MySOL is, 277
Web browsers, 64
Web hosts, 273
Web servers, getting for your weblogs, 39–44
choosing good hosting services, 42–44
choosing good IPPs, 42–44
weblog server jargon and definitions, 39–42
Web, teaching over, 332–333
critiques, 332–333
lectures, 332
news, events, and related links, 332
ongoing community, 333
Web, updating via, 95–96

Weblog, administering, 134–138
    banning IPs, 137–138
    deleting comments, 136–137
    editing comments, 136–137
    rebuilding files, 134–135
    uploading files, 135–136
Weblog, automated, 30–39
    preferring server-side weblogs, 36–39
    using hosted weblogs, 33–36
Weblog being right for you, 17–22
    consider your content, 17–18
    consider your goals, 18–22
Weblog Management settings, 198
Weblog-management software, 30
Weblog-management solutions, hosted, 33–34
    Blogger, 33–34
    LiveJournal, 34
    Manila, 34
    Radio Userland, 34
Weblog multi-entry templates, 224
Weblog netiquette, 250–251
Weblog pages, building basic, 52–56
    adding your first entries, 54–56
    creating pages, 52–54
    testing your pages, 56–59
    uploading your pages, 56–59
Weblog phenomenon, 9–11
Weblog server software, using special, 12
Weblog single-entry templates, 224
Weblog sites, publicizing, 297–316
    get listed and searched, 303–305
    headline syndication, 309–315
    how to be seen, 298–303
    link and ping, 305–309
Weblog software, 18
Weblog software and server, choosing, 25–45
    getting web server for your weblog,
      39–44
    types of weblog software, 26–39
Weblog software and services, 337–339
    domain name registrars, 339
    hosted blogging software, 337–338
    hosting companies, 338
    server-based blogging software, 338
Weblog software, types of, 26–39
    automated weblog, 30–39

    basic weblogs, 26–30
Weblog.php, 200
Weblogs
    adding to your, 102–105
    administering, 169–176
    basic, 26–30
    building community, 16–17
    configuring your, 199–200
    creating collective, 234–235
    dynamic collective, 17
    genesis of today's, 29
    headlines templates, 225
    hosted, 33–36
    and its formats, 5
    online journals and, 6
    preferring server-side, 36–39
    seriousness of, 318–322
    server jargon and definitions, 39–42
    technology doesn't define, 11
    updating, 14–16
Weblogs, add-ons for your, 271–293
    adding comments, 291
    adding image galleries, 288–291
    adding mailing lists, 282–286
    adding polls, 286–288
    Blogger editing tools, 291–293
    managing mailing lists, 282–286
    needing forums, 275–282
    setting up reply e-mail accounts, 272–275
Weblogs defined, 4–17
    new thing, 7–9
    updating weblogs, 14–16
    weblog phenomenon, 9–11
    weblogs are different, 11–14
    weblogs building community, 16–17
Weblogs, getting web servers for your, 39–44
    choosing good hosting services, 42–44
    choosing good IPPs, 42–44
    weblog server jargon and definitions,
      39–42
Weblogs, needing, 3–23
    call to action, 22–23
    get involved, 22–23
    weblog being right for you, 17–22
    weblog defined, 4–17
Weblogs, using, hosted, 73–114

Blogger, 76–89

business-like presence: Radio UserLand, 99–114

choosing hosted services, 74–76

community living: LiveJournal, 90–99

popular choice: Blogger, 76–89

Radio UserLand, 99–114

Weblogs, using in organizations, 317–334

ideas for organizational blogs, 323–333

making choices, 321–322

seriousness of weblogs, 318–322

Weblogs.com, 309

accepts pings, 308

Blogger doesn't ping, 308

Webring, 302

Website paths, 124

Websites

easiest way to identify, 5

ping, 307

Windows-based solution, Unix-based vs. Microsoft, 42

Windows NT-based server, 119

Writing

in active voice, 245

designing, and tweaking your blogs, 239–270

press releases, 314–315

quicker tidbits, 249

shorter articles, 249

stories, 106–107

Writing, improving your online, 245

consider your capitalization, 245

read back through your text, 245

using spell-checker, 245

write in active voice, 245

Writing voice, finding your blogging or, 241

X

XHTML-based conventions, 53

XML (Extensible Markup Language), 309

Y

YaBB (Yet Another Bulletin Board), 280

Yahoo!, 304

Yahoo! Groups, 284, 285

Yet Another Bulletin Board (YaBB), 280

INTERNATIONAL CONTACT INFORMATION

AUSTRALIA
McGraw-Hill Book Company Australia Pty. Ltd.
TEL +61-2-9415-9899
FAX +61-2-9415-5687
http://www.mcgraw-hill.com.au
books-it_sydney@mcgraw-hill.com

CANADA
McGraw-Hill Ryerson Ltd.
TEL +905-430-5000
FAX +905-430-5020
http://www.mcgrawhill.ca

**GREECE, MIDDLE EAST,
NORTHERN AFRICA**
McGraw-Hill Hellas
TEL +30-1-656-0990-3-4
FAX +30-1-654-5525

MEXICO (Also serving Latin America)
McGraw-Hill Interamericana Editores S.A. de C.V.
TEL +525-117-1583
FAX +525-117-1589
http://www.mcgraw-hill.com.mx
fernando_castellanos@mcgraw-hill.com

SINGAPORE (Serving Asia)
McGraw-Hill Book Company
TEL +65-863-1580
FAX +65-862-3354
http://www.mcgraw-hill.com.sg
mghasia@mcgraw-hill.com

SOUTH AFRICA
McGraw-Hill South Africa
TEL +27-11-622-7512
FAX +27-11-622-9045
robyn_swanepoel@mcgraw-hill.com

**UNITED KINGDOM & EUROPE
(Excluding Southern Europe)**
McGraw-Hill Education Europe
TEL +44-1-628-502500
FAX +44-1-628-770224
http://www.mcgraw-hill.co.uk
computing_neurope@mcgraw-hill.com

ALL OTHER INQUIRIES Contact:
Osborne/McGraw-Hill
TEL +1-510-549-6600
FAX +1-510-883-7600
http://www.osborne.com
omg_international@mcgraw-hill.com